TURKEY in the NEW CENTURY

Speeches and Texts Presented
at International Fora (1995-2001)

TURKEY in the
NEW CENTURY

Speeches and Texts Presented
at International Fora (1995-2001)

Expanded 2nd Edition

İsmail Cem

RUSTEM

First Published, 2000
Second Edition, 2001
The First Edition's Title "Turkey in the 21st Century"

ISBN: 975-97030-5-X

Cover design by Djochkoun Sami
Text design by Eylem Deliceırmak

CONTENTS

INTRODUCTION: *A New Approach to Foreign Policy*   1
1 - An analysis of Traditional Foreign Policy   1
2 - Reshaping Basics in Foreign Policy   20
3 - Shortcomings and Opportunities   40

CHAPTER I: *History, Culture & Politics*   49
1 - Coexistence of Civilizations and Cultures
    as a Means to Achieve Peace   50
2 -"Is Turkey Culturally Pulling Away from Europe?"   53
3 - A History, which provides for Opportunities
    as well as Problems   55
4 - Turkey, Europe, Eurasia   60

CHAPTER II: *Turkey & the World*   63
1 - Setting Sail to the 21st Century   63
2 - The Eurasian Dimension   67
3 - "Tour d'Horizon"   69
4 - The United States   72
5 - The Middle East   78
6 - Caucasus, Central Asia & Baku - Tblisi - Ceyhan   90
7 - For a Brave New Millennium   97

CHAPTER III: *Nothing Can Justify Terror*   103
1 - Over-Emphasizing Ethnicity Leads
    to Disasters in Europe   104
2 - An Anti-Islam Crusade?   109
3 - To End the Illegal Immigration   111
4 - Terror and Assasinations are not
    "Democratic Rights"   113
5 - Democracy, Linguistic Freedoms and
    the National Security Council   120
6 - A Choice to make between Terrorists
    and their Victims   124
7 - Those Who Encourage Terrorism   126
8 - An Appeal of a Different Kind   127

CHAPTER IV: *"If the Balkans Had Not Existed..."*   129
1 - "...The West Would Surely Have Created One..."   129
2 - Balkans of Euro-Atlantic and Euro-Asian
    Dimensions   134
3 - Balkan Countries Should Have More Say
    on Balkan Matters   135
4 - Economic Perspectives for the Balkans   139

CHAPTER V: *Greece & Cyprus*   143
1 - To be Fair in Cyprus   143
2 - Another Missed Opportunity   149
3 - An Act Of Self-Defence by Turkish Cypriots   150
4 - Q&A on Turkey, Greece, Cyprus   151
5 - Realities of Cyprus   158
6 - Russian S-300 Missiles: Latest "Fashion"
    in East Mediterranean   160
7 - What About the Turkish Minority in Greece?   171
8 - Problems and Achievements   172
9 - Through "Realism" and "Justice..."   176
10- Both Turkey and Greece have Gained
    from "Rapprochement"   181
11- "From Negative Anticipations
    to Positive Expectations"   186

CHAPTER VI: *The European Union*   189
1 - For EU, an Issue of Identity and Vision   189
2 - Scenarios for EU's Luxembourg Summit   192
3 - European Security, WEU and EU   196
4 - Turkey and Europe: Looking to the
    Future from a Historical Perspective   200
5 - EU's Conceptual and Political Horizons   207
6 - Making our Position Clear to EU   209
7 - An External Dynamic for Further Progress   214
8 - The Journey to Hope   217

CHAPTER VII: *Redefining Turkish Foreign Policy*   219

FORWARD

This book has a particularity: It consists of my articles published by American and European press, letters written to foreign colleagues, and speech made at international fora. Therefore, from the outset I apologize for some deficiencies in my English. Furthermore, I have translated into English some of my work, which was originally written -or spoken- in French.

Nevertheless, I thought that my views as presented to an international audience or to a foreign interlocutor might make an interesting entity. That's how this book came about. I have added a lengthy introduction to this second edition: "A different approach to foreign policy". This was translated to English by a professional. A few new items were added to the second edition.

"Turkey in the New Century" covers the years 1995 – 2001. This is the period when I was Minister of Culture, Chairman of the Turkish Group at the Parliamentary Assembly of Council of Europe and Minister of Foreign Affairs. I have tried to avoid repetition. Therefore, several among the articles are excerpts. There is, however, no editing which alters the essentials.

INTRODUCTION :
A Different Approach to Foreign Policy

This book explores the genuine contributions that Turkey in the 21st century can bring to humanity's quest for peace, freedom, economic development, and social justice.

For Turkey, the way forward —particularly in foreign policy— requires a new awareness of her own identity and history, of her assets and shortcomings. A nation whose foreign policy is alienated from its own cultural roots and historical past (as Turkey's has long been), cannot be a serious player on the world scene. Furthermore, in such an environment of alienation, it becomes possible for political and intellectual elites to develop 'colonial' mindsets, even in a country that has never at any time in its long history been a colony.

In probing Turkish foreign policy and Turkey's role in the world of the 21st century, my focus will be on history, culture, and a quest for renewal. Nearly four years of experience as Turkey's Foreign Minister have convinced me of the relevance of this approach. If, in this period, Turkey has achieved success in foreign policy, if she has increased her influence over a wider geographical area, and if she has pursued the interests of her own people more vigorously, the principal reasons must be the introduction of a historical dimension to her foreign policy and a renewal of its fundamental concepts.

1. An Analysis of Traditional Foreign Policy

A survey of the maiden speeches made by earlier Turkish Foreign Ministers establishes that almost all of them include pledges to the effect that "Turkey has a traditional foreign policy which will continue unchanged." Almost every new Foreign Minister has taken office with such words as if they were an 'inaugural oath of office' or a 'pledge of allegiance.' Regardless of the changes in parties, governments, or ministers, the promise has always been that "our established foreign policy will not change."

1

In practice, this attachment to 'that which is established' actually entails more of an attachment to the vices of that tradition rather than to its virtues. The tradition's virtues are ostensibly the three principles laid down by the founder of the Republic, Mustafa Kemal Atatürk: "Peace at home; peace in the world" (a policy that has been adhered to by nearly every government since — notwithstanding the Korean Conflict); The second principle is "to be a protector of oppressed nations;" while the third is the adoption of "a passion for independence as the basis of one's identity". Backsliding on the last two principles set in chiefly during the Cold War.

With minor exceptions, the errors caused by this adherence to an established foreign policy have maintained their effectiveness for half a century. Politicians claiming to follow nothing but "established foreign policy" become in fact the representatives of the reiteration of those errors.

In the past four years, significant changes have been made in this "established foreign policy", or, more correctly, in reversing the errors to which it has long contributed. It is due to the changes thus effected that Turkey's position in the world has also changed. In international relations Turkey has emerged as a country that is serious and influential, one that is aware of its own interests and of its own strengths, one that abides by its word, and one whose influence over a broad geographical region is increasing. We are only at the beginning of this renewal and there is still a lot to do. But already Turkey is witnessing the benefits of this change.

In other words, most of those long unquestioned policies that were made inviolable by repeated praise have been set aside. Generally accepted modes of behavior whose invariability was sanctioned have been eschewed. No respect has been given to the relief that these conventional wisdoms afford. On the contrary, there has been a clear break with traditional analysis and attitudes. In their place we have begun the process of constructing and implementing a new approach to foreign policy.

FOREIGN POLICY BEREFT OF A HISTORICAL DIMENSION: Turkey's traditional foreign policy was one, which may be best described as being bereft of a historical dimension. It lacked 'depth' with respect to time, and it lacked 'breadth' with respect to space.

What we had was a foreign policy that was alienated from its own roots, cut off from its own assets, indeed, divorced from the very elements that could nourish and sustain it. In this foreign policy's perception of the world and of itself, history was nonexistent. It was as if the historical experiences of centuries, as well as their civilizational assets and relationships, had never existed; or, if they did, they belonged not to Turkey but rather to some alien society. As such, they were not even deemed worthy of consideration. The fact of having lived together with many different peoples and societies for centuries; the fact of having shared equally in and contributed to a common state; the fact that the great majority of those involved shared the same belief in Islam -indeed, of having once even been the historical champion of that faith; the fact of sharing a language that has common roots and features with that spoken by more than a hundred million people in Asia: were all ignored in our traditional foreign policy. None of these facts were deemed to be of any geostrategic relevance.

The singularity of this understanding is that it confines itself to a very narrow time frame. It does not take into account even the whole of the republican period, much less the Ottoman centuries. That is why sensitivities for oppressed nations, as well as overtures to the Balkans or to the Middle East (such as the Balkan and Sadabad pacts of the 1930s) are absent in "traditional foreign policy". A history as vast as it is deep was dismissed. It is as if the genesis of Turkish foreign policy was considered to coincide with Turkey's relationship with NATO and the cold war.

In the process, Turkey's foreign policy was crammed into a straightjacket of some fifty or sixty years' time. All the priorities and advantages that might be had of seven centuries or a thousand years were deliberately ignored: indeed, they were disowned. Turkey's foreign policy voluntarily washed its hands of such enormous resources and deprived itself of them. Consciously and willfully, it circumscribed its own horizon.

Then, having been stripped of her entire historical legacy, including all those elements that were positive, the end-result was defined, exalted, blessed, and granted inviolability as 'traditional foreign policy'. Henceforth every new government that came to power would pledge that this established foreign policy would 'never be strayed from.' Thus guaranteeing that Turkey would take no interest in her own region and that she would distance herself from her historical geography. It was a foreign policy that turned its back on centuries of experience, a foreign policy that stubbornly persisted in regarding itself as an alien in its own historical context. This mindset manifested itself in many ways. For example, the attitude of 'Oh let's do keep out of Arab affairs,' every time someone uttered the phrase Middle East; together with fond hopes that the more Turkey distanced herself from Islamic societies or alienated herself from her own past, the more the West will 'like' her.

It is the addition of a historical dimension to the articulation of Turkish foreign policy that most distinguishes the past four years (1997-2001) from the previous era. This said, the contributions of earlier statesmen who were able to 'transcend the rule' deserve to be acknowledged here:

The first clear break with the 'traditional' took place in 1974 when Bulent Ecevit did the inconceivable and came to the rescue of the Turkish community on Cyprus. His decision to do so was of the utmost historical and strategic importance. After years of passivity, Turkey for the first time courageously rose above the position and role that had been assigned to her;

Turgut Ozal led the way in bringing the newly liberated Turkic states of Central Asia and the Caucasus onto Turkey's political and diplomatic agenda:

At a time when scarcely anyone else in Turkey was aware of what was afoot, Suleyman Demirel clearly saw that the fallout from the chaos of the breakup of the Soviet system was impacting on Turkey's geographic sphere of interest: this was especially true in Central Asia and the Caucasus, regions with whom Turkey shared strong linguistic and cultural affinities. Perceiving the great opportunities that these changes would bring, Demirel vigorously cultivated the friendship of both the newly forming countries in the region and of those who were regaining their independence;

One needs to take pains when trying to understand history and interpret it. This is particularly true for Turkey: When you have a history stretching back in time more than a millennium, you necessarily feel the weight of that long presence in every aspect of what you do. History is there, whether we like it or not. And history is a phenomenon that belongs as much to a country's 'present' as it does to its 'past' —all the more so when a country possesses the particular attributes that Turkey does.

A few examples will show why. Of the current members of the United Nations, some twenty-seven states have a shared history with Turkey. This is a figure equaled only by ancient Rome or maybe the British Empire. These states were once constituents of the '*Ottoman plenum*', for periods ranging from less than a century to over five hundred years. From the standpoint of endurance, no political entity since the Western and Eastern Roman empires comes even close to matching the Ottoman Empire's longevity. The majority of Turkey's historical links are defined not in terms of fifty or a hundred years, but in terms of centuries. Turkey's historical geography encompassed the Balkans, the Middle East, the Caucasus, and North Africa. Its roots, taking pre-Ottoman and Seljuk kinships into account, stretch back to the steppes of Central Asia.

There are reasons that make this fact more compelling and substantive today than ever before. For one thing, many of the independent states that emerged from the breakup of the Soviet system have their origins in societies with whom we share a history. For another, the economic and political dynamics of Turkey today make it possible to develop close relations with these new governments. Finally, economic interaction and new technologies have intensified the practical value of such links in today's world. In a context such as this, the advantages that possessing a common shared history make to the present become greater: Turkey's history thus becomes a cardinal element in shaping Turkey's present day role and foreign policy outlook.

Of course the record of a history of living together for centuries cannot be expected to be totally positive. For this reason, history does not just present us with opportunities, it also poses problems. Skill lies in being able to open the way for the first while limiting the impact of the second. The precondition for that is to make an accurate assessment of the current situation.

For all the peoples of different ethnicities, languages and religions who lived together for several centuries under an Ottoman

Turkish umbrella, the operative norm was one of peaceful coexistence, security, tolerance, and relative affluence, especially when compared with what existed elsewhere. Instability and hostility were aberrations, which were confined to the last decades of the Empire's six hundred years plus history.

What made centuries of stability, security, and tolerance possible was the pre-industrial nature of the Ottoman polity. The empire was the product of an age and of conditions in which the mechanisms of modern economic exploitation and modern classes had either not emerged or else could not develop. For economic, social, and ideological reasons, 'exploitation' in the classical sense —such as in the relationships between Britain and her colonies or in the Spanish and Portuguese looting of the Americas— is absent from the Ottoman Turkish historical landscape. Quite the contrary: in the accounts of the Ottoman fisc, the only province consistently generating more income than it received from the central treasury was Egypt. This, due to the Nile valley's role as a major grain production center. Ottoman financial support and investment flowing into Anatolia and the Arabian provinces in particular' was always more than what the treasury received in return. Moreover, Ottoman rationalism was able to see that a form of administration that was tolerant, fair, and impartial was not just in the best interests of the Empire's subjects, but of the central government as well. In return for the protection provided by the Pax Ottomanica contented subjects paid their taxes and the state flourished.

Such attitudes and the multicultural, heterogeneous, and egalitarian features of Turkey's history make it possible for those centuries of living together to have strong and, in many cases, favorable repercussions today. Her history thus provides an important foundation that Turkey can take advantage of in her international relations today. Contrary to a number of entrenched but mistaken suppositions in Europe, Ottoman conquests in the Balkans were won not against the region's peoples but against its feudal lords. At a time when the phenomenon of nationalism had not yet appeared on the historical stage, the Ottomans represented tolerance, security, and an order that was by early-modern terms relatively egalitarian. This was the main reason why Balkan societies embraced Ottoman rule. For their own part, the Ottomans skillfully publicized these attributes in the run-up to conquest and retained them afterwards. The decentralized nature of the newly established regime —especially in the Balkans and Central Europe— and the recognition of regional autonomies in the Muslim parts of the empire opened the way for cooperation and good relations.

Moreover, Ottoman culture was a 'synthetic' one: a fusing of many different elements coming from many different sources. This made it easier for different societies and creeds to live together while further strengthening the composite nature of the Ottoman state. This is why, for example, Islamic, Byzantine, Arab, and Persian traditions existed side by side in Ottoman art, architecture, and economics. This was true as well in the empire's military and governmental institutions. The language of literature, of court and government was a synthesis of Turkish, Persian, and Arabic elements. It reflected the heterogeneity and inclusiveness of the state. Likewise, the common cuisine, which still exists throughout the former Ottoman lands, remains as a poignant reminder of this shared heritage.

On the other hand, the nature of the governmental and military elites that ran the Ottoman state in the 15th to 18th centuries made it easier for different ethnic and confessional groups to live together in peace. These Ottoman elites were systematically —and almost entirely— created from *devshirmes* (conscripts). The source of the empire's military and civilian ruling class was Christian boys, separated from their families at an early age, converted to Islam, and trained in court schools *(Enderun)*. Upon graduation, these *devshirmes* took their places in government and military service according to their individual talents and abilities. The system ensured absolute equality and a level field for all players. The Ottomans' empire was run-and fought for-by a class of men who had been systematically shorn of their ethnic, racial, regional, family, and other backgrounds. The members of this elite were bound solely and directly to the sultan (which is to say, to the state) and they were his servants (kul), and his alone. This system helped prevent favoritism and bias based on ethnic or family considerations. For centuries, it kept the ruling class supplied with men who were not inclined to distinguish between different regions or ethnic backgrounds.

7

The system thus fostered a tolerant state and a ruling elite composed of individuals whose advance was based on merit. These were times when in the Balkans and Central Europe, the power of local feudal nobles retarded the formation of centralized states and led to an erosion of power. Lord Kinross, in his *"Ottoman Centuries"*, makes an interesting comparison: at a time when the Balkans and Central Europe were ruled by mostly incompetent aristocrats who had acquired positions through family privilege, the Ottomans were being governed by men who had started out as equals and rose through the ranks by fair testing of their competence. Lord Kinross calls this system, which functioned from the 15th century to the 18th, a *"meritocracy"*. This meritocracy and its encouragement of an equable approach to the diverse social groups in the empire was the most important element in centuries of peaceful relations between the state and a wide variety of ethnic groups.

This historical phenomenon contributed to a better understanding among peoples of all races and religions throughout the empire. The positive relationship, which lasted for centuries, provides in turn a favorable background that contemporary Turkish foreign policy can take advantage of throughout the region which once comprised the Ottoman polity.

The break-through achieved by Turkish foreign policy between 1997 and 2001 was the systematic and vigorous addition of a historical dimension to bi-lateral relations with these states which share a common Ottoman past with Turkey. That this had not occurred earlier was the result of a deliberate choice on the part of traditional foreign policy.

We are now witnessing the practical benefits of the inclusion of this decisive dimension to our foreign policy. Focusing on historical and cultural affinities has provided additional impetus in our relations with countries in the Balkans, the Middle East, Central Asia, North and East Africa. Analyses that take history as their point of departure are making it easier for certain realities to be perceived: quite often for the first time. Our new approach of including a historical consciousness has helped progress in certain sensitive topics. One such is the definition of minorities in Turkey. In addition to the relevant articles of the Lausanne Treaty (which we have said are not the be-all and end-all of Turkey's understanding), historical references were added to the argument. Specifically, we were able to demonstrate the existence of a seven hundred year old tradition of not making ethnic distinctions among members of the Muslim community, a tradition that is itself a reflection of the Ottoman-Turkish interpretation of Islam. This has helped others to a better understanding of this complex issue. (I will return to this subject when discussing the European Union.)

Quite a few of those states that I consider it fortunate for Turkey to have shared a history which are also ones that fought a 'war of independence' against the Ottoman Empire. Their own nationalist awakenings led to successful independence struggles against the Ottomans. Several such countries celebrate the anniversaries of the conclusion of their struggle against the Ottomans as their 'national independence days'. Among these are Bulgaria, Albania, Romania, and Jordan, to name but four countries with which Turkey today has the closest ties.

In assessing the prospects for Turkish foreign policy in the 21st century, old enmities and their consequences need to be analyzed:

In the 19th and early 20th centuries, three momentous changes occurred that affected the Ottoman Empire's relations with the rest of the world. The first was the appearance of nationalist movements in the empire's territories. The second was the policy of anti-Ottoman Western states to encourage, support, and sometimes even foment such movements to serve their own interests. The third was the helplessness of the Ottomans to do anything about this development. The outcome of these three factors coalescing is well known: guided, supported, or controlled by Britain, France, and Russia, some Ottoman ethnic groups rose in rebellion and the empire fell apart.

With the breakup of the empire and for reasons that are partly understandable, opposition to Turkey became a fundamental aspect of foreign policy for these newly-independent societies —a policy that some adhered to for longer than others. Countries that had only recently become independent interpreted in the worst light possible both the conditions that made their independence struggle necessary and the prosecution of the struggle itself. This was necessary in order to achieve unity at home and to strengthen —sometimes to create— a new sense of national identity. Therefore, clear benefits were to be had in keeping anti-Ottoman / anti-Turkish sentiments alive, even after independences were gained.

It is important to recall that the confrontation between the Ottomans and the revolting peoples occurred during what is, historically speaking, a very brief time frame. In most cases confrontation was limited to one or two decades in the last century of Ottoman rule. Nowhere in the world is there another example of such diverse ethnic and confessional communities enjoying centuries of such peaceful and durable relations among themselves and with the central authority, as was the case in the Ottoman Empire.

Historically, Ottoman rule was one based on mutual understanding and cooperation. Antagonism and conflict were the exceptions. That a blemish occurring in the final and brief stage of a centuries old relationship does not alter the realities of the overall picture. In most of these countries, though not in all, brief periods of strife turn into memories such as are to be found in everybody's historical heritage and in no way inspire lasting enmity. Today, realities and achievements are what survive.

The inability or unwillingness to perceive matters in their totality was one of the major shortcomings of traditional policy, particularly in the Middle East, where the common and positive experience of centuries was disregarded and short-term antagonisms were played up. This then was transformed into a justification to keep at a distance a region and a people whose significance for Turkey's interests is in fact paramount. Ignoring the positive aspects of the shared experience, Turkey made it easier for some European countries and Middle Eastern leaders to exploit the negative memories of the recent past: Thus, they were able to keep Turkish influence away from this strategic geography, to render its peoples more vulnerable, and to deal with them with a freer hand.

FOREIGN POLICY AND AN IN ADEQUATE APPROACH TO CULTURE: Culture provides a society with its collective memory, its basic mindset, and its patterns of behavior. Culture is also the mortar that binds the society together. In the development of any policy —but particularly in the shaping of foreign policy— a nation's culture and its self-perception are fundamental elements. The particular culture of a nation accrued in the course of history and its contributions to human civilization are among the crucial elements that create and enhance the nation's image. Cultural attributes facilitate or hinder the ability of a society to assert itself in particular fields. The authority of a foreign policy that has been developed in a deep-rooted culture matured in extensive experience cannot even begin to compare with those that do not have such attributes.

In this respect, Turkey occupies a unique position. She possesses an extraordinary background of culture and civilization, yet consciously and for quite some time, Turkey deprived herself of her cultural assets in their entirety. For years, Turkey's identity, as presented to her own citizens and to the rest of the world, as well as Turkey's internal and foreign policies, were erected upon a shallow cultural perception. In the main, Turkey's culture was contained in a very narrow time-frame, the cultural achievements inherited by modern Turkey from previous historical periods were considered to be non-existent. The fact that Anatolia was the cradle of civilizations was ignored. One also encounters an attitude that dismissed even pre-republican Turkish culture. It is to be pointed out that on its own, no policy —particularly no foreign policy— can be held responsible for the lack of cultural depth or for the absence of a historical dimension. Such shortcomings are first and foremost the produce of the ruling elites of Turkey's ideological, intellectual, and political development.

Deficiencies in the cultural framework have an impact on foreign policy. Shallowness in the common cultural outlook of a country manifests itself in two distinct manners: either as an uncalled-for and immoderate rejection, even denigration, of some foreign cultures; or, as an inferiority complex with respect to others. Colored by such underlying misconceptions, foreign policy is invariably going to be affected as a result. For example, societies representing Islamic culture have long been the targets of a negative foreign policy approach due to the cultural prejudices of Turkey's governing elites. On the other hand, foreign policy directed towards countries that share in Western cultural values tends to be excessively submissive. This is because of the unwarranted complexes that the same governing elites suffer in regards to the culture that these countries represent. Although Turkey has never been colonized, a strong inferiority complex that I define as a 'colonial mentality' exists in some Turkish political and intellectual circles.

11

In point of fact, all of the civilizations that have ever existed in our history or within our borders have together contributed to the shaping of our contemporary society. Turkey today is the joint product of those civilizations. An awareness of this truth would relieve Turkey's foreign policy of its cultural biases and complexes. It would also mitigate the stress of the cultural contradictions that plagued Turkish society in the 19th and 20th centuries. Overcoming cultural discrepancies is not easy but it is possible. Dialogue and peaceful debate in the last decade of the 20th century are evidence that steps taken in the right direction can lead to positive developments.

The legacy both of Turkey's Ottoman past with its renowned tolerance and of the secular republican revolution is this: a cultural outlook relieved of superiority and inferiority complexes is the prerequisite for cohesion in Turkish society. This will in turn have a decisive impact on Turkish foreign policy. To achieve these ends, all of the civilizations that have been a part of our history and our geography need to be reconciled with one another and with modern Turkey. In fact, they all contribute to the cultural roots of contemporary Turkey. We are not so remote as we tend to believe from Trojan, Ionian, Byzantine, or Seljuk civilization; nor is Ottoman civilization alien to republican Turkey.

History —be it social, political, or cultural— is not merely a lesson about the past. History's essential relevance is for the future. It is a vehicle for shaping the future and ensuring that the future develops free of the shortcomings of the past. Introducing to Turkey's foreign policy the cultural and historical dimensions that it was traditionally deprived of is the principal dynamic of the renewal achieved in recent years.

THE RULES OF THE GAME IN FOREIGN POLICY: Perceiving foreign policy in the form of 'idealistic' prescriptions is the primary characteristic of the traditional approach. Concepts such as 'friendly countries,' 'hostile countries,' 'sincerity', 'recognition of justified stances', abound. In a way, one could call it a 'foreign policy of abstractions:' 'The USA likes us, Russia doesn't.' 'This country is duplicitous, that one is sincere.' One foreign prime minister is 'a friend of Turkey', the other one 'an enemy' and so on and so on.

In fact, foreign policy is a mathematical equation of a country's interests. It is a matter of calculation. Foreign relations are the product of a dialectical process in which the internal and external factors that shape interests are in constant motion. Stances that perceive foreign policy as a static, rigid phenomenon and that define others within categories of 'eternal friendship' and 'eternal animosity' are destined to be satisfied with the minimum possible advantage. Unfortunately, that is how things were in Turkey for a long time.

The distinctive feature of Turkish foreign policy in the last few years has been a thoroughly realistic and flexible vision of the countries, policies, and conditions in Turkey's external environment. We have avoided any kind of abstract or idealistic evaluations. In foreign policy, there is no place for wishful thinking or for illusions. Success is dependent on realistic assessments. In a geography where tremendous interests are contending, the precondition for the success of an inter-regional power such as Turkey is realism.

Towards the end of the 20th century, a number of rather unpleasant realities of foreign policy began manifesting themselves. With the end of a 'bipolar' world in the 1990s, the need to look like something you are not was no longer felt as strongly as it used to be. A particular 'ethics' (or immorality) in foreign relations that was uniquely its own began to emerge. Taking this new aspect of foreign policy into account has proven to be extremely beneficial for Turkey.

In yesterday's world there were two opposing power centers that contended with each other, kept an eye on each other, and sought to gain the upper hand vis-à-vis one another. Each exposed the other party's weaknesses in an attempt to put it at a disadvantage. If one made a misstep, the other immediately moved into action. Not because it was overly partial to rights, freedoms or justice, but primarily to humiliate the rival. When Soviet tanks ran over Hungary or Czechoslovakia's Dubchek was overthrown, the USA and the West raised a ruckus. Certainly not because they had never employed such methods themselves when they felt them to be needed, but as a way of roughing up the other side. When the USA backed a fascist coup in Chile, it was the turn of the Soviets to play the role of freedom's champion. Just about everybody recognized the calculation underlying such 'moralistic' behavior and 'humane' concerns. But in the end, everybody was contained to a certain extent; there was a sense of mutual restraint. Dissuasion was not an empty word and each side was obliged to calculate the broader implications of its actions: If I do such-and-such, the other side will use it against me. As a result, each party kept itself under a certain degree of control. It had to.

At present, the balance that used to be based on opposing centers of power has changed. In the absence of bipolar power centers, the need for restraint has vanished. Everything is possible; all policy options have become conceivable. Something else —something very important— has changed: the role of moral factors and moral criteria has also declined. More likely, it has been realized that they're not as strong as they were thought to be, especially when they have to stand up and prevail on their own.

So far as one can tell, moral values were able to influence yesterday's delicate balances at least to a degree. Moral criteria did have some combative value: witness the French intelligentsia's opposition to the Algerian war and American students' struggle to end the Vietnam conflict. With the disappearance of bipolarism, all forms of behavior became 'acceptable' and 'conventional.' Nations may feel as much pity as they will for oppressed or slaughtered peoples. They may champion democracy to their utmost, but without the power centers of the past era that had to keep a wary eye on one another, morality have no more weight than the complaint of any benevolent, consistent individual.

For Turkey to be successful in her foreign relations, she needs to purge her traditional policy of all its abstractions and to rid herself of her habit of self-deception. Realism is the only approach that leads through the dangerous tangle of today's complexities.

FORCED ALTERNATIVES THAT NEED TO BE OVERCOME: Lying at the foundations of our traditional foreign policy were 'imperative choices' that had to be made from among 'imperative alternatives.' The alternatives could be summed up as 'Asian or European', 'East or West,' and so on. They incorporated an absolute dichotomy and an implicit and unquestioned obligation on Turkey's part to choose one or the other and to fully associate and align herself with that choice. At the roots of this mindset lay ideological and political balances based on interests. The allegedly 'imperative' alternatives and the contradictions and choices they implied were

14

considered sacrosanct. The most fundamental of these 'imperative' choices found expression in the dichotomy of 'Islam vs. secularism.' The foreign policy extension of the 'Islamic' side consisted of the 'Asian' and 'East' options; the 'secular' side had 'European' and 'West' to offer. In a real sense, the Islam vs. secularism dichotomy that plagued the country internally was being replayed in foreign policy and unduly influencing Turkey's view of the world.

Because this particular imperative choice (secularism vs. Islam) defines, to a large degree, mindsets, approaches, and domestic politics, it has shaped traditional foreign policy as well. But it is wrong: wrong as a hypothesis, as an analysis, and as a paradigm. The givens are misstated; the categories are misnamed; the stakes are misconceived. Conditioned to think within the framework of misleading notions, people's choices are handicapped. The result is that the inadequacy in the political superstructure (explaining all contradictions and choices within an Islam vs. secularism framework) permeates all aspects and all levels of social life. This blurs choices, degrades relationships, and misdirects foreign policy objectives.

In recent years, some progress has been made in transcending the artificial 'imperative choices' that are dictated by traditional foreign policy. This has already been quite effective in removing some of the stumbling-blocks impeding Turkey in her relations with the rest of the world. While that is another subject that I will be dealing with later in this book, at this point I want to touch upon the core of the issue: the 'Islam vs. secularism' dichotomy that so preoccupies people's minds and is exaggerated as to its relevance in both Turkey's domestic and foreign politics.

Defining the fundamental split in terms of an Islamic/secular dichotomy is demonstrably wrong, both objectively and politically. More than merely wrong, it is dangerous. This fault-line paradigm is the product of mainly Western academic and political circles and their perception of Muslim societies.

In the course of history, this approach and its implications have produced political dividends for its Western advocates: it was mainly used as a means to initiate and organize favorable indigenous political forces. Whether for ideological choices or financial reasons or because of a perceived need to man the ramparts against the 'other'

15

in their society, these indigenous power centers associated themselves with Western interests. Nowadays, however, the distinction tends to be recast as 'secular vs. non-secular' in analyses of Islamic societies.

Both as a definition and as an analytical tool, this categorizing is frequently observed in the Western media, even if no longer found so frequently among serious academics. This in turn impresses some Turkish politicians and media, who accept it at face value. Logically and intellectually however, it is not possible to regard this dichotomy as a principal element of Turkish political reality. There are three reasons why this is so:

1. The great majority of the Turkish people think of themselves as 'Muslim,' but they also readily accept and follow the basic precepts of secularism. The overwhelming majority of Turkish society does not consider that keeping the affairs of religion and state separate in any way conflicts with one's religious beliefs and practices. The findings of scientifically conducted surveys make it clear that Turkish society has no problem on this point. Of course there are some who sincerely believe it to be an 'either - or' issue: for them, one combines state functions with religion and thereby becomes a true believer or else he is not a real Muslim. For them, the two approaches are mutually exclusive. The number of such people in Turkey today who believe that this is a fundamental choice that has to be made is not significant.

2. Turkey's historical development does not facilitate divisions based on the 'secular versus Islamic' approach. In fact, it en compasses several factors that render such a confrontation in applicable. History in Turkey provides many examples and manifestations of tolerance for all religions. This is not to say that religion and state were separate in the Ottoman Empire; but what the Ottomans came up with was an original model in which the state kept the religious establishment by its side — and also under its strict control. This, in a way, assured the well being of an empire comprised of numerous ethnicities and religions. The particular handling of ethnic and religious matters by the Ottomans not only makes the Turkish reality different from the long-enduring Christian model, which generally assigned priority to the Holy Church, but also distinguishes the practices of the Ottomans and the Turks from those of other Islamic societies.

3. The days when the 'Islamic vs. secular' dichotomy might have been socially and politically effective are over and gone. There were times when the distinction made itself heard. The years of dire hardship when the republic was being forged were one. That was a time when Turkey's social structure was undergoing radical changes and those who opposed those changes or their consequences based their opposition to what they styled as 'straying from Islam and its precepts.' Later, other segments of the population were to proffer this 'straying' as the cause for their own destitution. Another instance of the 'Islam vs. secularism' dichotomy's raising its head was when 'Islamism' was used as a countervailing force against the rise of the Turkish left. The allegation that the split between political left and right was rooted in religious conviction; that 'the right favored religion and the left atheism', was exploited by the powers that be in Turkey from the 1950s to the 1970s. For its own part, some segments of the Turkish left even contributed to this fabrication themselves by falling into its trap and making the distinction an important plank of their political platform.

In the years since the 1970s, both the left in particular and progressive movements in general have managed to extricate themselves from this trap. At the same time, Turkey's democracy has been growing stronger and wiser and the criteria by which people may validly distinguish among political ideas and choices have become more sophisticated. Today Turkey is engaged in a process of communication in which democratic pluralism has become extraordinarily important. The 'Islamic vs secular' distinction today has lost whatever genuine influence it may have had for one reason or another in the past as well as the bogus influence that was attributed to it by power groups seeking to use it against their rivals.

But if that is so —if the 'Islamic vs. secular' dichotomy has never been a determining or permanent element of Turkey's past or present— why is it being constantly dished up before Turkey as if it were some kind of fundamental model for analyzing today's society? Similarly, why are its extensions —'East vs. West,' and 'Asian vs. European'— defined for such along period of time the basics of foreign policy?

A few reasons come to mind. Some of them are extrinsic, others are intrinsic:

1. One feature of the 'Islamic vs. secular' model is that the model stems from Western Europe's experience with colonialism. It is a handy template that is applied indiscriminately to any country in which there is an Islamic tradition and Turkey happens to be one of them. The assumptions on which the model is based however are quite at variance with Turkish realities, so it is not surprising that the model's application to Turkey leads to false conclusions.

One should also add that the practice of interpreting events in Turkey —or in any country with an Islamic tradition— in the context of a conflict between secular and non-secular forces makes it easier for Western politicians and diplomats to define categories that are convenient for Western interests, to identify 'partisans,' and to form alliances accordingly;

2. The reasons why inaccurate models based on false or nebulous definitions arise within Turkey on the other hand have largely to do with domestic politics. The 'secular / Islamist' card was an easy one to play once politicians realized that it could be used to distract attention from their own mistakes and also to garner votes.

An instance of this occurred when some members of the Refah (Welfare) party defined themselves as 'Islamist' and everybody else as 'secular' and then proceeded to present Turkey's fundamental problem as one of the former gaining the upper hand over the latter. By employing an abstract definition like 'Islamist' in conjunction with the sanctity and inclusiveness of the concept of 'Islam,' they sought to increase their political appeal and the number of their partisans.

Other politicians seized upon this model as a way of covering up their shortcomings and of diverting political attention away from valid criteria for making social judgments and decisions. Governments and politicians unable to come up with real solutions to such problems as the distribution of wealth, unemployment, in efficiency, inequality, and so on —as well as those who were discomforted by talk of such things— made use of this opportunity. They recognized the benefit, to their own political interests, in attributing Turkey's basic problem to an 'Islamist vs. secular' conflict.

When an abstract concept such as 'Islamist' is used as a criteria for political categorizing, the ultimate result is that it turns into an agent of mutual exclusion. When the press picked up and began elaborating on this model, and on its compartmentalized definitions,

18

the result was to divide people into hostile camps. Despite all the flaws inherent in it, and notwithstanding its relative unimportance in our history, the 'Islamist/secular' dichotomy still has power to attract adherents who cherish it as a major component of Turkish sociopolitics.

3. Obviously, there are and there will always be divisions in society and politics. Indeed, there should be: differences in interests, expectations, priorities, and solutions are what make democracy dynamic and fruitful. The essence of democracy is the freedom of diversity and dissent within the basic framework of democracy; the freedom to express and achieve, through political organizations and individual rights, people's views and wants. Democracy is the free competition of political movements that represent different interests: a competition whose final aim is to reach an overall, dynamic synthesis in which every political force makes a contribution commensurate with its strength.

The danger lies not in this one or another that party's ideals or policies that we happen not to agree with: what is dangerous is when dichotomies —in this case the 'Islamist / secular' one— that are artificial and archaic become the principal axis for ideological polarization; when their categorizing provides the centerpiece on the political stage; and when external analyses, domestic public opinion, and the media abet them. The natural socioeconomic and political contradictions of democracies such as 'labor/capital' or 'conservative/liberal' reflect democratically healthy differences whose resolution within the 'rules' of democracy is possible. 'Islamist / secular' and similar archaic models of division stand outside this democratic framework. They are alien to democracy and democracy to them. The natural methods of democracy are incapable of resolving the polarization that they initiate and for most of the time, the advocates of such models are not much sensitive about democratic frameworks in any case.

Turkey's traditional foreign policy trapped itself amidst the choices of 'European/Asian' and 'West/East'. Choices that were the extensions of fundamentally flawed analyses and polarization and that were proffered to foreign policy as imperatives. Foreign policy was invested, as if it were holy writ, with the belief in the absolute necessity of having to choose one or the other and of the absolute impossibility of any synthesis or multidimensional outlook. To the

19

degree that Turkish foreign policy has been able to move away from this traditional approach and arrive at new syntheses that are in harmony with Turkey's history, culture, and realities, it has been of greater benefit to the country and to others. That is the lesson to be derived from the changes that have occurred in Turkish foreign policy between 1997-2001.

2.   Reshaping Foreign Policy

My first press conference as Foreign Minister (July 14, 1997) defined the strategy that I wanted our ministry to pursue. Several new concepts and understandings were introduced at that time. One such was the announcement of our goal of becoming a 'world state.' So too was the declaration that Turkey is both a European and an Asian country and is not obliged to make a choice between East or West; that Turkey derives her 'European' dimension from her history and culture; that membership in the European Union is a goal for Turkey but not an obsession; that contemporary Turkey has an important part to play as a 'role-model' for societies with an Islamic dimension.

We have kept to this strategic vision. Whatever success I may have had or will have in office is due to the basic —perhaps ideological— framework that I presented at that initial stage. Following my first press conference, I further developed this framework, which I defined as an "ideological and conceptual renewal of our foreign policy ".

'The Eurasian dimension' is a new element that I have introduced to our foreign policy. I believe it to be a strategic asset and I deal with it extensively. In fact, Turkey has all the strategic, historical and cultural attributes, which provide it the opportunity to play a decisive role in the emerging Eurasian reality.

The following is the text of my first press conference:

A NEW VISION FOR AN ASSERTIVE COUNTRY
I. Turkey is a country with centuries of a unique historical experience, which encompassed millions of people on three continents. She is the successor to millennia of civilizations, which thrived on her actual geography. Turkey culminated her historical

development process in the present day's modern, democratic, secular state. Her responsibility now, to herself and to others, is to be cognizant of her identity and mission and to enrich her historical attributes with contemporary attainments.

Turkey is actually poised to reconsider her historical, civilization and strategic assets; to redefine her mission and to envision her contribution to the long march of mankind towards a more humane, more prosperous, and more equitable world.

The goal of present day generations should be to carry to the 21st century a country that has confirmed her attributes of a 'world state.'

A 'world state,' positioned among the major centers of the world and representing a unique blend of civilizational assets, historical experiences and strategic attributes. A 'world state,' one that is not a sole importer of foreign science and technology but contributes as well to science and technology. One that is not a mere observer of others' success stories but has its own achievements that sometimes make them envious as well. One that consistently develops its special relations with the regions with which it shares a common history. One that, in line with Atatürk's legacy, constitutes a role model for nations with parallel cultural backgrounds.

As the Ministry of Foreign Affairs, our mission is to evaluate global dynamics correctly and to bring the contribution of foreign policy to establish Turkey's role at the highest levels possible.

II. Turkey's strategic position, emanating from her history, culture, and geographic characteristics, provides her with means, which will put in use her inherent capabilities

Turkey's history has been molded through a constant interaction, communication, cultural exchange and trade with adjacent regions. Being a global power, the Ottomans influenced substantially all major developments in their huge neighborhood. They were in turn affected by the balances and developments in the world. The foundation of the future Turkish Republic in the early 1920s was primarily based on the masterly and realistic assessment of international equilibria. What history rendered as an 'achievable goal' was identified, its strategy was devised, and its mission was accomplished.

What is incumbent upon us now is to develop the 'syntheses' that are both beneficial to our Eurasian environment (Europe and Asia) and to our own interests; to detect appropriate avenues within global and regional balances; to provide foreign policy's contribution to Turkey's security and welfare.

III. I do not find appropriate the discussions over Turkey's 'location' in the world and over her 'identity.' I reject as false the presumption that we have to make a choice between 'The West' and 'The East,' between Europe and Asia.

Turkey is already European and has been for seven centuries. She is European, as well as being Asian: this is her privilege and her asset. She does not have any concern, problem or obligation to prove to others that she is European. Turkey declared to the world that she was European as early as 1453 and has remained European ever since.

If being European is a geographical definition, Turkey's history has transpired in a vast geographical area in Europe; a significant part of today's Turkey is located on the European continent. Geography-wise, Turkey is a European country as well.

If being European is a historical definition, Turkey's history was as molded in Kosovo, Bosnia, Edirne, and Manastir or any other Turkish European center as it was in Bursa, Kayseri, Sivas, Van, or any major Turkish city in Asia.

If being European is a cultural definition, then, in spite of some points that need further improvement, Turkey is a country that shares the values of democracy, pluralism, secularism, human rights, and gender equality: all of which constitute the basis of contemporary European culture as defined by the Council of Europe.

In other words, Turkey has no problem of needing to convince others to accept its Europeanness. Turkey's European dimension does not require credentials: it is a historical, geographical, and cultural fact.

Turkey does not have to make a choice between being Asian or European: Turkey has the privilege and the uniqueness of being both Asian and European. This is the source of our historical and cultural assets, of our geo-strategic advantages.

IV. Turkey has a privilege that is bestowed upon few countries: She has the distinction of being a 'role model.'

Among the countries —with a combined population of nearly 1.5 billion— that share the Islamic tradition, Turkey is the only one with a pluralist democracy, secular practices, human rights standards, gender equality, etc. Hence it is a role model.

Presenting the 'Turkish Model' to relevant nations as a unique and positive historical experience, as a paradigm of modernization, will be one of our objectives. This, of course, is not an export item. It is an additional and significant means of cooperation, a contribution of Turkey to the Islamic world.

V. Our Ministry of Foreign Affairs will formulate the policies of the forthcoming period cognizant of Turkey's richness in history, culture and of her strategic assets.

The Ministry will oppose negative attitudes, such as xenophobia, racial and religious discrimination, terrorism, and war. It will support peace, justice, human rights, and freedoms.

The Ministry of Foreign Affairs was one of the pillars of modernization within the Ottoman state. In modern times, it has contributed significantly to the foundation and development of the Turkish Republic. It will continue to do so.

Our ministry, with its experience, determination, know-how, and professionalism and with its historical role as a modernizing factor, has the capacity to fulfill its goals.

METHODS: There are three dimensions in the organization of foreign policy:

Classical diplomacy: The main target and the basic function of the Ministry of Foreign Affairs is to bring the contribution of foreign policy to Turkey's security; to attain "peace at home, peace in the world".

Economic diplomacy: The second function of our policies will be to provide the contribution of the Ministry of Foreign Affairs to Turkey's economic growth, to her external economic and commercial relations.

Cultural diplomacy: Finally, foreign policy is the essential tool to strengthen the image of our country in the world, to promote its culture and people, to enhance its prestige. 'Turkic languages' are expected to become the mother tongue of nearly 200 million people by the end of 21st century. This will provide for enhanced cultural cooperation and communication throughout a vast geography.

Focusing on these three concepts, we will develop our relations with the relevant institutions of our security and economy, labor unions, relevant associations, public and private entrepreneurial circles, the press, and the cultural and intellectual world. We will carefully take into consideration their experience, criticisms, and suggestions.

In the days following the press conference, I also announced a number of other pillars of the foreign policy that we would be following:

• Turkey's goal in the first decade of the 21st century is not just to become a member of the European Union but also to play a determining role at the heart of Eurasia; Turkey's membership in the European Union is a goal but not an obsession.

• Turkey's historical geography has a central place in its foreign policy;

• It is vital to redefine the concept of 'Western' and to eliminate from our relations with the West all the errors, complexes, and abstractions of the past.

• Historical and cultural dimensions will be introduced to our foreign policy;

• Contemporary Turkey is the simultaneous representative of seven centuries of Ottoman history and of the Republican revolution.

EUROPEAN UNION MEMBERSHIP: I consider EU membership for Turkey as a major goal but not an obsession. Full membership in the European Union is what we want Turkey to achieve. On our part, we shall exert every effort to gain that right as soon as possible. We shall keep a watchful eye on the European Union to ensure that it fulfills its political and financial commitments to Turkey. As the ministry, we are engaged in very intensive effort to realize our membership in the European Union. We shall continue to do so with increased diligence. Nevertheless, Turkey is not about to wait for an indefinite time.

Turkey will continue to accomplish the steps required for EU accession, while projecting her political and economic dynamism to every corner of the globe.

FOREIGN ECONOMIC RELATIONS: As economic cooperation and interaction between countries intensify, the causes for tension are reduced and the dynamics of peace grow stronger. I consider the contribution of foreign policy to Turkey's economic growth and trade development as essential. In line with this approach, we will assign special tasks to our missions abroad. They will function as an extension of our economy. Instructions are already being sent to our missions abroad.

As the Turkish economy has strengthened, the scope of its operations in the world expanded. Our ministry will improve the political infrastructure of economic relationships. We will explore new economic horizons, not to replace existing relations and preferences but to complement and diversify them. On the other hand, transporting Caspian oil and natural gas through Turkey is one of our primary objectives. This will not only provide safe transport for all interested parties but also will also serve our economic interests and satisfy our environmental concerns as well. Safeguarding the security of the Turkish straits is an integral part of this strategy.

THE CONCEPT OF THE 'WEST' IN TURKEY: A crucial element of reshaping Turkey's foreign policy is to explore the conceptual understanding of the 'West' and to determine its significance and function in Turkey.

The 'West' and 'Europe' are realities that Turkey has had to contend with for seven centuries. Turkey's historical development has been a never-ending interaction with the West, or to be more exact, with Europe. Our history with Europe has, to a large extent, been molded in relationships that have, for the most part, been ones of diametrical opposition with occasional bouts of compatibility. And it is not just a matter of the interaction with the West's peoples and with their armies and governments: there is also the influence of Western concepts and the occasional need to come to terms with them. Recent history also shows us that those who struggle against Western Imperialism end up, after emerging from the battlefield, advocating a model inspired by Western European institutions, which they adopt as the foundations for their own renewal. One of Turkey's interesting —and I would say positive— characteristics is that once a fight is over, Turks don't consider their former enemy as a permanent one. Nor they have any phobias about adopting aspects of their one-time enemies' systems to their own. This is probably an extension of our historical pragmatism.

25

ON BEING 'EUROPEAN': Throughout our history, the concepts, symbols, and practices of the 'West' and of 'Westernization' have sometimes been ideals and goals to attain, sometimes adversaries to overcome or ills to avoid. In a sense, though to a much lesser degree, they remain so even today. The renewal of Turkish foreign policy demands first of all that we correctly define the concept of the 'West' and set it in a proper perspective. This, in a sense, is where the accounts need to be settled. Indeed at this very moment, we are going through a new phase of this process: for, according to the expectations of some, we are going to join the European Union and thus will we 'become European.'

Are we really going to become European? Could it be that the goal of 'becoming European' is the product of an interpretation of history that is based on fallacies and thus of an approach that leads Turkey into error? Could it be an unwittingly accepted historical understanding that deprives Turkey of her assets and, therefore, diminishes her standing? Historical fallacies such as 'Turkey, to aspire to be European' will go on causing harm so long as they remain fallacies thought to be valid. Myopia along the historical dimension muddles our vision of the present. Is Turkey really going to become European by joining the European Union?

Or could it be instead a case of a country that is in fact already European by virtue of her geography, history, and her contemporary attributes, joining a group constituted by a few others, which also happen, like her, to be European?

There is a world of difference between these two perceptions: both in their substance and in their consequences.

Historically, those who governed Turkey —I am thinking particularly of Sultan Mehmed II Fatih and his successors— certainly always thought of themselves as European. Indeed Mehmed II styled himself both as 'Sultan of Islam' and as 'Caesar and Emperor of Rome,' the latter being a title directly inherited from the Byzantine emperors, and he included this title on the coins and medals struck in his name. 'Europeaness' and 'European culture' are much more a constellation of values nowadays than geographic attributes. Modern Turkey is most certainly a part of that.

The West's assessment of Turkey is closely linked to Turkey's own self-definition. For far too long, Turkey's own views

26

and understandings of herself have misled the West in its assessments. We've become a country that deifies the West and thus becomes neurotic about it. Here, the psychological dimension is particularly relevant: 'The West is superior to us,' 'The West is better than we are,' 'We're no good,' etc. Turkey conditioned herself to believe this nonsense. At the same time, and again for far too long, Turkey has segregated her present from her past. Because of this compartmentalizing, which couples the previous assertion on how inferior Turkey is to the West, we were strongly overcome by inferiority complexes that affirm that 'Our history is deplorable,' 'We're historically backwards'. The end-result of all these self-inflicted complexes was a longing 'to copy the West and get it right and thus be numbered among the Europeans'. This was understandablycoupled with alternating fits of immoderate reactions to and unjustified accusations against the West. Out of this commotion emerged a perception of the 'West' that translated itself into a 'love / hate' relationship.

Turkey's foreign policy has been seriously afflicted by all these attitudes. Others defined Turkey according to terms of reference that Turkey herself had put in place. They thus formulated their policies on false presumptions that Turkey herself declared on her character, history, culture, aspirations: 'becoming European,' 'getting Europe to accept us,' etc. Europe was understandably misled by the unfounded discourse that Turkey had about herself.

What the foreign ministry today is striving to contribute to Turkey through the medium of foreign policy is to purge the country's foreign relations of all their misperceptions and misconceptions. Its aim is to give a correct picture of Turkey not merely to foreign observers but to the Turkish people as well.

ON MEMORY AND CONSCIOUSNESS: What played a key role as well in delaying the much-needed renewal of Turkish foreign policy was an overall shortage of memory. It is likely that there is no other country that derives as little support from its own historical assets as Turkey manages to do. In the initial phase of the republic, there were understandable and even justifiable reasons for a temporary policy of disengaging the present from the past: for a transitional and intentional loss of memory in other words. But there is no such reason for this situation to persist in the present day.

27

Turkey is a society that pulled itself into the modern world through revolution. There is a peculiar —indeed universal, and in a sense inevitable— logic to revolutions: in order to create the future it is necessary to break with the past. Turkey's republican revolution necessarily and naturally followed this path. The experiences and distinctive assets provided by history were shunned in order to shape a new order. That is the reason for the consistent efforts during the early republican period to isolate Turkey from her past and to define the past in terms of a limited time frame and a narrow cultural scope. Given the compelling circumstances of the social and national renewal that was the foundation for the republican revolution, this was a rational choice.

What happened however was that this break with the past was perpetuated long after any such policy ceased to be either a revolutionary necessity or an intelligible choice, even after the republic had become an acknowledged and accepted fact of life. The prevailing view that took hold was that Turkey was a country that had no historical depth, that lacked a unique cultural identity, and that had never, in its history, been a 'European power.' It was, in other words, a Johnny-come-lately peering in from beyond the European pale.

Such misguided attitudes naturally hamper Turkey's ability to function at every conceivable level. They also facilitate and mediate the process whereby Turkey is distanced from and even deprived of any historical / cultural priorities that she might take advantage of in her foreign relations. Equally natural is the pursuit, by some for their own ulterior motives, of policies aimed at encouraging Turkey to forget both her own past and the trump cards that her past has dealt her. The upshot is that a society that made it clear to the world already in the 14th century that it was a European power ended up in a tragicomic situation in which it has to struggle to be acknowledged as European. This abnormality is what I believe we have at least partially remedied by our renewal of the country's foreign policy.

Turkey today is coming to the realization that to reconcile oneself with history and derive strength from historical and cultural assets is no longer 'reactionary.' It is, on the contrary, a crucial element of holding one's own in today's world. For a society to take an interest in its own history is tantamount to its taking an interest in its own future. Studying history contributes to a better assessment of both the present and the future. As in the issue of 'Europeanness,' it is the sure method to avoid frivolous analyses and approaches.

The present is more than just 'today:' it needs to be seen and understood in its historical context. Doing so will fortify Turkey's efforts to renew herself and will also add weight and strength to her mission and role at the international level.

ON THE WESTERN MODEL: Historically for Turkey, the concept of 'West' or 'Europe' has always incorporated elements that Turkish society opposes as well as those that it cherishes. After the 18th century however, the concept acquired a new dimension: that of a 'model' for Turkey's progressive elements. Unfortunately this opened the door to a polarization between those who were for and against the West. The model paved as well the path to the weaving of a tissue of illusory 'benefits' and equally illusory 'evils' around the opposing perceptions of the West,' and —ultimately— to conceptual pandemonium.

In order to design Turkish foreign policy and foreign relations in the 21st century, it is essential to accurately identify what the symbolic meaning of the 'West' is for Turkey and to determine what place the 'West' should have in the model that Turkey has set for herself.

Elevating Turkey "to the level of contemporary civilization" is a specific challenge in Turkish history laid down by Atatürk himself. The concept summed up in the phrase "contemporary civilization", which is often and wrongly misunderstood as 'Westernization,' has been generally misinterpreted. What the progressive elements of the Ottoman period — the Young Ottomans and the Young Turks— and what the leaders of the War of Independence and the founders of the republic understood by the phrase "contemporary civilization," was never properly clarified.

"Contemporary civilization" was certainly not 'the West and nothing but the West,' nor was it 'the West and everything that it incorporates.' To assert such a thing would be doing a grave disservice not only to the progressive movements of both empire and republic but also to all those who have aspired to share in progress and change. The founders of the republic most certainly were not thinking of the European Imperialism and injustices with which they were intimately familiar when they used the phrase "contemporary civilization".

29

While many of the basic criteria of contemporary civilization are to be found in the West, they exist outside the West as well. This leads to the question: What features and criteria does the West bring to the definition of "contemporary civilization?" The West is, in a very real sense, the principal benchmark by which "contemporary civilization" is measured. It has earned that status because of the sensitivity that it is today able to display towards human rights, because it has bound human relations to principles of personal liberty and mutual respect, because it created legal and political infrastructures and mechanisms that can make these ideals a reality, and because of its special attention to rationalism and productivity.

A West which ignores these values and advances others in their place, which commits Vietnams, which abets massacres in innocent countries, which displays racism and xenophobia, or which applies double standards is of course still "the West": but it is not "contemporary civilization".

ON 'BECOMING' WESTERN: There is a need to question Turkey's assessments of the West and a need to reevaluate the Western —or European— issue from a historical perspective as well. This will contribute to Turkey's positive relations with the West and to a correct self-definition. The historically and culturally non-Western societies that have develop a healthy conceptual relationship with the West have a common trait: they exploit the distinctive features of their existing identities, using them as a basis for the development of their 'modern' characteristics; they most certainly do not do it by totally replacing their historical / cultural identities.

A society manifestly does not have to be in the west in order to be defined as 'modern'. Similarly, neither being Western nor even being a member of the European Union is a prerequisite for economic or social development. The cultural language that one speaks may be different; historically inherited symbols and communally recognized heroes and settings may be different; one may, in a word, be different. But those differences don't make it necessary to forgo the values such as democracy, individual freedoms, secularism and rationalism that are the symbols of Western —or, more accurately, of universal— civilization. What makes these values easier for one to absorb, however, is a consciousness of one's

30

own cultural assets and inherent values. In other words, it is not a matter of 'becoming Western' (a hollow and meaningless expression if ever there was one) but rather one of accepting a range of values and approaches that Western civilization has contributed and that are superior because of their universal validity. To share in and to contribute to human civilization, one must first be one's own self.

There is a common misapprehension that one needs to avoid: if Turkey is to be part of the European Union and be respected in her relations with Europe, it won't be because Turkey, for example, 'resembles the Belgians' or has 'become Italian'. Quite the contrary: Turkey's membership should be desirable for the EU precisely because she has identity and historical / cultural dimensions that are different from those of Western Europe, and, because these differences can bring additional dynamism to Europe and make it easier for Europe to further broaden its horizons and range of experiences. What possible additional contribution could a Turkey whose cultural identity suggests that of Portugal, or whose historical dimension is that of Luxembourg, make to Europe? To put it another way, the problem is the following: if one ignores its own cultural language, its own cultural symbols, and its own cultural background because it wishes to join a different cultural discourse, it is going to be that much more difficult to share in that discourse. One loses not only one's own originality but also the very things that make one attractive to others.

Obviously, none of this should be taken as an excuse for cultural chauvinism: it is instead an argument that we need to seek and find within ourselves what we can contribute that can be of universal value. When talking about the European Union for example, we should be asking ourselves questions like 'What genuine contributions are we to make to Europe's great cultural assets, to its great intellectual syntheses, to its intellectual quests?' If all we think about is what we will gain from this relationship, then we will have to be content with the absolute minimum.

Imagine if you will a Turkey vibrantly aware of her history and culture rather than dimly oblivious to it, channeling the power and virtues of her genuine identity into universal cultural syntheses... That is where the problem lies: the problem is not a 'Western question', it's a 'Turkish question'. Its causes are in Turkey. And so are its solutions.

31

ON THE CONSEQUENCES OF BEING A 'FRONTIER OUTPOST':
After the Second World War, Turkey acquired an international
function that ceased to have validity when the Soviet Union broke up
nearly half a century later. As a result of this change, there was also
a qualitative change in Turkey's interaction with the West.

After 1950, all of Turkey's institutional and political attentions
were focused on a specific mission, which had been given to Turkey
and with which Turkey identified. That mission was to be the West's
—NATO's-'frontier outpost', guarding the West's frontiers against the
Soviet threat and keeping an eye on dangers that might emerge on the
alliance's southeastern flank. Turkcy's political and institutional
apparatus and its development were shaped in line with and
according to the dictates of this fundamental mission.

When one looks at Turkey's system of government, political
structure, dominant ideology, values, and concepts from the 1950s
onward, a common denominator becomes obvious: the overall setup
—and each and every element of it— is an extension of the
particular mission of being the West's frontier outpost. Our penal
code, our view of the world, our limited version of democracy, our
prohibitions, our politics, our political parties, our foreign policy, and
even our fears and our mental landscapes were colored by a view —
by an acknowledgement— that 'We are the West's frontier outpost.
This is our mission. Turkey is the West's stronghold against the
Soviets.' And all of Turkey's attributes were developed accordingly.

In nearly all of Western Europe, the years after the Second
World War were a period during which the partisans of freedom and
democracy gained increasing momentum and support: a process that
was seriously retarded in Turkey, mainly because of the will of her
ruling elite and of the exigencies of her particular international
mission. There were concerns that the existence of even mildly
democratic freedoms could lead to a clamor for more and also to
unseemly arguments over the advisability of the mission and thus
impair its effectiveness. It is a matter of record that, for as long as the
Cold War went on, those in Turkey who championed Western-style
democracy, freedom, and politics, or criticized NATO or the United
States were accused of being 'Soviet stooges' and 'Communist
sympathizers' and that more than a few of them were tried, found
guilty, and imprisoned.

ON THE BREAKING OF THE MANTRA: By the end of the 1980s, the process that broke up the Soviet empire also reduced Turkey's geopolitical value. That is an event of crucial importance in understanding not only where Turkey stands today but also what Turkish foreign policy should be. During the Cold War, when Turkey's friends and enemies wore conveniently recognizable labels, the country had an acknowledged function and a 'traditional' foreign policy and it enjoyed a position of no little importance. Then suddenly something changed and with it, Turkey's world collapsed: the reason for the existence of the country's accepted function as a frontier outpost no longer was there and so, it seemed, Turkey's "external value" suffered in kind.

Then Turkey began noticing that she was increasingly becoming a target of criticism. People and institutions, which, in the past, would never have said anything negative about Turkey or taken actions detrimental to her interests, were suddenly sporting altogether different colors. During the Cold War for example, it would have been inconceivable for any of Turkey's neighbors to challenge the United States and NATO's beloved and vital ally. Furthermore, none would have dared to harbor and nurture terrorists to be unleashed upon her. When the Soviet Union broke up and Turkey's basic function of being the West's frontier outpost became meaningless, the value of Turkey's coin among its allies was seriously diminished and one after another our neighbors began behaving in the most uncommon and disconcerting ways. The most striking instances of this change are to be seen in the examples of Syria and Greece, both of which became principal supporters of separatist terrorism in Turkey.

Another manifestation of this change can be seen in the West's perception of Turkey's democratic credentials. No democracy is perfect and there are certain aspects of Turkey's democracy that I personally criticize. Could it be that these shortcomings didn't exist in the old days when Turkey still had value as a frontier outpost? They most certainly did. If anything they were much worse and even more ingrained. The picture of human rights in Turkey during the 1940s, 1950s, 1960s, 1970s, and even the 1980s cannot even begin to compare with what it is in post Cold War Turkey. During the Cold War, conditions on this front in Turkey were incomparably bleaker. But

33

somehow they never became a subject of attention at the international level. Certainly the American, French, or British governments never made them an issue; neither did most other governments. In fact, in the early 1980s, a time when democratic rights in Turkey were probably more violated than ever and democracy itself was put on the back burner for several years, even the most respected organs of the West's so wonderfully free press managed to promote Turkey as 'a model country' which was held up as a model for others tofollow. Just consider Turkey's image at this time: the military had stepped in; political parties and politicians were banned; but the West saw Turkey as a country on the right path and encouraged it as such. Because Turkey was performing a function vitally important to the West's security interests at the time, the notion of criticizing Turkey for its record on democracy and freedom seems not to have entered anyone's agenda. Because of Turkey's status as a bulwark against the Soviet threat, such problems were blithely ignored.

But when Turkey's strategic value declined and its traditional function expired, Western diplomats and public opinion suddenly began making noises about 'democracy' and 'human rights'. Even our 'closest ally' — the US — began leveling increasingly heavy criticisms against Turkey. The Council of Europe turned Turkey into a target for taking pot-shots at. At a time when Turkey was actually making a progress towards more democracy, the same West that had once regarded all the country's faults as normal had suddenly mutated into evangelists of human rights and democracy-at least where Turkey was concerned.

With the end of the Cold War as we approached the 1990s, Turkey's forty-year-old 'mantra' was broken:

Confronted by this sudden change, Turkey's first reaction was one of shock. With their concepts of right and wrong, friend and foe in confusion, people began asking questions like 'What's going to become of us?' The proliferation of unknowns provoked anxiety. There were strong feelings of alienation and insecurity at both the individual and the societal level.

Unjustifiable and wrong as they might be, constitutionally imposed prohibitions, their expression in counter-terrorism laws and intellectual crimes, restrictions on political and trade union activity, and all the other blemishes on its democracy at least had a certain

34

logic, a 'rational' to them when Turkey was a cold war outpost. Turkey had based all its 'strategic value', all its 'external value', foreign policy, and all its *raison d'etre* on global balances that were now becoming obsolete.

With the end of the Cold War, Turkey's traditional internal and external balances, structures, and attitudes were left without anything to prop them up. As the Berlin Wall came down bringing the world it represented with it and as a new world order was being formed, Turkey suddenly found herself in a void. That was because she had fallen into a kind of complacency: in the past era, Turkey knew that if anyone ventured to do anything nasty, America would tell them to get back into line. Western European allies would watch out for their NATO partner. But now the mantra to which Turkey had become accustomed was broken. The country was caught unprepared for the emerging world and its new conditions. It was almost impossible for a country whose legal, political, and values systems were reflections of its long established role to acquire a function in this new world.

With the end of this era, the problems and the solutions confronting Turkey were daunting. The task she faced was how to reform a democracy, a legal system, economic habits, political institutions, a clumsy way of governing, and relations with Western Europe and with the world —all of which had been tailored under the conditions of a world that no longer existed-in light of the changing demands of a new world.

While it is too early yet to make a comprehensive assessment of the situation, a tentative one is possible. The post Cold War period in which Turkey's geostrategic value was reduced did not last as long as many anticipated. The reason was that there were quite a few external factors making it possible for Turkey to acquire for herself a function that was as important as and more benign than the one she had had. After a spate in limbo during which it looked as if Turkey had lost her significance, the country's importance and external value rose again mainly because of global strategic changes: changes that were closely linked to the demise of the Soviet empire and the information revolution. Unlike during the Cold War, when Turkey's function allowed the country's democratic and political shortcomings to be glossed over, the new process in a sense provided Turkey with a much better opportunity to deal with these flaws.

ON TURKEY'S RAISING VALUE IN THE WEST'S EQUATION: Turkey's economic, political, and strategic relevance under the world's changing conditions have been undergoing a reassessment in many think-tanks. According to these new assessments, Turkey's importance waned following the end of the Cold War, but then geostrategic conditions began to change and Turkey began to acquire new dynamics. As a result, Turkey's 'external value' rose. There were three main reasons for this:

1. Quite a few of the 'new' or 'recently independent' countries that appeared in the geography of the former Soviet empire in the Balkans, the Caucasus, and Central Asia were those with which Turkey has historic and cultural ties. This provided Turkey with an opportunity and a relative advantage and it is a matter of record that Turkey has since developed strong political and economic relations with the great majority of these nations. In nearly all these countries, Turkey ranks either first, second, or third in terms of foreign trade, foreign investment, or infrastructure development. The discovery of energy resources in areas with which Turkey has historical and/or cultural affinities (especially in the Caspian basin and Central Asia) further increased Turkey's strategic value.

Another important factor is to be seen in Turkey's developing military ties with these new countries and in the fact that Turkey commands the biggest military force in the region extending from the Balkans to the Caucasus and Central Asia. This is not just having more artillery and tanks than anyone else: Turkish military officers are providing training in nearly thirty countries and those of the former Soviet realm make up an important number of them. Furthermore, several of these countries' own military officers and cadets are being trained in Turkey's military academies. In some instances, officers who have been trained in Turkey already make up a significant part of the chain of command. Turkey's role in the militaryestablishments of the new Balkan countries and in the Caucasus is strong. In 2000, security cooperation agreements were concluded with a number of Central Asian republics and joint mechanisms have been developed.

Turkey's political, economic, and military role in the former Soviet territories has already heightened the country's geostrategic importance. In the 21st century, Turkey will continue to be a decisive factor in this part of the world.

2. Turkey launched a proactive foreign policy that sought to make the strategic changes and the emerging economic environment work to her advantage. The renovated foreign policy we initiated in 1997 systematically mobilized Turkey's historical and cultural assets, putting them to work to nourish economic and political relations. The result was a growing influence in the Middle East and other Islamic countries, as well as in the Balkans and the former Soviet Central Asia.

In all of these areas, Turkey has found greater scope for action the more she divorced herself from the prejudices, misconceptions, and mostly psychological limits that prevented her from playing an influential role in the past. The more she pursued this new and correct line of approach, the stronger Turkey's strategic position became and the more she counted in global balances.

3. The third reason for the increase in Turkey's value on the international stage was the transformation of the Turkish economy into one of the biggest and most dynamic in a huge region extending from the Balkans to the Caucasus and Central Asia and from North Africa to the Middle East.

In 1997 the country sustained a political crisis and a change in government in the wake of protracted tensions and doubts over whether the existing regime should be allowed to survive or not. Despite all of this —and this was the surprise— the national economy posted real growth measured as 7% of GNP that year. In 1998, some measures were taken to reduce, even if only by a small amount, the grotesque inflation from which the country has been suffering for years, and yet the Turkish economy grew by nearly 6%. 1999 was indeed a bad year but that can realistically be blamed on the disastrous Marmara earthquakes. In 2000, the country got its inflation down from 64% to 34% while implementing an IMF-blessed stabilization program and still the economy grew by 6%. It should be added that these results, especially those in 1997 and 1998, were achieved at a time when Russia, Turkey's second biggest trading partner, was going through its own economic and financial meltdown.

Turkey's procrastination in making much-needed economic and administrative reforms resulted in a severe financial crisis in early 2001. While this was a blow to short-term expectations, the strong industrial infrastructure provided expectations for an overall recovery.

37

Where the Turkish economy comes up short is in the fact that the country doesn't produce enough of its own technology and also in the unfair distribution of the benefits of its economy. The Turkish economy is certainly in need of rationalization and greater productivity and it also needs to learn how to combine efficiency with social justice; but it's an extremely dynamic economy. Moreover —at around two hundred billion dollars GNP— it's also a big one. When the 'unregistered' economy is factored in, as economists are in the habit of doing, the result is a real figure of around three hundred billion.

At this point I want to digress briefly to touch upon Turkey's position in the 21st century in light of some of the parameters drawn by the Organization for Economic Cooperation and Development (OECD) for the years 2010-2020. I'm quoting them from a book, Turkey & The World: 2010 - 2020 prepared by Orhan Guvenen and Yaman Baskut with the help of experts from the Turkish Foreign Ministry and from the State Planning Organization.

According to the OECD, the principal factors that will shape the world in the 21st century are population, technological development and services, the impact of the global economy's developmental potential, environmental issues, the exploitation of natural resources (especially water), and changes that take place in the development of energy resources, transportation, and consumption. The OECD developed a model taking these factors and countries' average annual growth rates for the last 22 years into account in order to take a snapshot of the future based on the assumption that those growth rates would continue for the next two decades. Looking at Turkey in the first twenty years of the 21st century, this is what the OECD sees:

- In 2010, Turkey will be the second most populous country in Europe; in 2020 it will be the most populous, with 83 million ranking ahead of Germany at 76 million and of France, Italy, and Britain at about 60 million each.
- In the categories of technological progress, Turkey will still be weak in research and development, making rapid progress in exploiting computer technology, and highly advanced in modern business management techniques.
- In the area of transportation, Turkey will be a key country. She will be an active participant in five of the ten top-priority projects that will be keeping Europe busy in the 21st century (Germany/Middle East, East/West, Balkans/Turkey projects).

Other projects in which she will be a player include highways and railways between Europe and the Caucasus/Asia, the extension of the TEM system into the Middle East, and the extension of the Black Sea highway into the Caucasus. In a sense, all of Europe's main links with the east will be passing through Turkey.

- On the economic front, there are two scenarios. The first is that global conditions will be "middling"; the second is that they will be "favorable". In the "middling" scenario, which is taken to mean that the global conditions prevailing over the last 22 years will be sustained, the average rate of annual growth among all OECD countries will be 2.3% in 2000-2010 but Turkey's will be 3.8%. In the 2010-2020 period, the OECD average will be 2.6% and Turkey's average 4.9%.
- In the "favorable" scenario on the other hand, the OECD average is still a low 2.6% in 2000-2010 but Turkey's rises to 4.9%; and in 2010-2020, the OECD average edges up to 3% while Turkey's soars to 6.2%.
- One of the most important indicators of modern economies is "purchasing power parity": a way of comparing currency conversion rates that eliminates the differences in price levels between countries. As calculated today, Turkey's PPP is only a third of the OECD average. This gap is expected to close substantially by 2010. By 2020, Turkey should just about reach the OECD average: the OECD averages in 2010 and 2020 are USD 26,000 and USD 31,500 respectively. By the latter year, Turkey's PPP is expected to be USD 30,500. Now consider that figure again in light of a projected population of 83 million and one can see the signals of one of Europe's biggest economic players. (Even at its present, Turkey ranks 17th in the world, according to the World Bank.)
- By 2020, Turkey's foreign trade should be ten times what it is today. To achieve that, the country's trade needs to grow by around 10% a year. Considering that Turkey's export trade in goods and services increased an average of 10.8% a year in 1987-1997, this is not an unreasonable expectation.

As Mark Parris, former US ambassador to Ankara, said in 1998, Turkey is destined to be not just an economic force in Europe and its own region but also to be a world-class player in the global economy of the 21st century.

39

The profile that emerges of Turkey in the 21st century is that of a country taking good advantage of the world's changing balances: a country whose growing economy and greater political awareness increasingly advance its international position.

And that is why Turkey's geostrategic value is growing.

TURKEY AND THE WEST: In assessing the interaction of Turkey and the West and relations with the European Union, there is one more issue to be addressed: it's true that the majority of Europeans don't approach the subject from the standpoint of 'Islam vs. Christianity'. But it's also true that many do not consider Turkey as 'one of them' either. On the historical level, there is an important reason for this: for centuries, Europe west of Turkey considered Turkey as the main threat to its own civilization, beliefs, and attitudes. Some of the effects of this historical conditioning still survive today. Beyond that however, there is also an exaggerated, distorted image of Turkey which is widespread in Western Europe and from which anti-Turkish, anti-Muslim and xenophobic movements or fascist parties draw some of their strength. These are simply facts of life in Europe today. Turkey certainly has acted slowly on some issues related to democracy and human rights; but these shortcomings are exaggerated with an attitude that is little short of hostile. This in turn is used as grist for propaganda mills. Some spur such unjustified propaganda because of perceived conflict between Turkey and their own interests; others may simply be following suit for no particular reason.

Be that as it may, we must acknowledge that European public opinion does not yet perceive Turkey as a genuine element of European unity. We ourselves need to make a greater effort if this is not to remain the case; but Western Europe needs to change as well.

3.   Turkey Today and Tomorrow: Shortcomings and Opportunities

Is Turkey on the way back to being the "Sick Man of Europe" as she was perceived in the 19th century and as some would like to see her?

ON SHORTCOMINGS AND FLAWS: Turkey has never at any time in her long history been anyone's colony. How then can one explain 'the colonial mentality' that bedevils so many, especially those in some political, business and media circles? Is Turkey a hapless traveler headed for the narrow horizon she tailored for herself? Is she doomed to ingratiate through a discourse she feels obliged to follow?

This mentality takes many forms. You see it in warnings to the effect of 'Mind your step and don't displease your betters'. Those who insist on seeing Turkey in the second league or who declare that Turkey is incapable of any influence, purpose, or achievement, display the same mentality. This attitude prevails in Turkey's lack of self-confidence, her inability to recognize opportunities and in a chronic effort to appear docile and humble.

Can inadequacies that have persisted for so long, really be overcome? For example, will the foot-dragging over governing the country in line with rational principles end? Will Turkey's traditional organizational models and attitudes be purged of their shortcomings, be it in government, or in the economy, or in politics? Will serious-mindedness be inculcated in a society that willingly makes exceptions to its own rules, thus opening the door to different sets of standards being applied to different people? Will management and control systems that belong to an era when things were so much simpler be eliminated to cope with the complex demands of today? Will the empowered but also responsible citizens that the modern world requires be encouraged and supported?

Societies that fail to turn politics into a race in which different interest groups contend by producing solutions, end up not with solutions but with empty words and demagogy. An argumentative style comes to dominate politics in which some parties appear to function not as solution finders but as obstacles to solutions. As we set out, we must speed up the fight for equality, provide all children and youths with equal opportunities, and combine values such as rationalism and productivity with those of social solidarity and justice. We must quickly mend the flaws and shortcomings in our democracy and realize that development is not just a heap of numbers and that real progress in a society involves art, culture, and a respect for nature and the environment as well.

Every aspect of the human horizon is expanding: from the extension of liberties to the protection of the environment; from social equality to the encouragement of diversity and participation. These changes are going to make the 21st century an age of democracy and human rights. At a time when societies are going to be judged on the basis of such criteria as these, forcing Turkey to number among the 'disabled' would be the greatest injustice one could do to the country.

Turkey must not shy away from the great challenges posed by its past and by its present. Outdated attitudes and ineffective governmental / political mechanisms must not delay Turkey's progress on the international plane.

ON ASSETS AND SOLUTIONS: Do the stumbling blocks and shortcomings mentioned above give the complete picture? Are they all that Turkey can be?

Or could Turkey, as a country whose economy for years has ranked as the fastest growing in the OECD, whose 29 members include the world's richest economies and generate three-quarters of the world's wealth, be one of the stars of the 2000s? This is a Turkey on the threshold of resolving the nightmare of terrorism and of finding the resources she needs to finance the completion of the Southeast Anatolia Project. A Turkey weaving a new and complex web of diplomatic and economic relations with the Far East, with Africa, with the Balkans, with her Middle Eastern neighbors, with America, with Western Europe, with Russia, with the Caucasus and with Central Asia ...

Turkey embarks upon the 21st century with a new sense of her global mission. Turkey's function as a 'bridge' to which we historically and justifiably attached so much importance will become a thing of the past in the 2000s: Turkey is moving away from being simply a 'transit corridor' or a 'bridge over which Asia and Europe trade with one another and move their goods'. Instead, Turkey in the 2000s will become increasingly more a 'terminus' and a 'destination' country.

In other words, Turkey's basic function ceases to be that of transporting or delivering energy, raw materials, and goods after receiving them from east and west. She becomes more and more a country that consumes, processes and with her added value, exports such inputs.

42

The 21st century began by giving signals that a large part of Caspian-origin energy will be processed in Turkey, consumed in Turkey, and delivered to the West through Turkey. The eastern Mediterranean coast of Turkey, with the existing Kirkuk-Yumurtalik and the prospective Baku-Ceyhan links, will provide a major energy terminal and outlet for Middle Eastern, Central Asian, and Caspian oil. These developments, coupled with peace and stability in the region, will provide Turkey with a role as a world-class state situated on strategic crossroads.

If Turkey takes proper advantage of the years ahead; if she clearly identifies her goals, sets out with policies that have philosophical and ideological depth, and makes courageous choices, then the distance she must travel will certainly be shorter than what is anticipated.

Conditions and realities are changing in Turkey and around the world. Continent-spanning new geostrategic balances are emerging. In this new age, information and communications technologies make it possible to compress into a few years developments that it took others centuries to discover and realize. This is a confluence of factors, which, if properly understood and insightfully exploited, will impart tremendous momentum to Turkey. Turkey is the representative of a historical experience that is centuries —indeed, millennia— old; of a geography that has given birth to civilizations; of a republican revolution that serves as a paradigm of modernization for oppressed nations. As Turkish society becomes more politically and historically aware, and as her economy develops, she will see ever-expanding horizons in front of her.

Turkey's influence already extends over a broad region. Turkish society and foreign policy today have finally begun to sense and even to understand what an immense advantage it is to share a common history with twenty-plus independent countries and their peoples. Also, how cultural and confessional affinities add impetus to every sphere of endeavor from economics to the arts. Furthermore, that she is uniquely poised to serve as a genuine model for modernization in societies with Islamic traditions, and finally, that there is great benefit to be had in discarding outmoded complexes into the trash can of history and enjoying the privilege of being both European and Asian.

We are at a juncture in time when these realities are being related, debated and their value reassessed. Through a very dynamic process of self-questioning, Turkey is renewing her democracy, economy and her foreign policy. With the redefining of her foreign policy since 1997, Turkey is now able to stand out in the international arena as a genuine and influential actor, as a player with an identity that is unique and strong. Within this promising environment, the dynamics of Turkey's aspiration to be a Eurasian power center are taking shape. Eurasia is the union of Europe and Asia, two continents that are becoming increasingly more interdependent and complementary in the new realities of globalization and technology. Eurasia will be the powerhouse of global development in the 21st century thanks to its growing energy resources and to the rapid growth in trade opportunities.

In this process, Turkey ceases to be a suburb or an outpost of Europe. Turkey of course is European and has been so for the last seven hundred years. But her horizons are not limited to that. Standing at the beginning of the 21st century, Turkey is confronted by two great goals that are equally important: the first is to become a member of the European Union; the second is to become a decisive center in a Eurasia that is no longer just a geographical concept but is on the way to becoming an economic, social, and political reality. These goals are not at all contradictory: in fact, they complement and reinforce one another. They are goals which, conscious of her identity, Turkey can achieve using her historical/cultural dimension as an axis of her development. In the vast geography extending from the Balkans to North Africa, the Caucasus, Central Asia, and the Middle East, Turkey has the most vigorous economy, the strongest army, and —notwithstanding some shortcomings— one of the few deeply-rooted democracies.

Turkey will achieve her twin goals to the extent that we acknowledge the 21st century as an age of democracy, human rights, development, and social justice. These will be the fundamental criteria by which success and progress are measured. To the extent that we develop rationalism, productivity, and social justice as elements that complement one another and to the degree that we mobilize all the advantages that history, culture, and economics bestow upon Turkey, these goals will become more attainable.

44

ON THE MERITS OF OVERRIDING TRADITIONAL POLICIES: Turkey's redefined foreign policy, formulated out of a will to make a fresh start and to renew, has yielded positive results in a remarkably short time. A few examples are in order here:

Through the renewal of her foreign policy, Turkey has made more progress in the direction of the European Union during the last four years than she achieved in the previous four decades. Let me make this point clear because it is important: the EU's acknowledgement of Turkey's candidacy for full membership at the Helsinki summit was no coincidence. It was a direct outcome of foreign policy moves that Turkey has made since 1997. A key element of our foreign policy was that EU membership was not something that Turkey was obsessed with. Turkey made it clear that she rejected the vague position that had been proposed for her at the Luxembourg summit (1997) and in effect put on hold political dialogue on sensitive issues.

On the other hand, probably for the first time, the EU was reminded of the huge strategic advantages that Turkish accession would provide the organization. There were occasions where it was pointed out that Turkey's historical links were unique and that through Turkey, the EU would have access to different civilizations, cultures, geographies and opportunities. In addition, because of Turkey's candidacy and membership, the communal boundaries of the EU would be moved east of Turkey from their present location in the Balkans and the Aegean. In a statement that he made after the acknowledgement of Turkey's candidacy at Helsinki, Gunter Verheaugen, the commissioner responsible for expansion of the European Commission, made it clear that these considerations were instrumental in the Helsinki decision.

By having freed itself of the thrall of the "friend / foe" compartmentalizing of traditional foreign policy and by convincing everybody that she seriously meant what she said, Turkey has increased her influence both as a factor of dissuasion and as a peacemaker. One immediate result was the dislodgment of the terrorist organization from Syria followed by a breaking of the logjam that stymied friendly relations with that country. The same determined approach made it possible for the Greek and Turkish foreign ministers to come together officially for the first time in over forty years and initiate a process which, for all its difficulties and its ups and downs, has been and will continue to be to the benefit of both sides (in just the first year of this rapprochement, there were increases of nearly 50 % in the two countries' bilateral trade and bilateral tourism revenues; a number of joint-security measures were introduced in the Aegean and in Thrace).

Decisiveness and self-confidence enabled Turkey to abandon the 'federation' model for Cyprus (which, in its substance, worked against Turkish interests) and led to the proposal of a new and much bolder idea, that of 'confederation'. The same decisiveness convinced both the Cypriot Greeks and Greece to forgo all their blustering and to abandon a plan to install S-300 missiles on Cyprus.

The addition of a new historical dimension to foreign policy made it possible to dispel the chill that used to plague Turkey's relations with countries lying within its historical sphere, especially in the Middle East, the Gulf, and North Africa. Turkey has regained both strength and respect in countries whose societies are predominantly Muslim. Moreover, Turkey has done this at a time when she was also expanding her relations with Israel. A striking evidence of the changes that had been wrought is to be seen in Turkey's new role as a facilitator, with the full confidence and assent of both sides, which contributes to the cause of peace in the Middle East. Former President Demirel's inclusion among the 'five wise men' assigned the task of investigating the sources of the violence wracking the region is yet another example of the confidence Turkey now inspires in the Middle East and in the world.

Additional examples of the merits of abandoning traditional foreign policy could be given. At the roots of them all is the redefinition of foreign policy that we have enacted in recent years.

ON THE HARMONY OF CIVILIZATIONS: The foreign policy that we pursue does not see its mission as a front-line warrior for this or that civilization which is supposedly in conflict with another. Quite the contrary, I see Turkey's geostrategic function as one of bringing civilizations together.

In July 1997, I summed up Turkey's foreign policy goal as that of becoming a 'world state' in the early 21st century. Over the last four years, a strategy has been developed that will take Turkey to that goal. Policies have been identified, and quite a lot of progress has been made in this direction. Correct analyses and choices have made it possible for Turkey to take advantage of the new political balances and opportunities that emerged with the end of the Cold War. Turkey has added to her foreign policy the extraordinary advantage of representing seven centuries of history as well as a secular republican revolution. The historical dimension that for so long had been ignored was at last restored to the formulation of Turkish foreign policy.

We have driven home the recognition that foreign policy is not just a topic of interest to a small coterie of elites. Rather, it touches directly upon people's daily bread and our children's future.

Turkish foreign policy is being shaped by these approaches and by an appreciation of the centuries-old store of culture and history that we have shared and sometimes created in common with other peoples. In addition to enhancing Turkey's security and her geostrategic value, this foreign policy has systematically strengthened the foundations on which economic relations can be erected.

Taking these elements, analyses, and convictions as its starting point, Turkish foreign policy questioned itself; evaluated its centuries of universal experience; redefined and renewed itself in support of progress for Turkey and for all.

CHAPTER I :
History, Culture & Politics

*** *I have always considered history as the decisive factor in defining Turkey's past and her present. I believe it's our most valuable asset. I also believe that we have never made good use of our historical and cultural specificities. I tried to bring up this point in some of my books and essays. Actually I am making ample use of this asset in designing our policies. In fact, the much-delayed introduction of the "historical dimension" to our geo-strategy is what I consider as my modest contribution to Turkish foreign policy.*

Turkey is a country that has much to gain from her historical role and cultural particularities. This is why I have often used culture as a means to facilitate foreign relations. Given that we are a people who participated in the formation of several great civilizations and that we have a huge historical geography, which endured centuries, I believe this advantage should be put in practice in our present day endeavors. I try, and so far we had nothing but positive results.

"Identity" is another issue that encompasses historical and cultural aspects. The proper understanding of it's identity is essential for a people which has contributed to several civilizations and which underwent their particular, sometimes conflicting impacts. I have always argued that Turkey, given her historical and civilizational realities, should have an encompassing approach towards her identity. It seems totally wrong to define our identity solely on the basis of one particular culture, as "Western", or "Islamic" or whatever. And, not many nations have the advantage of having a "multi-civilizational" characteristic. This, again, is what I try to put in use in our foreign policy formulation.

*I dealt with some of these points in a speech I made at the conference of the "Assembly of Turkish-American Associations", in Washington D.C., to an audience of Americans and Turkish - Americans. I was Minister of Culture at that time.****

1. Coexistence of Civilizations and Cultures as a Means to Achieve Peace

Turkeys Ottoman past is justly considered as the historical model for tolerance. In order to appreciate this characteristic and to draw some lessons for our present day societies, one should try to answer "Why the Ottomans were tolerant", "Why, in general and relative terms, they displayed institutions and approaches which were the most tolerant in their times?"

In fact, a contradiction is bound to draw attention. The Ottomans had every apparent characteristic and reason to constitute an intolerant society rather than a tolerant one:

The Ottoman Sultan from the 16th century on was considered the Caliph of all Moslems and the Ottomans were the spearhead of Islam. Throughout their history, The Ottomans mainly fought nations of Christian belief. The state's "reason d'être" was to expand the realm of Islam, using means of war when necessary; to promote Islam and to be its guardian. Furthermore, Islam was a doctrine of State as well, encompassing all aspects of life.

Given this background, one would think that the Christian subjects of the empire, as well as other minorities would be oppressed, persecuted and treated as spies and potential enemies of the State. It's the exact contrary that came to being. Why?

I don't underestimate some of the inherent positive characteristics of the Ottoman ethic and the role of humanitarian aspects of Muslim religion that the Ottomans cherished, but there should be other factors contributing to the high degree of tolerance that prevailed throughout centuries.

One of these factors seems to be a simple but decisive one: The Ottomans were tolerant because being tolerant was the only way of life that would permit them to be a great and strong empire and to live in peace within their own borders. They were tolerant because they had a huge benefit in being tolerant. The Ottoman mainstream wisdom was able to detect this basic reality and, supported by religious and ethical motives, turned it into an institution of tolerance.

In fact, varying through the centuries, Christian subjects of the Ottoman state represented 30 to 50 percent of its population. The State had to be in peaceful terms with such a huge population.

Furthermore, these non-Muslim subjects, exempted from military service, paid a special tax for this exemption. This counted much in the State budget. The Ottomans, contrary to some widespread beliefs in the West, realized much of their conquest in the Balkans fighting the feudal lords rather than the people. In order to procure the passive compliance of the Balkan peasantry, they had to be presenting a rule of tolerance and of peace. This, they did superbly, both before and after the conquests. It should also be noted that the Ottoman culture was one of a highly synthetic nature, which, for its own sake and survival, had to promote tolerance. In fact, Islamic, Byzantium, Arabic and Persian elements coexisted in Ottoman arts, architecture and in the economic, military and administrative institutions. The literary language as well as the administrative and court language was a highly synthetic one. It is almost impossible for an average contemporary Turk to understand this language. One might also add that the ruling elite of the Ottomans, the meritocracy of 15th to 18th centuries, was systematically and solely composed of converted Christian Ottoman children.

Given all these facts and factors, the Ottoman tolerance finds its explanation in materialistic terms as well as in ethical or spiritual considerations. The historic bottom-line that might serve as a reference to our present day societies might be something as the following: First, being tolerant brings no harm to the tolerant majority; second, vis-à-vis a tolerant majority, the minorities have little cause for rebellion; third, cultural interaction and cultural coexistence provide the main means to achieve a tolerant society.

Departing from these observations, it might be assessed that tolerance in present day societies might be sought through a new cultural approach - in Turkey, rather through an old approach: One which would try to conciliate with each other and with contemporary Turkey all the civilizations that thrived in our history and in our geography. This seems to be a major point: Neither the Ionic or Trojan or Byzantine civilizations are alien to us, nor the Ottoman civilization is alien to Republican Turkey. In fact, these civilizations present in our history and in our geography shaped our contemporary society. And it's the predecessors of our present day society that helped the shaping of those civilizations. This consciousness should help to alleviate the tensions produced by the diversity of civilizations and cultures that characterize our society in the 19th and 20th centuries. The sensible approach should be to end the mutual negation of cultures, western, eastern, religious, secular, Republican, Ottoman or whatever, and to promote their coexistence. This is not an easy goal to achieve, but it is a feasible one. In the last decade, experiences of dialogue and of peaceful encounter prove that steps taken in this direction produced encouraging results. They contributed to a better understanding and presumably to a more tolerant society.

The legacy of our Ottoman past, which is recognized to be the historical model of tolerance, is short and clear: Tolerance is primarily a product of rational choices and necessities, achieved through the peaceful coexistence of cultures and through the reconciliation of civilizations. This, our ancestors were able to realize, this we should do our best to realize.

Contemporary Turkish Republic should consider its identity as the expression of all cultures, which have thrived in our land; as the possessor of a great cultural heritage that can be traced to Ion, Byzantium, Central Asia, the Seljuks and the Ottomans. In a historical dimension, our present day republic should be the representative and bearer of all these cultures that flourished within our geography. Thus, what seems to me as the main factor of identity of Turkish culture might appear in a clearer vision: To be an original culture and to be specific to our geography on one hand; and, on the other, to be the cultural expression, the means of cultural dialogue and interaction, sometimes of synthesis, of a much wider geography extending from Central Asia to the shores of the Aegean, to the Balkans and to Central Europe.

History, whether social, economic, or cultural, is not solely a study of the past. In fact, it is a study conducted on the future, it is a means to shape the future and to provide for a brighter and happier world for generations to come.

To this end, the Ottomans contributed their sense of tolerance.
(Speech at the 16th annual Convention of the Assembly of Turkish American Associations, Washington, D.C., September 1995)

* * *

2. "Is Turkey Culturally Pulling Away from Europe?"

Following the formation of a governmental coalition led by the "Welfare Party", considered as representative of the religiously sensitive policies, raised a lot of question marks in the West: "...Was Turkey changing course, was she evolving towards an Iranian model?" I was asked by a prominent cultural publication, "...if Turkey were culturally pulling away from Europe? "In fact, parallel concerns were observed in our own public opinion. Rather than "pulling away from Europe", the concern was Turkey's secular system.Well, the motivations and goals of political parties are sometimes an issue for discussion. On the other hand, Turkey's basic constitutional choices are strong enough not to be affected by political changes. I have difficulty to discuss the probability of Turkey drifting' away from a particular cultural category, for I do not agree with the general definitions of our cultural identity, which, from my point of view, is complex and can not be categorized by one, single term

-I- The advent to power of a party which represents religious sensitivities as well caused a flurry of questions and hesitations both in Turkey and in the West: About Turkey "...*culturally pulling away from Europe*".

The indecisive outcome of December 1995 elections brought the somewhat religiously motivated Welfare Party (RP) of Mr. Erbakan to a dominant position in the coalition formed with Mrs. Ciller's True Path Party (DYP). The two parties have respectively 21 % and 19 % of total votes, which provide for a majority of 53 % in the parliament. The Government was formed in July 1996.

Political developments that have a cultural dimension are sometimes difficult to explore. This is especially true for Turkey where a complex cultural identity prevails. Over-simplifications and categorical terminology are often misleading: Defining the Turkish culture or cultural identity in a concise way by calling it "Westernized", "Islamic", "Secular" and the like, does not contribute for clarity. Neither for a realistic evaluation of recent political events, which are linked as well to cultural systems and symbols.

53

-II- The *relevance*, *scope* and *limits* of the actual phenomenon, sometimes described as "Turkey culturally pulling away from Europe" might be better assessed through a historical approach.

The present culture of Turkey reflects several civilizations, from Hittite to Ottoman. This diversity provided for a unique blend of culture. The imperial heritage of multiplicity is reflected in the present-day cultural identity of Turkey: An identity that cannot be defined in uni-dimensional terms. Furthermore, the Islam values and the West European values have coexisted since 19th Century. This historical symbiosis between Western Europe and Turkey contributed to the interaction of cultures and life-styles.

To state "Turkey is culturally pulling away from the West" would be misleading; for Turkish culture has never been a "West-European Culture". The same goes for "drifting away from Islam"; for Turkey, throughout its millennium of existence, was never a conventional "Islamic Culture" in the general sense of this terminology. Our culture has numerous inputs from different civilizations that thrived in our geography through millennia of history. The uniqueness of her culture explains Turkey's differentiation with other countries of Islamic background, as well as it's rather smooth transition to a secular State.

-III- These historical facts and factors might not be clearly defined in the perceptions of the individuals. Nevertheless, in the Turkish case, they constitute the *common cultural denominator* that strongly affects people's approach to life, to politics, their fears and their aspirations. I believe that it's the same subconscious common denominator, shaped by their cultural heritage and by centuries of experiences, which draw the limits to any form of cultural and political domination; or, rather, to a will for such domination.

In this context, a political action that aims to destroy the unique blend of cultural identity of Turkey, or, willingly or unwillingly, sets free the dynamics of destruction, is bound to be limited in its effects. The coercive domination of one of the cultural dimensions of Turkey over another had been tempted in past centuries and has always proved to be of a contained and transitory character.

I would therefore conclude that what we are observing in present-day Turkey is partially an understandable -if not justifiable- political attemp of those that consider themselves handicapped in their presence at the cultural synthesis of the country. And, partially, a radical, insensible effort to gain dominance by the negation of another cultural dimension; an attempt that has already proved itself to be weaker than what was anticipated and which is already failing.

The cultural "problematique" in Turkey is to enhance the values of *"democracy and human rights"*. Turkey should make a greater effort in this sense; through its actual government, as it should have made it through its previous governments...

(Published in the Quarterly Review of "Institut fuer Auslandsbeziehungen, Stuttgart" (February 1997)

* * *

3.   A History, which Provides for Opportunuties as well as Problems

United Nation's General Assembly offerss to foreign ministers a forum to present an overview of their policies. It is an occasion as well to have bilateral meetings. 1997 was my initial attendance. From 1997 to 2000, I consistently broke my own "record" by organising bilateral talks with as many as 35 foreign ministers in five assembly days. In 1997, there was some curiosity about the newly formed Turkish coalition and the foreign policy that I was to implement. I sketched briefly our goals and parameters. As I write my speeches myself, this was not the usual kind that they used to have from Turkish foreign ministers. There was an attentive audience and later I had several questions from my counterparts. My insistence on history as the main source of our present internal and external issues drew the attention of Arab foreign ministers and of Europeans as well.

-I- As we approach the new millennium, we realize more clearly the impact of our culture and history on our foreign policy. We observe that our current issues and our opportunities have a definite historical tone, that they are mostly the legacy of the past seven Centuries. And as we ponder the role that Turkey should play in the next millennium, it seems that this mission, to be most beneficial for us and for the countries around us, should be defined in line with our history and with the particular cultural fabric of our people.

I will first try to elaborate on history and culture, and then move on to contemporary factors to explain the policies that we are currently developing:

When we say "Turkey", we are talking about a nation, which coexisted with the nations in its vicinity, within the same political entity, from the 14th to the 20th century. This was a coexistence, which has had its share of historical problems, opportunities, tolerance, strength and hope. This provides the present day Turkey with characteristics of a *World State*, having a strategic influence over vast geographic and cultural regions. Turkish foreign policy initiatives have a significant impact on a wide geography, from the Balkans to Central Asia, from the Middle East to the Mediterranean, the Caucasus and the Black Sea. In addition, Turkey's NATO membership, her "Customs Union" and links with the E.U. also makes Turkish foreign policy a significant factor in West European affairs. This of course is an interactive phenomenon; all these regions have a direct impact on Turkey, on its external relations as well as on its domestic development.

In fact, Turkey is linked to several other countries either by cultural affinities, by a mutually shared history or by its former role as a spiritual leader. We speak the same language with about 100 million people in Western and Central Asia. We also shared with the Balkan, Caucasian, North African and the Middle Eastern peoples the fate of the same political entity, with its ups and downs through the seven centuries of her existence.

This historical background is the main source for several problematic issues -and for vast opportunities- that actually lay before Turkey. For example, all current issues of rather not-so-positive relations with our southeastern neighbors, or problems in the Aegean, present themselves mainly as ongoing issues related to historical causes. On the other hand, the same mutually shared history provides for unparalleled opportunities to promote understanding and to develop economic and cultural relations.

Political sociology points out the strong relationship between a nation's cultural identity, its cultural attributes and its respective competence in various vocations. The contribution of past civilizations to a given nation shapes her cultural fabric, which in turn pre-defines a set of values affecting the common patterns of individual and social behavior. From a historical perspective, the Turkish Republic is the representative and bearer of all civilizations that flourished within its geography.

-II- As the Foreign Minister of the new Turkish government -in office since three months- I am trying to make a thorough analysis of the historic and cultural set-up linked to our present strategic role. We aim to use Turkey's cultural and historical affinities as major inputs to our international relations.

Within this framework, I have identified 5 main assets to support our foreign policy objectives:

1. *Historical asset* and its revaluation; the modern crossroads of the East and the West.

2. *Cultural identity*, the privilege of being a European nation, as well as an Asian nation.

3. *A thriving economy*; great potentials of industry, trade and tourism.

4. Proven *parameters of stability and peace* in a huge and most disturbed geographic region, which holds the major energy resources of the world, as well as enormous economic prospects.

5. *"The Turkish Model"*, the main, if not the only experience in the world of a country with Islamic traditions, which has adopted pluralist, democratic institutions, human rights, secular laws, gender equality.

Turkey is a country with a rich and vast Islamic background, which provides for one of the major components of its cultural identity. And Turkey, through Atatürk's leadership, forged a modern republic, reconciling the past with the future; religious traditions with secularism. This was not an easy task and still creates some transitory problems. Nevertheless, through this unique experience, Turkey now constitutes an inspiring "model", a hope and a vision for the nearly 1,5 billion Moslems in the world.

-III- In keeping with these five assets, we adopted some priorities and policies. I will cite a few examples:

Special emphasis on Turkey's Historical Geography: Located at the crossroads of the three continents and several regions, including the Balkans, the Middle East, the Caucasus and Central Asia, Turkey has an effective role in the maintenance of peace, security and stability in its wider region. We lived together with peoples who actually constitute 26 contemporary independent States. Today, the historical and cultural attributes of this vast geography, more than ever, find their expression in Turkey's foreign policy.

"Large-scale economies" that Turkey can further develop its economic relations with, and with whom we wish to expand our trade, have been targeted.

Within this context, the United States, Japan, Russia, India and China were taken as priorities and several new initiatives were also undertaken. Trade and information centers are being established in Moscow and Shangai. On the other hand, Turkish diplomatic missions throughout the world are now working jointly on a plan, which promotes economics as a major diplomatic concern.

In keeping with Turkey's historical role, The Baku / Ceyhan Pipeline project which will carry the Caspian oil to the Mediterranean is also on the agenda. This project will revive the old Silk Road. We worked hard to provide the foreign policy input needed to initiate this endeavor and realize that the pipeline will further enhance Turkey's strategic position.

Improving our relations with our neighbors is another priority. When I took office, observing that we were not on best terms with several neighbors, I thought that some of the fault should lie with us. We thus adopted and declared the principle that if one positive step comes from the other party, we will respond by two.

Actually, we have initiated a dialogue with two southeastern neighbors, with whom we have problems. Diplomatic relations with Iran will soon return to normalcy. Iraq used to be a major trading partner in the Pre-Gulf War Era; totaling some three billion dollars per year. This went down to a few million. Now it's on the rise again. Relations with Syria are tense as usual, but a few positive signs seem to be emerging. Relations with Greece, where obstacles and opportunities lay side by side, have been problematic for quite a time. But if something has already hit the 'bottom', it can only go up! Russia has always had a special place in Turkish foreign policy, since the Ottoman times. This is mainly due to the geo-strategic positioning of the two countries; and to their specificity as representatives of two great and unhampered civilizations.

A return to normalcy and the reintegration of Iraq to the international community are of vital importance for all countries of the region. We support the preservation of the independence, sovereignty and territorial integrity of Iraq.

Turkey has been complying with the UN sanctions regime imposed on Iraq. On the other hand, it is obvious that the main victim of the sanctions is the Iraqi civilians, the children in particular. We believe that the sanction regime should be scrutinized to relieve some of the sufferings of the population. It is a fact as well that the sanctions have produced totally unforeseen and negative effects on the economies of third countries. Turkey stands at the forefront of those countries, which have been directly and most adversely affected by the imposed embargo. This unacceptable situation reminds us of the very pertinent remarks of the former Secretary-General of UN: "Sanctions are a measure taken collectively by the United Nations to maintain or restore international peace and security, the cost of which should be borne by all member states and not exclusively by the few who have the misfortune to be neighbors or major economic partners of the target country." We expect the Security Council to expeditiously consider Turkey's application to the Sanctions Committee, and take appropriate action.

-IV- *A new government, a new beginning:* We are a new government, not a "care-taker" one, but one determined to reform the administration and the economy. In spite of it's minority status in parliament, a strong government; with firm popular and public opinion support.

We are conscious of the role of a consistent, rational, creative foreign policy. We feel, more than ever, its historical and cultural dimensions; their capacity to provide us with some of the best opportunities for promoting peace and security in our greater region. It is then our task to cast aside historical differences and to embrace our historical affinities. And to lay grounds for common aspirations and shared achievements.

At the dawn of a new millennium, we are confident that Turkey will have a leadership role in her wider region. She will continue to be the bridge, the communicator and the peacemaker. Turkey, since centuries have provided a safe heaven for the discriminated and persecuted masses of immigrants, for those that were in desperation. On the eve of a new millennium, we are ready to face our new challenges and to promote freedom, stability and development in a region both blessed and tainted by the remnants of history.

(Speech at the United Nations General Assembly, New York, September 1997, excerpts)

* * *

4. Turkey, Europe, Eurasia

***The interaction of these three separate but interlinked entities is a recurring theme in my discourse: I had declared that our two foreign policy goals, to be reached within the first decade of the new century, were "...to become member of the European Union" and to constitute "...a pivotal, decisive center of the emerging Eurasian reality". In fact, those two goals are not contradictory, but complementary. This, I know by experience as well: During my years in office, we developed substantially our relations with the Balkans, Middle East, Caucuses and Central Asia. Generally speaking, the regions I define as our "Historical Geography". The more we improved our performance in these regions, the valuable we became for our Western partners. The same goes the other way around: Once we became candidate for accession to E.U., our statute and role in Eastern geographies was enhanced. Turkey is probably one of the few countries that historically and culturally can claim to pursue these two goals simultaneously.

In this interview I gave to l'Express, I pointed out as well Turkey's genuine contribution to E.U. At the Helsinki Summit of the European Union, December 1999, Turkey was declared to be an official candidate for accession. This is a strategic decision by E.U., which transforms her into a genuinely multi-cultural, multi-ethnic and secular organization.***

As to her history, culture and geography, Turkey is both European and Asian. This does not constitute for us a dichotomy, but rather a most valuable asset.

It is precisely for this unique experience, accumulated through centuries in Europe and Asia, that my country displays a particular mission: At the dawn of the new century, Turkey is a paradigm of modernization for Eurasian peoples who aspire for social change within a pluralist and secular democracy.

Historically, Turkey is a Eurasian power. Our history is molded as well in Central and Eastern Europe as it is in the Middle East, in the Caucasus.

Istanbul, the European metropolis, sees its influence being felt in an expending geography. Istanbul, which shelters several musty-cultural and national-national institutions is on her way to become the "Capital" of Eurasia.

In fact, within the framework of the "galloping" globalization of our times, to assign clear-cut borders to our old continents -and to our perceptions- becomes obsolete. The decision of Helsinki Summit that recognized Turkey's candidature, is in a sense "revolutionary" for the European Union: Instead of clinging to virtual boundaries which are destined to become obsolete, EU rejected the idea of a Europe defined on ethnic and religious terms. The European Union, after Helsinki, has become a "secular project" with a clear "global dimension".

Our world goes through radical changes. "Geography" as such now turns into a "concept" that initiates and carries out increasingly broader visions. It is not there to limit our perceptions. In this new environment of ever-growing interactions, some concerns and considerations become vital for the well-being of nations: The democratic principles of a state, of a system, of a government; the aspirations and the way of life of citizens; the consolidation of human values, etc. This is how I perceive Europe in the 21st Century. We are determined to make Turkey a part of "this" Europe, which is a "vision", not a geographic, ethnic or religious definition. We are to contribute to this "vision" our own historical experience, our cultural assets and our socio-economic dynamism.

After all, it is wrong to idealize "Europe" and acclaim property rights on all values that human history has produced. Instead, it is to be acknowledged that human values are the produce of millennia, of all peoples and all geographies. It is to be acknowledged as well that some peoples in some other continents were at times comparatively more active than Europe and Europeans in their contributions to human values. The reality to note is the unique nature of human values, which are universal and do not belong to particular civilizations -in plural-, but to the "human civilization" - in singular. Ataturk once noted that "...there are scores of countries, but only one Civilization..."

I am trying to define the strategic posture of Turkey within this conceptual framework. Our particular history and culture are assets we intend to further expand. And from this unique experience, both Europe and Asia might derive relevant points to enrich their own development.

(Excerpts from the Interview given to l'Express, Paris, May 2000)

* * *

CHAPTER II :
Turkey & the World

1.   Setting Sail to the 21st Century

-I- The termination of the Cold War at the end of the 1980's is a turning point in the 20th century. A transformation with vast global ramifications is taking shape. Global balances once more overturned, are being re-established. Although the emerging setup many talk about has yet to be clearly defined, its goals have more or less become visible: democracy, supremacy of law, respect for human rights and fundamental freedoms, adoption of liberal economic practices and peaceful settlement of disputes.

Today, while the world is preparing itself to set sail towards new horizons, it is also faced with a series of resurfacing problems, such as social inequality, ethnic nationalism, racial discrimination, xenophobia and terrorism. In other words, we are living hope and despair all in one and at the same time.

Arguably, there exist currently two opposing major trends. One is the integrationist effort represented by several emerging regional or even continental organizations, such as the European Union. The other, "ethnic nationalism" and "xenophobia", which challenges peace and harmony, among and within countries. It seems that the interaction between these two opposing trends will in broad lines characterize the initial phase of the 21st century.

Although developments of gigantic proportions are in the making in Asia, in the Pacific Basin and in the American Continent, European politics and security still remain to be at the heart of global balances.

Europe is putting on a new appearance. New security architecture with transatlantic ties is emerging in Europe. They claim as well to embrace the interests and the obligations of major international actors like Russia. With the new expansions of NATO and the European Union (EU), we seem to be inching closer to the prospects of eliminating the centuries-old divisions in Europe. Hopefully, one day we will define this continent as "whole and free." We aspire to put into practice the concepts of "security for all" and "prosperity for all" in Europe.

Turkey, in the aftermath of the Cold War, has assumed a new geo-political and strategic role at the center of a geography stretching from Europe to the center of Asia. To our north, Russia is still a powerful country engaged in a historic transformation and a new working relationship with the West. To our south, we live with all the tribulations of the Middle East.

I do not find a discussion on Turkey's "true location" relevant; whether she is European or Asian; whether she is in the Balkans, in the Caucasus or in the Middle East nor is there any need to choose "one or the other", for Turkey is the embodiment of them all. That is our uniqueness, our richness and our strength.

-II- Integrating with Europe in its political, defence, economic, social and cultural institutions is one of Turkey's priorities.

There is one remaining major European institution in which Turkey has yet to have her place; that is the EU with which she has an "Association Agreement" dating back to 1963. On her part, Turkey is conscious of her delay and will continue to make improvements. We shall urge the EU to comply with her contractual obligations and to use the same standards and criteria as with others. Without turning it into an obsession, Turkey will continue to do all the work necessary for accession to EU membership, while projecting her political and economic dynamism to other geographies as well.

In this context, Turkey will continue to make effective contributions to such regional and multilateral co-operative schemes as the Black Sea Economic Co-operation, the Economic Co-operation Organization, COMCEC, (Standing Committee for Economic and Commercial Cooperation of the Organization of the Islamic Countries) Balkan and Mediterranean cooperation fora and the D-8, most of which were initiated by Turkey.

Turkey wishes to increase and diversify further her strategic ties with the United States, which has a special place in her foreign policy considerations. In a number of geographies, both Turkey and the U.S. have particular interests. This provides a basis for cooperation.

As the Turkish economy strengthened, the scope of its operations in the world has expanded. We will improve the political infrastructure for new economic openings, not to replace the existing ones, but to complement and diversify them. In this context, closer relations will be sought with countries with large-scale economies like India, Russia and China. A concerted effort will be made to improve economic ties with the American continent. The same approach will be adopted towards the Pacific Basin.

Respect for the independence, sovereignty and territorial integrity and co-operation based on mutual interests constitute the bedrock of our policy towards our neighbours. Non-interference in internal affairs, border security and co-operation against terrorism are among the other criteria. Terrorism, it is one of the worst scourges of our century. International co-operation in combating terrorism will continue to be one of our priority issues. The contribution of countries to this co-operation will be regarded as an important yardstick in our evaluations. It is in our tradition to respond generously to those who approach us in a friendly manner. It would be but natural that unfriendly behavior receives the response it deserves.

-III- We wish to elevate to the highest level our historical and close relations of friendship and co-operation with the Balkan countries. We support the existing multilateral co-operation schemes aiming to promote peace and stability in the Balkans.

The Caucasus is in our immediate neighbourhood. It is also the bridge to Central Asia. The preservation of the independence, sovereignty and territorial integrity of the Caucasian countries and the peaceful elimination of the existing internal and external disputes is key to the peace and stability in this region. To ensure that the main pipeline to transport Caspian oil to world markets will pass through Turkey is one of our primary objectives. This will provide a safe and continuous line of transportation to the West, and will also meet our environmental concerns. In this context, I should underline that safeguarding the security of the Turkish Straits is vital. We will not let the Turkish Channels turn into a "pipe-line" for the growing output of Caspian oil.

We shall further develop our co-operation as equal partners with the Central Asian Turkish Republics to which we have a close affinity. We attach great importance to the preservation of their independence, sovereignty and territorial integrity. We shall continue to support them in their economic and social development within democracy and in their drive towards integration with the international community.

We wish to further develop co-operation with the Islamic world. We are determined to invigorate our historical relations of friendship with the Arab countries. Our positive relations with Israel will continue to grow. We consider this to be a contribution to peace and stability in the region; it is not directed against any other country's interests. Turkey hopes that the obstacles to the eventual success of the Middle East Peace Process will be eliminated. To this end, we are ready to provide our centuries old experience in the disputed geography.

To our north, Russia is a valued partner. Economic relations with Russia have flourished recently to the benefit of both countries. Trade, contracting services and tourism are rapidly developing and opening up new horizons. It is to be hoped that the reflexes of the past are totally abandoned so that this favorable atmosphere may have repercussions on collaboration in other areas, both at regional and international levels.

Despite the fact that the existing disputes with Greece remain unresolved, the climate of goodwill created in the margin of the NATO Madrid Summit (July 1997) hopefully will provide the framework for positive developments in our relations.

Heavy armament with sophisticated weapons in the Greek Cypriot part of Cyprus creates a security problem not only for the Turkish Republic of Northern Cyprus, but also for Turkey herself. The EU's insistence on opening negotiations with the Greek Cypriot Administration for full membership, in total disregard of the international agreements on Cyprus, is overshadowing the continuation of U.N. sponsored talks between the two parties. Turkish Cypriots will continue to enjoy Turkey's political and military guarantees emanating from international agreements on Cyprus.

These are some of the thoughts on current policy issues that I wanted to share briefly. During our administration, I will be keen to conduct a transparent foreign policy, peace-oriented and characterized by realism, pragmatism, consistency and continuity.

Turkey is ready to cooperate with all countries willing to make the 21st century the most peaceful and the most prosperous times ever.

("PERCEPTIONS", September-October 1997 (II-3), Ankara)

* * *

2.   The Eurasian Dimension

In a short preface I wrote for a book that our ministry published, I tried to present my strong belief that Turkey's strategic future is linked with the emergence of Eurasia. I further developed this view in theory and in practice. It was rather in perceptions that this was more difficult to realize. In the dominant Turkish politico-intellectual circles, any reference but the European one, but the "Western" cult, was considered to be close to sacrilege. Today, I may claim that the two complementary dimensions in Turkish foreign policy are finally established. But some intelligentsia was so reluctant to leave behind their old clichés, so unwilling to understand...

If foreign policy is built upon a balance of power, the nature of this balance is certainly changing: We no longer live in a world where sheer military force is the major determinant of a country's international status. The new paradigm sets the stage for a new kind of power - one that rests on economic vitality and persistence. As the world is becoming a truly global marketplace, economic factors coupled with historical, cultural and political assets shape a country's role for the next millennium.

Given these attributes of the contemporary power game, the decisive element is a country's ability to make optimal use of its comparative advantages. Turkey, with a multitude of opportunities, is poised to be a significant player in the coming decades.

Contemporary Turkey aspires to be the leading economic and political actor in Eurasia. We envisage an international mission that is no longer peripheral and confined to the outskirts of Europe. Our mission envisions a pivotal role in the emerging Eurasian reality.

This is where we stand now, and for several reasons:

1) The central stage of the next millennium, many observers agree, will be Eurasia, broadly defined as the geography stretching from Western Europe to Western China. Given the trends in production, communication and information technologies, Europe and Asia will form an integrated whole, interlinked and interdependent. Both will gain substantially by being part of the same entity. Furthermore, much of the next millennium's economic development will take place in Asia; the advent of new energy sources and communication corridors bears witness to this emerging reality.

2) The Post Cold-War political framework witnessed the re-appearance or re-confirmation of several independent states. Out of the multitude of those "new" states, almost all - in the Balkans, in the Caucasus or in Central Asia - are those with whom Turkey shares a mutual history, religion or language. This provides Turkey with a new international environment of historic and cultural dimensions. Furthermore, these new nation-states quickly embarked upon the task of rebuilding their economies as well as opening them to foreign investment and competition. Turkey, as a long-standing actor in these geographies, has become a vital partner in their economic restructuring.

3) This strategic change corresponds with a new consciousness in Turkey. The role of a shared history and of parallel cultural characteristics is highlighted and put into practice in all spheres of our foreign policy. It is worthwhile to note that there are twenty-six countries with which we shared for centuries a common history, a common state and a common fate. This background provides for strong economic relationships and a unique platform for political cooperation. In this vast socio-political geography, Turkey, having the most dynamic economy, most advanced armed forces and the longest running democracy, has optimal conditions to contribute to stability and to enjoy the opportunities presented by the new "Eurasian Order." By virtue of its historical and cultural attributes and its privileged identity, European as well as Asian, Turkey is firmly positioned to become the strategic "Center" of Eurasia.

This brings the present analysis to the subject that this book addresses: Based upon the parameters proposed by the OECD and the average statistical data from the last 22 years, this study attempts to give an objective picture of Turkey for the years 2010 and 2020, within a comparative framework.

Some of the conclusions point at a country, which not only possesses the capabilities for a pivotal role in Eurasia, but has the economic means as well. Whereas in the past, Turkey was mainly recognized for its strategic contribution to NATO, it now distinguishes itself through its economic vibrancy, its entrepreneurship and foreign trade. Coupled with a new foreign policy combining economic progressivism with historical and cultural affinities, Turkey is riding the wave of a new economic momentum, transforming its former regional role into a global one.

Talking or writing on Turkey, I know that I might not be considered an "objective commentator". Nonetheless, I would claim that we are discussing a case of "realistic aspirations": Of a centuries-old civilization, of an organizational wisdom which helped the middle ages to transform into the modern centuries, of a country and nation which represent both a unique historical experience and the assertiveness of the Republican era.

History is not lived in vain. Yesterday provides the theory and shapes the present day; the present day puts theory into practice and defines tomorrow. Our societies, coming from their distant past, will carry their own dynamics of development into the coming millennium. I believe in a future that is brighter for humanity. I believe as well in Turkey's contribution to this future.

(Preface to "Turkey & The World, 2010 - 2020", Ankara, August 1998)

* * *

3. "Tour d'Horizon"

In this sub-chapter and in the following ones, I am trying to address different issues, through excerpts from various interviews. The interviews were scattered in my first three years in office. This facilitates to track the evolution of events and of their interpretation. The following is an excerpt from the introduction that the two interviewers had inserted to their article.

TDN: Turkish Foreign Minister Ismail Cem has stated that in the handling of the Kosovo conflict, it was a mistake for the international community not to involve the Balkan countries even to the decision "shaping" process, let along the decision "making" process. The self-acclaimed "Contact Group" had as participants neither the Balkan countries nor politicians with insight into the Balkans.

Cem said he had criticized this attitude right from the beginning and had warned against its possible consequences. "I kept raising this point at every opportunity. I warned that solely countries with no Balkans experience were making decisions on this very particular and delicate issue."

The Minister added that most recently, at the latest NATO meeting where the developments in Kosovo were being discussed, he had said that it was time for self-criticism: "If people with insight into the Balkans, if Balkan countries themselves had been involved in the process right from the beginning, then, at least some of the very serious mistakes could have been avoided and perhaps the scope of the conflict would not have expanded so far".

Cem's persistent criticism that Turkey and Greece should not been ignored in handling the political dimension of the problem has paved the way to the inclusion of both the Turkish and Greek Foreign Ministers in the so-called "Friends of Kosovo" group, established by UN Secretary-General Kofi Annan to assist him.

Cem stated that the Greek Foreign Minister Papandreou had expressed his content with Turkey's approach to the Kosovo problem. "Nevertheless", Cem continued, "...the Greek refusal to allow Turkish troops to transit Greek territory on way to Kosovo as irresponsible behavior."

The Kosovo problem, Cem said, has displayed to all NATO allies that Greece, as a NATO partner, was not a country one could rely on. Underlining this point, Cem further complained that, it was difficult for Turkey to understand how the British Foreign Minister or a senior U.S. official could thank Athens for its "contributions regarding Kosovo".

"Unfortunately, interests may come before ethics or commitments" he commented, "But we shouldn't ignore that in the long run, when issues and actors are evaluated in NATO with a broader perspective, every body will be knowing each other much better".

Refuting claims that there were tensions between the ethnic Turkish and ethnic Albanian Kosovars, Cem said: "We are not discriminating between ethnic Turks and ethnic Albanians there: For 500 years we shared a common history as citizens of the Ottoman Empire, we shared the same destiny. We were equal subjects of the same empire. No one was privileged over others.. No one was a second-class citizen. We regard them historically as our people... All of them, all Kosovars, without any distinction."

Talking about Turkish-American relations, Cem said in that ties between Ankara and Washington have strengthen over the past few years. "...Nevertheless, both Turks and Americans should understand that the two countries may not always see eye to eye on every issue. On particular issues, it is only normal that the two countries have different priorities.

At a time when the seven leading industrialized countries (G-7) and Russia have started pressing for a solution to the Cyprus problem, and when the UN Secretary-General has announced his intention to call for a Summit on Cyprus this fall, Foreign Minister Cem has asserted that external pressures and impositions render a Cyprus settlement more difficult.

In an exclusive interview with Turkish Daily News editors, the Foreign Minister stressed that Turkey disapproves of such pressures.

Cem defined the scope of the Cyprus talks as an exercise "in search for a model that would bring the two states together through a reconciliation between the two peoples of the island".

Reiterating Turkey's "full support" for Turkish Cypriot President Rauf Denktash, Cem stated that Ankara believes that a confederal settlement on Cyprus best fits the existing conditions:

"Unless the existence of the Turkish Republic of Northern Cyprus (TRNC) is acknowledged; unless the equal existence of the Turkish Cypriot State on the island is accepted; unless the right to sovereignty of the Turkish Cypriot people is acknowledged; unless the Greek Cypriot side abandons its claim of being the representative of the entire island, including the Turkish Cypriots, no outcome can emerge from any meeting. If these were to be achieved, a settlement would have been within reach," Cem further stressed.

"We want to be on friendly terms with Greece", the Foreign Minister said, "... a country of 65 million people cannot have policies of enmity against a neighbouring country of 10 million. We seek peace and friendship. But we cannot sacrifice our vital interests for the sake of peace and friendship"

(Introduction by I. Cevik and Y. Kanli, to the Interview given to Turkish Daily News, Ankara, June 1999 - Excerpts)

* * *

4.   The United States

***Now, speaking about the world's only remaining superpower, the United States, you recently had talks there, you attended the latest United Nations meeting (September 1998). How do you view the leadership of that country, particularly after the Clinton-Lewinsky affair?*

I am of the opinion that the United States is leading the world into the 21st century, mainly with her internal creative dynamism and her revolutionary achievements in disseminating information and knowledge. I believe these are the main factors in her leadership. I also believe that U.S. will continue her leadership in the next century. One might define the U.S. not as a 'superpower,' but a 'super generator of knowledge and information'. As for the second question, personal affairs do not affect the leadership qualities of a country.

*** *Is the United States still a leading factor in our relations? Take the Bakü-Ceyhan Pipeline issue for an example. Is the United States' support still continuing ? What we hear is that the United States is now in a wait-and-see mode. She might be in favor of delaying or slowing down the process.*

If we mean the US administration, no, I don't agree. The U.S. government is supportive for the Baku-Tblisi-Ceyhan. We have frequent consultations. They see this project as one which is vital for strategic U.S. interests. As for U.S. companies, this is a different matter. The companies see the energy issues through a commercial optic. This is natural. There is harmony of interests with U.S. government; and, I hope, such a harmony will appear with the interests of companies as well. (August 1998)

*** *The United States of America is present in almost all events taking place around us, such as in Kosovo and Cyprus. In the States, Clinton says: "This fall (1999), I would like to see a development in Cyprus." The United States has a significant role in the G-7 as well. What are the recent developments in Turkish-American relations?*

We have mutually achieved quite a progress during the last two years (1997-1999). Two years ago, we had a number of significant problems. Today, our relations are at their peak.

Turkey and the United States are not comparable, neither in size nor in capacity, I am well aware of this. However, Turkey and the

United States both have interests of global nature. Turkey is, in fact, a multi-regional country. I would not use the term "regional power" to describe Turkey. "Regional power" would mean Turkey is a power in one region; a powerful country in the Balkans, for example. Or, Turkey is a "multi-regional" power. It is a power in the Balkans, the Middle East, and the Caucasus... She has strategic and economic interests in Central Asia, Northern Africa... The United States as well has a multitude of interests and concerns. It is impossible for both countries to see eye to eye on all issues. Some times and on some issues, perceptions, interests and policies of the two countries diverge.

When we think of northern Iraq for example, the priority of the United States government is to topple the present regime, no matter what the costs are. In principle, the U.S. would not like to encourage the disintegration of Iraq especially if this brings harm to Turkish interests. But, her priority being the removal of Saddam's regime, she would go along with any means to reach this end, even if she is sensitive to Turkish concerns. Our priority, on the other hand, is to protect the territorial, national and political integrity of Iraq. As in this case, perceptions, priorities and interests sometimes differ.

I totally disagree with U.S. policies on Cyprus. There are other areas where we would like to see a change in Washington's policies. I consider the U.S. policy on Greece detrimental to peace in the Aegean. She sometimes encourages Greece to be intransigent. On the other hand, there are several areas where Turkish and U.S. policies converge. Energy issues, the Caspian Basin, Central Asia, some European issues, for example.

In general, Turkish-American relations are progressing on solid ground. With respect to economy, we have certain demands. We want the trade barriers, "the quotas" to be lifted. Perhaps I am boasting a bit, but in a difficult year like 1998 for, we managed to expand our exports to the United States by 12 %. But when I consider global figures, the situation is not all that bright. There is still a huge deficit in our trade with the United States. When you add military procurement to that deficit, things become even worse. We have just paid hundreds of millions of dollars for a helicopter purchase from an American company. We paid that sum because the helicopters were worth it. But when you add military purchases to the total of our imports from

73

the United States and compare them with our exports, there is a huge imbalance. Therefore, we ask all restrictions, quotas and such barriers, to be lifted. We want the American market open to competition by Turkish products. After all, isn't this the trade policy that the Americans are telling everyone else to pursue?

(Interview given to "Turkish Daily News" Ankara, June 1999 - Excerpts)

TURKEY AND U.S. IN A GLOBAL CONTEXT: Turkey was a comparatively latecomer to the new continent. But the U.S. diplomatic presence was one of the first established within the vast borders of the Turkish-Ottoman Empire: The first binding document between the two parties was in fact a Trade Agreement, signed in 1829. The first U.S. consulate was established in Izmir in 1831 and the first US Ambassador arrived in Istanbul in 1843. The first Turkish Ambassador assumed his position in Washington by 1867. Meanwhile, several US consulates were established throughout the Empire. At the time, this was a far stronger representation than any West European power.

Throughout the past two centuries, we had times of difficulty but, overall, our relationship stands as an example of stability in foreign relations. In fact, the three qualifications that would best fit U.S. - Turkish relations would be: Consistency, Predictability, and Reliability.

Inter-Regional and Global Roles: One can correctly assess that the understanding between U.S. and Turkish foreign policy is not just a matter of ideals. It is deeply rooted in realities and interests. Looking at current U.S. strategic priorities, we can easily name the Balkans, Bosnia, Macedonia, Kosovo; the Middle East with its oil reserves and its Israeli - Arab conflict, the problems of Iraq, security of the Gulf; the Caucasus and Central Asia with their huge energy and other natural resources; East - West corridors and the lingering Azeri - Armenian conflict. In all these regions and countries stakes are high and the political and economic future of Eurasia is molded. Well, they have one common denominator: They are all part of Turkey's historical and cultural geography.

I have named regions, regional concerns or disputes. But each one of them has far reaching global consequences.

Obviously, these geographies, together with Western Europe and the United States, constitute the main focus of Turkey's present-day foreign policy. And they point at a huge area of mutual concerns and mutual interests for U.S. and for Turkey. In fact, they constitute our common agenda.

Balkans, Middle East, and Caucasus: I would like to elaborate on some of these issues:

First, the Balkans: The volatile conditions persist. The Dayton agreement is still challenged. Kosovo is open to all kinds of negative developments. Macedonia is fragile. Yugoslavia still uncertain. Turkey is deeply involved in all Balkan matters. The Balkans is a geography where all European actors might have particular interests and preferences for a certain country or ethnicity. Errors were committed through the Rambouillet peace accords and in the subsequent handling of Kosovo. I believe that U.S. involvement in the region should not loose momentum. U.S., an objective party that has no special link with any country or ethnicity in the region, has a distinct and constructive mission, one that should not be restricted, but on the contrary, expanded. I welcome today's excellent statement by President Bush, supporting Macedonia's integrity and urging all parties in the Balkans to be more conciliatory with one another.

The situation in the Middle East and in its shattered peace process has come to a critical point. If events follow a similar path into the future, there will be more bloodshed in Israel and Palestine; turmoil in the neighbouring countries; upsurges of radicalism in all Arab nations. This will create further pressures on moderate governments.

During the last six months and responding to demands by both parties, Turkey became involved in the peace process, trying to facilitate the efforts for a final settlement. We are probably one of the very few countries that both Israel and Palestine have full confidence. Obviously, we are the country, which has the deepest insight to this region and towards the psychology of its peoples. What we actually observe is a critically deteriorating situation. I believe that the U.S. should persist in her role of contributing to resolve this problem. And that she should do this objectively, acting in an even-handed manner.

I believe that the appropriate approach for us all is to support a simultaneous quest to bring down violence and to work out a path to a final settlement. Unless there is a light at the end of the tunnel, a light for both parties, it is very difficult to expect a positive development.

Finally, the Caucasus and the Azeri - Armenian conflict: Turkey firmly supports the Baku-Tblisi-Ceyhan project. This will provide a secure outlet for energy resources. And it will contribute to the sovereignty and democratic development of regional countries. Given the navigational difficulties and the persistent increase of hazardous tanker traffic in the Turkish Straits, any economic prediction for further sea transportation of oil is highly risky. There are millions of people and millenniums of culture on the shores of Turkish Channels. It is obvious that security and environmental restrictions will objectively prevent the swift passage of oil tankers.

On the other hand, the Nagorna - Karabagh issue, which is a concern both for US and Turkey, should be handled in a way, which would not result in creating instability within the two countries involved. This would be disastrous politically and economically both for the parties and for the region and conducive to infiltration.

Euro - Atlantic Dimension; NATO - EU: The second category of Turkish - American interests is our Euro - Atlantic cooperation. NATO is pivotal in European defense. We support the development of the European Union's defense organization and we are willing to participate intensively. But we do not want this development to decrease the role of NATO.

In regards to our quest for full membership in EU, the US has been most supportive. I can say that the recent developments are encouraging. In fact I arrived yesterday from Brussels, where I presented the Turkish National Program for the Adoption of the Acquis. Turkey is determined to become integral part of EU. We have two strategic goals, to be a central, pivotal country in the emerging Eurasian reality and to be a member of the European Union. EU membership will further enhance the two dimensions of our identity, our particular and invaluable asset, which is, being both European and Asian, encompassing cultures of many great civilizations.

National Economic Program: I would also like to briefly comment on the recent economic difficulties that we face (March 2001). I'll keep it brief for I know that you have elaborated extensively on this subject.

Turkey's legal and administrative setup, as well as some of her political and economic outlook has been out of synch with the pace of her development. This has created a serious gap. The legacy of the past becomes dangerously obsolete as the necessity for change develops.

This contradiction and its main product, are of a global nature which have occurred in various countries. What we observe is the distortion of the markets by inflation, corruption and mismanagement, in both public and private sectors, resulting in crises. I cannot refrain from remembering a 1998 issue of "Foreign Affairs", which had as its banner, "The Corruption Epidemic". In fact, ill begotten gains, archaic financial institutions and mismanaged public or private companies are not specific to Turkey. The search for good governance is high on today's global agenda. The additional burden in Turkey is that we currently lack the adequate capital formation to swiftly overcome this crisis.

What we do have, though, is a clear acknowledgement that things have to change and a strong will to change them. When I look at the past, I see several reasons to be pessimistic. But when I look at the future, I see more reasons for hope and optimism.

My colleague Minister Dervis has given a comprehensive and expert account of recent developments. He explained to this audience the ways and means to tackle the current economic problems and to bring them to an end. I am confident that the national economic program he outlined will overcome the acute shortcomings, which we face.

I see this critical juncture and this negative experience as an opportunity to upgrade to a more rational, efficient and just economy. An economy which aims at sustainable growth. This will provide the individual with the social environment necessary for his development in the fullest sense.

U.S. and Turkey: Necessary Symbiosis: After these rather long analysis of US - Turkish relations, one might define it in terms of symbioses. Besides our common values of democracy and freedom, we have interests which overlap in numerous fields and regions. Turkey, besides her euro-atlantic mission, is focused on several regional issues, which have far reaching global consequences. We are a multi-regional power, dealing with several geographies. The US is a global power, encompassing all geographies. Looking at the positive results of our past relationship, one can confirm the necessity of maintaining and further enhancing the cooperation of our two countries. In fact, one can correctly assess that we have never let the other down, and as U.S. and Turkey, we have always been true to each other.

At the dawn of this new century, a new world is emerging; a world of freedom, of justice and of equality. I believe in United States' and Turkey's growing roles in this emerging hope.

(Speech at the Conference of American - Turkish Business Council, Washington, D.C., March 2001)

* * *

5.   The Middle East

IRAQ & NORTHERN IRAQ:***If we look to Iraq, and particularly to the recent agreement (October 1998) signed in Washington between the rival northern Iraqi Kurdish factions, Turkey seemed to be disturbed. Why do you think that thaw took place?*

To call this a 'thaw' might be exaggerated. There is no change in Turkish policies. We have concerns and we are very cautious. Though U.S. have acted with good intentions, her last initiative might spark some negative consequences. I think Turkey's concerns have been taken into consideration, but not sufficiently.

We might speak of two possible approaches: Either pursue your own policies, or adopt the policies of others. If you implement your own policies, you are more likely to diverge, at some points, from others' policies.

Turkey is sensitive on northern Iraq. For the past year, she has been considering her own interests, along with those of the United States and of Britain, within the framework of the Ankara Peace Process. Relations are further improved with Barzani's Kurdistan Democratic Party (KDP). Lately, Turkey began to formulate policies more in line with her proper interests. I don't mean that our interests in the region contradict those of the United States, but divergences might come up. Given the conflicting dynamics of northern Iraq, this is normal.

(Interview given to TDN, October 1998)

78

***The Iraqi Kurdish groups were brought together in Washington (June 2000) . And this time representatives from Turkey also attended the talks; however, no progress was made. Turkey had expressed some reservations regarding the previous Washington accord (October 1998) between the Iraqi Kurdish groups.*

Washington and Ankara have different priorities. This does not mean we hold contradicting positions. The Washington talks were held between two regional groups. They are discussing issues relevant to the land where they live and for which they fight each other. They have their priorities as well. We should not expect that everything develop as we anticipate. Nevertheless, Turkey would not permit a chaotic situation to emerge along its borders.

***The leader of the Patriotic Union of Kurdistan (PUK), Jalal Talabani, was in town several days ago. Did he bring some observations and suggestions in regards to the Kurdistan Democratic Party (KDP) which has been increasingly irritating Turkey, mainly over the Turkomans and the outlawed Kurdistan Workers' Party (PKK)?*

Basically, Talabani wants to improve relations with Turkey. He came to Ankara to communicate his intent for developing existing relations and to inform us about measures which his party has taken against separatist terrorism.

You have asked about the KDP and their treatment of the Turkomans. The Turkomans rank high on our list of priorities in northern Iraq. We have been pursuing a policy of goodwill in order to create opportunities for cooperation that will benefit everyone in the region. But I do not think our policy produced positive results. We are now re-examining our policies and we will not refrain from self-criticism. But the existing facts are dim: Turkomans in the KDP-controlled North have been and continue to be oppressed. 85 % of all Turkomans live in the South, controlled by Iraq, but they too are oppressed. Hence, they are under pressure both from the KDP and from Baghdad. These are the realities that we will have to change.

(Interview given to TDN, August 2000-excerpts)

NEIGHBOURHOOD FORUM: ***At a moment where American bombing of Iraq seemed eminent, we prepared a plan to ease the tensions and to provide Iraq, our neighbour, an opportunity to make a conciliating move. I asked U.N. Secretary General Kofi*

Annan for his views. We were both at Davos, World Economic Forum. He made encouraging remarks. In a week, I had a plan, "The Neighbourhood Plan" ready and having agreed on the dates, I was on my way to Baghdad. It was February 4, 1998. I tried my best to persuade the Iraqis to make a move. They were quite content that such a concern and a display of friendship emanated from Turkey. They were excellent hosts. But they kindly refused to cooperate. That was a pity; the Americans bombed Baghdad a few weeks later. The neighbourhood initiative had a very positive impact on other neighbours of Iraq, the plan helped to enhance the image of Turkey in the Arab world and provided support for the policies we were initiating at the time, to foster better relations with the Middle East. I still think that an opportunity was lost and I still believe that this plan can work, even today. The "Neighbourhood Initiative", as it was called, had the following proposals:***

Principles underlying Turkish Neighbourly Peace Initiative (in addition to defusing the "February Crisis"):
1. Prevention of the reoccurrence of crises in the region,
2. Preservation of Iraq's territorial integrity and political unity,
3. Need to address all questions that have emerged following the Gulf Crisis of 1990/1991,
4. Elimination of terrorism from the region,
5. Elimination of weapons of mass destruction as referred to Security Councils Resolution 687. (Turkey does not posses and does not intend to posses weapons of mass destruction and is gravely concerned by their proliferation in several countries of the region.)

Turkish initiative is based on the prerequisite of Iraq's full compliance with UNSC resolutions.

Turkish Neighbourly Peace Initiative consists of three overlapping circles:
1. Turkish - Iraqi bilateral relations
2. Iraq's relations with its immediate neighbours
3. Regional cooperation

Turkish - Iraqi bilateral relations developing within parameters of the UN regime.

Immediate neighbours should take steps to encourage and facilitate Iraq's full compliance with relevant UN resolutions.

Regional cooperation consists of confidence building measures (CBMs) in the political realm and confidence building projects in economical areas.
CBMs can be developed on universally accepted concepts:
- Respect for sovereignty and territorial integrity,
- Non-aggression,
- Non-use of force,
- Inviolability of borders,
- Non-interference with internal affairs.
A document or declaration of commitment based on above principles to be agreed upon by relevant countries could be produced.
Confidence building projects can be formulated based on the following concepts:
- Projects for economic cooperation
- Projects for enhancing economic interdependence among the countries in the region. (Examples: electricity interconnection, communications, transportation projects, transit trade)
(4-5 February,1998)

SYRIA: "DAMASCUS MUST ACT ON PKK": *** - *Foreign minister Ismail Cem has said that Turkey is not willing to initiate a war with Syria, but that she is determined to compel Syria to put an end to her support for the terrorist Kurdistan Workers' Party (PKK). In an exclusive interview with the Turkish Daily News, Cem underlined that Turkey had not prepared a particular strategy to increase tension with Syria and that her recent reaction was spontaneous, since the Turkish people had "run out of patience." Commenting on the timing of Turkey's hardened attitude, Cem said that Turkey had been late in forcing Syria to halt its support for PKK terrorism. The foreign minister was not particularly concerned about a probable Arab solidarity with Syria but urged the Arab countries to limit their backing for Syria at a level that does not bring about support for terrorism. Cem said that Turkey did not have any problem with the Syrian people. He indicated that Turkey's relations with Syria could be normalized after Turkish demands are met.
*** The crisis with Syria is the most controversial issue nowadays. Is there really a crisis? The media is warmongering. But diplomats and military officials say that there is no atmosphere of war, but just a difficult situation, which should be overcome. What is your assessment?*

At a certain moment, it seemed as if Turkey had got accustomed to the ongoing assaults of terror supported by Syria. As if she took it like an inevitable way of life. A total alienation. Now Turkey has displayed a new determination. This is not a pre-conceived development. Suddenly we realized that the situation had gone beyond all limits. We had reached the limits of patience. The significant thing is that we, the whole nation, the parliament, the government, united and declared that 'enough is enough.' All interested countries should take this seriously, for we are determined to get over with Syrian support to terrorism. We will see whether or not this will lead to a crisis, or beyond.

***Do you think that the timing was correct? Israel says that Syria was just about to get used to the peace process, talks were going on with the Palestinians; that nothing should happen to Syria at the moment... The Americans have implied that the timing is not good. Others say that the aim is to divert attention from domestic disputes. What is your comment?*

The suggestion about domestic reasons is irrelevant. Turkey's reaction is understandable. It did not happen as a result of a pre-calculated timing. Turkish people had displayed for years a remarkable patience and it had reached the point of explosion. Our reaction has nothing to do with the concerns of the Americans, the Israelis or the Palestinians.

Actually everybody, the Syrians, other Arab countries, international media as well ask the same question: *Why now? What has changed?* This is precisely the point, in fact nothing has changed. Ours is a reaction to the fact that nothing changed and that nothing changes. And "...why now?" Well, I say 'Why did we not do it earlier?' This is my response to those who ask 'Why now?' Just think of it -how many lives might have been saved, how many billions of dollars might have been spared if we had shown this determination 10 years ago? If Turkey does not show determination today, 10 years from now another foreign minister will look back and ask me, 'Why didn't you do what was necessary 10 years ago?' Well, though with a delay, Turkey has such a determination now. It is not easy. Naturally we do not have any fixation on starting a war. But we are determined.

*** *We have an array of anticipations from Syria -to stop supporting Abdullah Ocalan, the PKK...*

With President Demirel, we explained to President Mubarek and Foreign Minister Musa (of Egypt) our concerns and our resolve to take strong action. In fact, we are informing all interested parties and organizations. What we say is not news for anyone, neither for the Turkish public. In short, Syria should halt its support for separatist terrorism and put an end to this ongoing problem between our two countries. If she does not, well, that's her concern. We are determined to act, unilaterally, if necessary. This is where we stand.

*** *Despite being occupied by Syria, Lebanon also has a role in this situation. Where do you think Lebanon stands? Is Syria the sole enemy?*

In almost all cases where there is a mention of PKK enjoying a permanent safe-haven, this place is defined as 'Syria' or 'Lebanon territories occupied by Syria.' There is no reference to Lebanon. I should clarify one more point: We have no problem with the Syrian people. The Syrians are our brothers. They always had friendly relations with the Turkish people. Our problem is with the Syrian administration, with the mind-set that is currently governing Syria.

****Turkey to some extent neutralized PKK in Iran. Iran gave assurances. Through agreements with Barzani and other measures, the PKK was not as active as before in Northern Iraq. Was the only remaining problem with Syria?*

No. But, it is clear that Syria harbours the bulk of the organization and provides main logistic and communication facilities.

*** *If Ocalan were forced out and sent to a third country, would this solve the problem?*

Syria should end its support to the separatist - terrorist organization. She has to do this with determination, clean herself from this disgrace. Once she achieves this change, there is no reason why positive relations between Syria and Turkey cannot be established. It is in the interest of Turkey to have the best possible relations with Syria. I am not optimistic, but I hope. First, Syria has to solve this problem.

*** *And later, the water issue and others, can they be discussed?*

The imminent problem is terrorism and we are focusing on this crucial subject.

*** *Some Arab governments claim that Turkey has a strategic alliance with Israel; that this targets directly Arab security. Might Turkey's last stance on Syria be interpreted in relation to these presumptions ?*

Some Arab circles, which use this unfounded allegation, try to create for themselves a political leverage. They know very well that there is no military alliance between Turkey and Israel, that Turkey is not a threat. What they aim at is to discredit Turkey in order to contain Turkey's growing role in the Middle East. To that end, they make-up stories to deceive their public opinion, to alienate their people from Turkey. Anyway, Turkey does not need Israel's assistance to deal with a neighbour who harbours terrorism. Israel is clever enough not to involve herself in a crisis between Turkey and Syria. But these realities will not change the rhetoric of some Arab circles. They are not concerned about realities; on the contrary, they are trying to distort realities.

******Ghaddafi says that he supports Syria. What is the level of relationship that we have with such countries, especially with Libya?*

The countries you define as 'such countries,' if their approach to Turkey is friendly, we reciprocate. The Middle East policy we are implementing since a year has already yielded positive results. One can't change everything overnight, but our well-intended initiatives had an impact within the Arab world. However, this does not mean that the Arab countries will support us when we have a problem with Syria. Arabs nations, understandably, have an inherent solidarity. Eventually, they would be supportive of Syria. But I do not anticipate an exaggerated support. Probably they will react realistically. We should be ready for any consequence. United Nations Security Council might issue resolutions critical of Turkey. We may face pressure from third countries. But, we have taken a decision and we are implementing this decision.

*** *Will Turkey send envoys to countries in the region to explain Ankara's position ?*

I have sent letters and documents to foreign ministers of Arab countries. We plan having special envoys as well. We'll make every effort to explain. But we shouldn't over - estimate the impacts of such efforts. There is no place for optimism in a conflict situation.

(Interview given to 'Turkish Daily News', October 1998)

TURKEY AND SYRIA AGREES TO FIGHT TERRORISM:
The special security meeting held between Turkey and Syria has been
completed today (20 October 1998). The agreed "Protocol" has been
signed by the heads of delegations, our Deputy-Undersecretary Ugur Ziyal
and Syria's Major General El-Hasan. I will make a brief assessment:

Through this protocol, Syria has undertaken several
commitments in regards to Turkey's security concerns. At the
meeting in Adana, Syria had a positive approach that we consider as
constructive and promising. The same constructive approach is
expected to subsist in the implementation phase. We will carefully
watch to see how Syria implements the agreement and fulfils her
commitments.

The agreements reached at Adana have been evaluated today at
our ministry. I presided a meeting of high-ranking officials of the
relevant authorities. We have concluded that the Adana Protocol
provided for positive concrete results, which would now need a close
follow-up.

I believe that a promising framework has been achieved. First,
I would like to congratulate the distinguished staff of Ministry of
Foreign Affairs and the representatives of other institutions who
attended this meeting. Together with Ambassador Ugur Ziyal, they
made an invaluable contribution to a better understanding between
the two neighbouring countries. This issue has a turbulent history of
fifteen years behind it. During the last two weeks, more is achieved
to solve this problem than what was possible in the past fifteen years.

Though I still maintain my cautious approach, I do not
underestimate the result we have reached. After this point, I hope that
the commitments will be fulfilled and a problem, which has cost
Turkey so heavily, will be solved once and for all.

*** *Is there a meeting between you and Mr. Shara on the
agenda? An inspection mechanism, which would ensure that the
parties would keep to the agreement, was under consideration. Was
this issue actually agreed? Was there any other issue on the agenda
besides terror? There are statements propounding that the terrorist
leader (who was forced to leave Syria) is in Moscow?*

The point here is not the question as to "who is where", but that
terror now looses a crucial logistic base. The Syrians have addressed
the issue earnestly. I cautiously declare that they have fulfilled our

expectations. The Syrian side has pledged that the organizers of terror will not be sheltered in their country and that they will no longer have access.

No other subject apart from terror has been elaborated. We had nothing on the agenda except terror. In my declaration prior to the Adana meeting, I had stated that to suppress support for terrorism was the precondition to any further dialogue with Syria. There are several items in regards to inspection mechanisms through which Turkey can follow and judge the extent of the implementation.

There is no meeting planned with the foreign minister of Syria. As I have already mentioned, at this stage we have a satisfactory development. We now expect a sincere implementation of the protocol.

I hope that what we achieved through the Adana Protocol will pave the way to a thorough change. We look forward to a new understanding of neighbourhood. Both Syria and Turkey have great interest in forging new political and economic relations.

***An item on the Adana protocol refers to a possible cooperation with Lebanon. Can you elaborate? On the other hand, has Syria put an end to the support it provides for PKK?*

Syria has already obliged terrorist leaders to quit her territory and the Adana Protocol is put into force with good faith. I am not saying that every problem has been solved and that the terrorist organization in Syria has been totally annihilated. However, a promising start is at hand. Other countries as well are in a position to judge the compliance of Syria with her Adana commitments: Together with Turkey to eradicate terrorism from the region. This does not mean that every problem has been solved and that we have an easy job ahead of us. This is a process and we look forward to positive developments.

An item in the Protocol suggests that Syria, Turkey and Lebanon should come together on a platform of cooperation. There is a mutual understanding between Syria and Turkey on elaborating such a project. We know that Lebanon is going through a political change and we will later see if this is feasible. (Press Conference, Ankara, October 1998)

***Have our expectations risen after Beshar al-Assad came to power in Syria?*

86

Too early to say... Since the agreement signed between Turkey and Syria in Adana (Fall 1998), our relations have taken a positive turn. I do not have a particular complaint with respect to Syria, though that does not mean that we have solved all our problems. Cooperation on security has been relatively successful, but we still have grounds to cover.
(TDN, August 2000)

IRAN: ***We always seem to have ups and downs in our bilateral relations with Iran. What is the latest situation, as the 2000 nears its end ?*

The problems that we have with Iran are on security issues. We have partially resolved some, but I cannot say that they have been eliminated. The Iranian Ministry of Foreign Affairs seems to have a constructive role. However, we sometimes face situations that stem from the peculiarities of the region and of the Iranian reality, and confront negative developments that does not seem to be directly linked to the Iranian Government. We have, with Foreign Minister Kharrazi, reached an agreement on a security mechanism; every so often we obtain positive results. However, it is too early to say that we have resolved our problems. Armed terrorists still find shelter in certain parts of Iran.

ISRAEL: Turkey has common historical, geographical and cultural relations with the Middle East. Generally there is a positive interaction between her and the majority of the regional countries, including Israel.

The Turco-Israeli relations have developed in various domains. Our economies are of complementary nature. We have several agreements, which provide the legal basis for our economic, commercial, scientific and military cooperation.

But these agreements should be considered in their appropriate context. We always made clear that the military aspect of our co-operation with Israel is of "defense industries cooperation agreements" and "military training agreements". We have parallel agreements with some twenty countries, some of which are members to the Islamic Conference Organization. Certainly, our military cooperation with Israel is not directed against any third country.

I have explained intensively our position to the Arab world, through diplomatic channels as well as through the Arab media. I have said time and again that our friendships are not items for trade-off, neither bargaining chips: We shall never compromise our friendship with Arabs to gain favors with Israel; and we shall never degrade our relations with Israel in order to be on better terms with the Arab world. I can realistically claim that since about three years that we pursue this policy, the concern of certain Arab countries have dissipated to a large extent.

(Speech delivered at the 52nd General Assembly of the United Nations, September 1997 - Excerpts)(Interview given to Turkish Daily News, Ankara, August 2000 - Excerpts); (Interview given to l'Express, Paris, May 2000 - Excerpts);

THE PEACE PROCESS: Events have recently taken, rather unexpectedly, an unfortunate and dangerous turn. The Israeli settlement activities in the Occupied Territories, which take place despite the relevant United Nations Security Council and General Assembly resolutions, as well as the provisions of the peace accords, and the abhorrent terrorist activities have placed the Peace Process under a very severe strain.

It is in the best interests of all concerned to act with restraint and not to take any action that may completely derail the Peace Process. We urge the parties to do their utmost to establish mutual trust, otherwise it would be impossible to attain the objectives of the Peace Process.

(Speech delivered at the 52nd General Assembly of the United Nations, September 1997 - Excerpts)

THE WAY AHEAD IN A VIOLANT "PEACE (!) PROCESS...": I am honoured and pleased to address the Atlantic Treaty Association. I will try to elaborate on some characteristics of the enlargement concept of NATO and I will then briefly touch upon a most unfortunate development in the Middle East, with far reaching consequences. (...)

The interdependence of geographies and regions is a key factor in providing security for us and for others. In the construction of a new Europe, the concept of "neighbourhood" is essential. In fact, in today's globalised environment, happenings in the neighbourhood generally have direct impacts on each of us.

I want to share with you some of my country's concerns, which originate in our Eastern neighbourhood. That is to say, the Middle East.

The escalation of violence in Palestine and Israel poses a crucial threat to the region. It will have far reaching effects on the overall stability of a vast geography extending beyond the Middle East. It will certainly have a negative impact on the economies of the Euro-Atlantic sphere.

1) One might assess that the actual situation is probably the most explosive one since the Arab - Israeli war of 1973. In the seventies and eighties, the superpowers, which had an effective influence on the parties, provided a safety factor as well. The 1973 war drew to an end when Brezhnev and Kissinger met in Moscow. Unlike previous crises, no superpower can simply turn the present crisis off.

2) The explosion of violence that we are witnessing in Israel and Palestine is more than a setback in the peace process. It displays a major change, the collapse of the political centre and the destruction of a *modus vivendi*, certain coexistence between Israelis and Palestinians. The moderates in both camps have lost their bets, at least for the time being. It's the radicals who actually are carried to the forefront.

3) The same negative trends are growing in the Arab world. Even the most rational circles are adjusting their course in line with the popular reaction. Furthermore, the Lebanese border is open to all kinds of provocation, even to explosion.

4) The reality now is the following: Each new day of violence renders the return to normalcy more difficult. And losing the perspective of normalcy sustains the spread of violence. The inevitable psychological and political escalation that builds up discards any "partial" or "temporary" solution.

5) Given the actual situation it would sound ironic to speak about peace, but it seems that only the final peace settlement might bring an end to the escalation of violence. It was once thought that the parties could end violence and pave the way for the resumption of the peace process. Now it seems to be too late. This is the reason why Sharmal-Sherif summit failed to produce any substantial result. It's rather the other way around: It seems that only an immediate and final settlement can end the ongoing violence.

Well, this is a development, which takes place far from NATO's immediate concerns. But it is a major concern for Turkey, who, for five centuries shared the same history, the same state with the peoples of the region. Furthermore, we are one of the rare countries that enjoy the equal confidence of both the Israelis and Palestinians. Before the recent events and upon both parties' request, we were able to make some modest contributions to the peace process, facilitating a better understanding on certain sensitive issues.

Actually, nothing as such would bring about a positive contribution. It's simply too late. Only a prompt, radical decision for final settlement might change the dramatic course of events.

As the Atlantic Alliance, we have set up an example on how nations can get together and face the challenges of a new era. How they can work together to transform themselves and their political environment for a better future for all.

We have achieved this end and we are proud of it. Some years ago, this might have booked as far-fetched ideals. But even ideals that seem to be out of reach sometimes are realized. Let us all hope that what seems to be a distant dream given the Middle Eastern reality turns out to be feasible as well. And soon.

(Speech at the General Assembly of the Atlantic Treaty Association, Budapest, November 2000, - excerpts)

* * *

6.   Central Asia, Caucasus & Baku-Tblisi-Ceyhan

CENTRAL ASIA: *** *One of the most significant regions is Central Asia. For instance, there are many problems in Uzbekistan and Kazakhstan have started imposing visa requirements on Turkish citizens. When we examine this region, we currently see several problematic areas. How do you evaluate Turkey's policies with respect to Central Asia?*

I see Turkey's policies with respect to Central Asia as having gotten over the "teething" stage and they are now in the process of maturing. Over the past ten years we established a sound basis for political, economic, cultural and military relationship. We have been successful. We firmly supported their independence, provided economic aid and we were present whenever there was a need. Now, I believe we are all ready for a new phase in our relationship; a phase which will be less intuitive and less informal perhaps, but which will grow in its intensity and substance, in the quality of its means and mechanisms. We are already taking the first steps.

Just recently, I discussed the basis of a new kind of relationship with foreign minister colleagues. I visited Azerbaijan, Kyrgyzstan, and Kazakhstan. The Georgian FM was my guest; the Turkmen FM will be in Ankara at the end of August. I will host a working luncheon in New York, on the margins of UN, to my colleagues from Central Asia and the Caucasus. I shall visit Uzbekistan in early October.

All colleagues and the presidents and prime ministers with whom I shared my views to initiate a new phase in our relation, were interested and very supportive. In fact, we have mutually reached a level where we can now leave the over-emphasis on idealistic concepts and concentrate more on interests, on plans and details.

I was conversing with the Kazakh Foreign Minister, he suggested that we bring a new impetus to Turkish-Kazakh relations. "Let us set up an organized work- plan which is both systematic and structured; initiate study groups and inject new life into our relations," he said.

We are already observing positive developments with Kazakhstan and Kyrgyzstan. Countries of Central Asia and Turkey do have their differences, but I think they stem from misund erstandings. I believe we are going to take positive steps to rectify our relations with Uzbekistan. I hope that with my Uzbek counterpart, we will soon be able to make a new beginning.

***Of course, Russia's political influence in the region is still considerable. When Putin was elected into office, he put Russia on the "attack", so to speak. It is suggested by certain circles that Russia opposes both Turkey and the United States; that Turkey is playing Russia and the United States off against each other; and that through this, Turkey is assuring certain advantages. They believe that Turkey has taken the lead. Would you agree with them?*

Not on all aspects. However, your analysis has certain valid points. It might be assessed that Russia does not have the vigorous leadership it has had in the Soviet past. However, the pre-Putin chaos seems to be coming to its end, and this is a rather significant development. Present Russia, compared to Yeltsin times, is taking more initiatives. She is more concerned with what is currently going on around her and with what she calls her "near-abroad".

In regards to Central Asia and the Caucasus, yes, the United States and Turkey are pursuing policies that are somewhat parallel. We have a close cooperation. During our first bilateral with Ms. Albright in Washington D.C. (December 1997), we devised the components of a plan which had a strategic dimension as well. We have therefore been in close contact on both political issues and energy policies, such as the Baku-Tbilisi-Ceyhan project and the trans-Caspian natural gas transport. "...Have we had to put up a fight with Russia for all that has been achieved to date?" No, definitely not.

Russia and Turkey are two great civilizations. They are two assertive countries and, quite naturally, are engaged in peaceful competition in several sectors, both political and economic. This reality should not be overlooked. But there is no question of us pursuing a policy of hostility towards Russia or any other policy that will force the Central Asian and Caucasus countries to make a choice between Turkey and Russia. I have always defined the independence and the security of Central Asian - Caucasus countries as our top priority. With the unfortunate but valuable experience we have in combating and defeating terrorism, we now share our experience with those who are facing similar threats.

Turkey is the leading economic power and a major political actor in a vast geography encompassing the Caucasus and Central Asia. She is already well established in trade, industry and construction business. Consequently, we are far ahead of everybody else on the economic front. In fact, Turkey is the only regional country that can pay cash for her present and future imports of natural gas. Besides our strong cultural links, we have as well established military cooperation with several regional countries. I can say that our overall position is one which has consolidated foundations. We expect constant developments.

***What happened to the Caucasian Stability Pact that was proposed by former President Suleyman Demirel?*

The concept and draft ideas are being discussed. The reactions we had to our proposal is generally very positive, encouragingTurkey to pursue her efforts. They underline though that to resolve the Nagorno-Karabagh dispute is cardinal for progress. We know that it would be rather difficult to continue working on the Pact as long as the problem in Nagorno-Karabagh persists. We are, nevertheless, pursuing our efforts. Probably we had a good idea, for I see that now the European Union as well is initiating work for such a pact.

We are now developing a new conceptual framework for the East - West energy corridors. We previously spoke of "Caspian Basin energy resources". We now speak of the Caucasus and Central Asia as a whole. The reason is simple: Each day new reserves are discovered in the region, particularly in Kazakhstan. Latest news is that rich natural gas reserves have also been discovered in Uzbekistan.

In September 2000, Kazakhstan will have reliable estimations on its natural gas and oil reserves. The Kazakhs will probably discuss with the Azeris what the prospects are. In turn, we will probably hold talks with the Azeri and Kazakh authorities. We will discuss, hopefully, newly discovered oil and natural gas resources. These will considerably increase the feasibility of the Baku-Tbilisi-Ceyhan pipeline. In this "joint" Caucasus - Central Asia geography of energy resources, Turkey will have a pivotal role, both as a transporter and as a major consumer. Furthermore, it is to note that a memorandum of understanding for the transport of natural gas from Asia to Europe was signed between Turkey, Greece and the European Union.

AFGHANISTAN: Afghanistan is another conflict area where the international community has so far been unable to help bring about a just and lasting solution. At present, the national unity of the Afghan people is at stake. It is most unfortunate that the confronting factions are fervently pursuing the military option. The immediate goal of the international community should be to convince the parties that all efforts for military domination are doomed to failure, and that, the only way to achieve peace is through dialogue and the establishment of a broad-based representative government. Regrettably, one of the major obstacles to convincing the factions that a military solution is un attainable is the continuing supply of weapons, equipment and ammunition. Plus, the military involvement from outside.

My country has close and historical ties with Afghanistan and the Afghan people. We feel very strongly about the independence, sovereignty, territorial integrity and national unity of Afghanistan. We will continue to support the United Nations' efforts for the preservation and consolidation of these fundamental assets.

THE CAUCASUS: The Caucasus, as a gateway between East and West, attracts worldwide attention politically and economically. We attach highest significance to peace and stability as well as to the preservation and consolidation of the independence, sovereignty and territorial integrity of the countries of that neighbouring region.

In this context, it is vitally important to bring about a just and lasting solution to the conflict between Azerbaijan and Armenia on the basis of international law. The Nagorno-Karabakh dispute still stands out as the principal obstacle to peace, security and enhanced cooperation in the region. More than one fifth of Azeri territory remains under occupation.

We support the basic principles of a peaceful settlement which have been adopted at the December 1996 OSCE Summit at Lisbon by the Chairman's Statement. All parties concerned should carefully consider the efforts made by the OSCE / Minsk Group. As a member of the Group, Turkey will continue to contribute to these efforts.

We welcome the recent meeting held in Tbilisi in August between the parties of the Georgian/Abkhazian conflict, and the signing of a statement by the leaders, on the peaceful and mutually acceptable solution of the conflict. In this regard, I would like to stress that Turkey is committed to the sovereignty and territorial integrity of Georgia within its internationally recognized borders.

*** *You mentioned concerns related to the Caucasus, and what was happening in Chechnya. What are your main concerns: Russian hegemony in the region?*

It's not really Russia that worries us. In the Caucasus we have one real problem, which hinders development: Armenian occupation of Azeri territory. We worked hard to get the two parties together on a plan of reconciliation. We cooperated with the US on the issue.

There were times when it seemed almost as though an agreement was in arm's reach. We were hoping, even planning to have a joint statement of reconciliation by the two parties at the

OSCE meeting in Istanbul (November 1999). Then came the assassinations at the Armenian Parliament. We did not lose hope and tried to contribute to a new path to reconciliation. But now it seems that there is a deadlock. This is our concern in the Caucasus. The Armenians know that in case of reconciliation with Azerbaijan, they too would benefit from our support.

Then there's the spill-over effects of Chechnya. The Georgians have some 8,000 - 10,000 refugees from Chechnya. There were some harsh statements by Russia and Georgia about the refugees, which might have led to a dangerous confrontation. The risk is not yet totally over.

We do of course have vested interest in the pipeline bringing Caspian oil through Turkey to the West. And though Chechnya does not affect those projects, stability in the Caucasus is a plus. That's why I am concerned.

THE CASPIAN AND "BAKU / TBILISI / CEYHAN" PROJECT:
***How important is the Baku-Ceyhan pipeline to Turkey's regional role?*

It would add an extra.

*** *The Baku-Ceyhan is also being used, it is claimed, to change the situation in Bosphorus, for Turkish gain. Do you want to renegotiate the Montreux Treaty for instance?*

Our concern is the heavy tanker traffic: The Turkish straits, the millions of people living in the region, several civilizations' assets and the natural environment are all under serious threat. The rational limits of traffic in the Turkish straits are already surpassed. Physically, we are not able to afford any more. If additional oil transport through the Turkish straits is envisioned, it is obvious that substantial difficulties will occur. Not that we will create this extra difficulty, not that we will overlook the Montreux Treaty, but physically this traffic will have to be carefully organized, monitored and eventually, it will become very slow. These are conditions, which will hurt economic concerns of oil producers and oil transporters.

*** *Was there a disappointment with the reaction of the US oil companies? Did you expect the US to push its companies more?*

The US government is doing its best. But of course the oil companies are private enterprises, looking for profit. They might have other scenarios. We shall see how it goes. But it seems that with Baku - Tbilisi - Ceyhan there is still a problem about the transit fees. It is not settled yet, though Turkey, Azerbaijan and Georgia seem to be close to a conclusion. Once this is agreed, it will be a question of financing. There are several options. I think the project will develop successfully.

Someone once told me that building a pipeline is like building a motorway. When you have a new motorway, in the first stage, motorists have a tendency to shy away. But by time, all cars resort to this convenient new option. This is the case with Baku - Tbilisi - Ceyhan.

***Some commentators have been predicting that the fundamentalist threat will now shift to the Caucasus and Central Asia, away from the Middle East. What evidence do you have of this, and how much does it worry you?*

I take equally relevant the fundamentalist threats developing in Western, Central and Eastern Europe. All threats of this kind in all geographies should be a common concern for us all.

*** *Recently a report that the United States had asked for a feasibility study for an alternative pipeline for Caspian oil that will go through Bulgaria, Macedonia and Albania. There are claims that Turkey could be bypassed?*

In foreign relations, everything is possible. But for the time being, I don't detect such a will. As for the feasibility study, was it the U.S. administration or the companies who demanded such a study? There is a difference. Anyhow, if the companies think that such a pipeline would be cheaper to transport oil, that's their preference. I cannot say whether it will or will not realize. On the other hand, there are substantial developments with regard to the Baku-Tbilisi-Ceyhan pipeline. Agreements, and some serious headway have been reached. Will it be finalized? I certainly hope so. But we tend to exaggerate developments related to Baku-Ceyhan. Baku-Ceyhan is not a project that would yield large profits to Turkey. We were making around $ 200 million per year from the Iraqi - Turkish pipeline. That was all. Baku-Ceyhan might bring in something around $ 250 million. This is not of great economic significance.

What is essential for us is the strategic link Baku-Ceyhan provides for Turkey, and, for the West through Turkey. This strategic choice will bring together all the Caucasus and Central Asia around the same strategic project. It will facilitate the development of democratic institutions in a huge geography. Baku - Tbilisi - Ceyhan provides as well the secure East - West corridor for the valuable energy resources. On the other hand, we are very much concerned by the increased tanker traffic through the Bosphorus and the Dardanelles. This has already created imminent danger. Within the framework of the Montreux Treaty, we are going to deploy all means to limit the intensity of this traffic. Millions of lives and millennia of cultural history will not be put to further danger for the sake of extra-profits to oil companies. The Turkish channels will not be turned into a "pipe-line".

There is oil in the Caspian, but oil exists in the Middle East as well. If conditions change in Iraq, Iraqi oil will be transferred to the West through existing Turkish pipelines. Baku-Tbilisi-Ceyhan pipeline is of course very important for us. Its strategic value for Central Asia and the Caucasus is immense.

(Interview given to M. Howard and published by "Odyssey", Athens, March - April 2000, Excerpts) ;(Interview given to "Turkish Daily News" Ankara, June 1999 - Excerpts); (Interview given to I. Cevik, broadcasted by "Kanal 7", Istanbul and published by Turkish Daily News, Ankara, August 2000); (Speech delivered at the 52nd General Assembly of the United Nations, September 1997 - Excerpts); (Interview given to "Turkish Daily News" Ankara, June 1999 - Excerpts)

***

7.   For a Brave New Millennium

-I- It seems that all speakers in this last session of United Nations in the 20th century display a common tendency: We all try to assess the achievements and inadequacies of this century, which goes by. And we formulate hopes for the next millennium. Well, I will try to do my part.

As we look back at our century that is about to end, three categories, which within themselves comprise both achievements and failures, might be discerned:

1) The 20th Century achieved remarkable technological / scientific capabilities, but,it did not put them fully to the use of humanity. Instead of mobilizing all its force to build, protect and enhance life, this was used to a large degree for the destruction and extermination of life.

2) The 20th Century achieved enormous accumulation of wealth but used it for one fifth of the world population and deprived the rest from benefits of economic growth.

3) The 20th Century achieved enormous intellectual depth but throughout the century, intellectual distortions as fascism and racial discrimination, as well as policies and politics on ethnic lines caused the extermination of millions.

This brings up the challenge which we face: What is to be initiated, to be inspired, to be organized by the UN, so that it further brings the contribution of an international organization to forge a more rational and more humane century, in the millennium that begins?

No easy responses, of course, but I will try to formulate some elementary suggestions:

First, a very strong drive to limit the ongoing sophistication of means to kill. Not to impose certain limits solely on the demand side, but on the offer as well. An effective convention, which would be morally and politically binding, as, for example, the European Human Rights Convention. An undertaking to contribute to human welfare, to environment, to life, for every deadly weapon produced...

Second, a drive to accumulate an international fund, an organized and morally binding plan to donate a given fraction of national income, to geographies which for centuries were forced to contribute to that wealth and to that income. Not a charity, but an orchestrated effort for development projects to be internationally financed.

Finally, a coordinated, resolute plan to purify minds and souls from the distortions of discriminations of all kinds, from racism, from totalitarianism, from policies and politics on ethnic lines. A concrete legal setup to condemn publicly and to punish universally all parties and countries, which to a smaller or larger degree follow discrimin atory lines, countries that in their legislations or practices reflect those unfortunate distortions.

98

The General Assembly, which you preside, Mr. President, marks the last to be held in this century. We are about to turn a new leaf in history. It is also a time to adjust our priorities and determine our agenda for the next Century.

Our global challenges hereafter, whether political, economic, social or environmental, will continue to require our concerted efforts. As the main world forum for international cooperation, the United Nations will continue to be the focal point of our collective work. Its effectiveness will depend on our willingness to make it an indispensable tool for our global responds to our global dilemmas.

-II- A little over a month ago, one of the deadliest earthquakes of the century struck the northwest of Turkey, which is the most populous region of the country. The devastating quake claimed more than 20.000 lives and thrice as much wounded. It left nearly half a million homeless.

This tragedy has been a source of immense anguish for the Turkish nation. We continue to tackle the humanitarian and economic dimensions of this disaster.

We have, nevertheless, derived great fortitude from the exemplary display of solidarity and the swift response of the international community to rally to the assistance of Turkey. In fact, through this tragedy, the best qualities of human nature were displayed. Namely, the capability of the human being, and of nations, to share the other's agony; to share its burden; to contribute to its reconstruction.

I would like to convey the profound gratitude of the Government and people of Turkey, to the international community, the United Nations system, all organizations, institutions and agencies, along with the numerous volunteers and individuals that stood with Turkey at its most trying hour. You were most friendly, generous and efficient. Your young men and women were with us, searching for survivors under the rubble and sometimes risking their lives to save our lives. In fact, all countries, all peoples rushed to bring humanitarian, medical, technical, and financial aid. All members of the international community displayed a tremendous solidarity. We are grateful to all of them. We shall never forget them.

The Turkish Government has mobilized all its human and material resources to alleviate the suffering. We concentrate all our energies to overcome the consequences of this human tragedy.

The continued support of the international community in this arduous task remains crucially important.

Taking into account the solidarity displayed by the international community in the face of the earthquake we endured, we believe it would be appropriate for this organization to take a further step with regard to natural disasters. This would also be in keeping with the enhanced role of the United Nations in the new era. That is why my country, together with Greece, which also suffered a similar calamity recently, is introducing a draft resolution to the General Assembly on this subject. We hope that it will receive your full support.

-III- Poised, at the epicenter of Eurasia, Turkey aspires to broaden the circle of cooperation and shared prosperity in her region through initiatives for economic development. At the crossroads of civilizations, she continues in its traditional role of connectingcontinents and bridging differences between cultures and peoples.

Turkey this year will be the host of the last summit of the century. The OSCE Summit to be held in Istanbul in November will set stage to important decisions. These will define the future security and cooperation architecture of the Eurasian landscape.

In this geography and in the course of the last decade, we have witnessed the appearance or -confirmation of several entities as independent states.

With the great majority of them, we share our history, or faith, or language. At some instances, we share all three important attributes. As a matter of fact, the end of the Cold War provided Turkey with a changed international environment where historical and cultural dimensions are highlighted.

-IV- We have seen more than enough that inertia and disinterested reflection breeds only pestilence. Indeed, the confrontation in Kosovo has been brought to an end only with such resolutely pursued initiatives.

We are committed to the vision of a peaceful, democratic, and prosperous future in southeastern Europe, and we will continue to bring forth our resources and contribution to that end. The need for a large-scale and long-term stabilization and reconstruction program for the entire region, and more urgently for Kosovo is evident.

100

We therefore welcome the establishment of the Stability Pact for Southeastern Europe. In this context, it is important that the agreements and arrangements on Kosovo are fully implemented along with the maintenance of support and assistance to Albania and Macedonia.

On the other hand, the wounds opened by the Bosnian tragedy are not yet completely healed. The provisions of the Dayton Peace Agreement must be strictly observed and implemented.

The tragedies in the Balkans have taught us to be absolutely cautious in addressing conflicts among nations. We do not have the luxury of selective memory. We cannot afford pursuing virtual objectives and plans, which do not correspond, to the realities and to the aspirations of all peoples concerned.

In this context a case in point is Cyprus. Indeed, a just and lasting compromise in Cyprus can only be based upon the existing realities. There are two separate peoples, two separate states in Cyprus. These two states should be able to solve their differences through their own free will. On our part, we believe that the confederation proposal made by the Turkish Cypriot side can serve this purpose. It provides the basis for realistic and viable solution in Cyprus.

-V- Turkey is actively involved in the efforts to secure peace and stability in Southern Caucasus, in the Middle East and in Central Asia. We participate substantially in their democratic and economic development.

We are encouraged by the recent progress in the Middle East Peace Process. Once mutual tolerance and understanding start to fully reign over this region, her natural and human resources of this region, and the great wealth of wisdom it embodies will be sources of strength. My country, at once a European and Asian nation, will continue to actively support the aim of reaching peace and security in the Middle East.

Likewise, cooperation can lead to the wealth and prosperity for the peoples of our wider region the wealth and prosperity; because they are as well endowed with rich human and natural resources. Balkans, Caucasus and that Central Asia will witness substantial economic development during the next decades. Turkey, lying at the hub, will become an energy terminal in its own right, connecting in more than one sense of the world, the wealth of the two parts of Eurasia, witnessing their increasing interaction. We are determined to take part in this great journey and see the mega projects of the next century erected in our country and region. At the crossroads of continents, we will bring in our contribution to bridge differences between cultures and civilizations.

-VI- Two months ago Turkey and Greece initiated a dialogue. High ranking officials of foreign ministries held two rounds of talk and explored the possibilities of promoting cooperation in the fields of tourism, environment, trade, culture, regional cooperation and the fight against organized crime, illegal immigration, drug trafficking and terrorism.

Both sides agreed that there is a scope for further cooperation in these fields and identified specific projects to this end.

Turkey has the political determination to carry the dialogue process beyond its current framework and spread it to other fields.

It is our belief that there are no insolvable problems between Turkey and Greece so long as the two countries have the good will and the political determination.

-VII- The compelling lesson to be drawn from 20th century is that we must all place human values at the top of our priorities. We must overcome ethnic and religious divisions that stand in the way of human progress. The well-being of men and women, their right to a dignified life and the security and prosperity of nations must take precedence over all priorities.

Whether it is to halt aggression and uphold international law, to arrest crimes committed against humanity, to purge societies of racist and xenophobic tendencies, cultural and religious intolerance, to combat international terrorism or to provide humanitarian assistance, to bridge the gap between the rich and the poor, to secure sustainable economic and social development for all nations, we should mount a massive international coalition against all threats to international peace, security and prosperity.

We must all share in the responsibility of averting human misery and making the world a better place for all of its inhabitants, present and future.

(Speech Delivered at the General Assembly of the United Nations, September 1999)

* * *

CHAPTER III :
Nothing Can Justify Terror

I believe that West-Europeans have a share in the responsibility for the ethnic and separatist terrorism that Turkey faced in early 1980's and in 1990's. This does not relieve Turkey's political leadership of her own responsibility, due to mismanagement. Nevertheless, the Western political elite and media, by their misunderstandings and prejudices, sometimes by their animosity, contributed fully to the tragedies that Turkey went through. From 1987 to 1997, I was one of those who tried -sometimes in vain- to explain and to persuade my colleagues at the Parliamentary Assembly of the Council of Europe, Strasbourg. From 1997 on, I pursued this "mission" as a foreign minister. "Terror" has been a consistent subject in my work at international fora. Turkey was made a target of separatist terror, of ethnic, sometimes racial substance. Furthermore, terror organization had the general complaisance of some West European publics, the political, financial, logistic and military support of some Western or Eastern countries. The toll that this brought about was thousands of innocent lives. I have to underline that most of the times I had to deal with colleagues who were completely unaware of the realities, knew nothing of Turkish historical development, of the conceptual understanding of "minorities" in the Ottoman interpretation of Islam, etc. On the contrary, they generally displayed nothing but prejudices and a repetition of the claims of the terrorist organization and their affiliates. To be fair, I have to add that I could - during my ministry - convince some of my European Union colleagues to look into realities and to see through different optics as well. On the other hand, since late 1980's, I tried as well to make the West European colleagues understand that their support to ethnically oriented policies in other countries enhances ethnical politics among their own people. What we actually observe is the rise of xenophobic and sometimes fascist trends in Western Europe.

1. Over-Emphasizing Ethnicity Leads to Disasters in Europe

My intervention to discuss some aspect of a "Draft Resolution" at the Council of Europe, displays some of the unfounded claims that we faced; as well as some of the basics on Turkey. I believe my letter of March 1997, summarizes a period of misunderstandings and, from my viewpoint, the biased approaches of some West Europeans.

I have gone through the "Introductory Memorandum" that Mr. Haggard sent me and I would like to formulate some initial comments. I hope to make a thorough study as well and will present it to you later. I believe that my remarks and suggestions might be of relevance to your work, underlining some specific aspects, which might have been overlooked by the rapporteurs in the preliminary draft. I would also like to draw attention to some assertions that need to be checked before your work is finalized.

I thank you for your kind evaluation of our assistance to the rapporteurs during their contacts in Turkey. I hope your forthcoming visit proves to be helpful as well.

1) The ratification of Protocol No 11 had been taken up positively by the government. It is supposed to reach the Parliament soon. Nevertheless, given some of the late decisions by the Court, as in the case of "Loisidou", which declares Turkey responsible for presumable violations of human rights in regions outside the jurisdiction of the Turkish Republic, have generated doubts and criticism (which I find generally justified) about the Court.

2) I agree that prosecution of members of parliament should be conducted with the greatest concern. Furthermore, neither parliamentarians nor non-parliamentarians should be convicted for their political views. But your statement about the DEP case contains some factual errors and needs to be re-checked by our rapporteurs:

The four DEP deputies that you are referring to were not sentenced under Article 8 of the anti-terror law and because of their political views. They were charged and sentenced under Article 168/1 of the Penal Code, which deals with membership and assistance to separatist armed gangs. The European Commission of Human Rights and the Court is actually examining their cases. Their allegations as to the "absence of fair trial and denial of free expression" were declared unjustified by the Commission (23 May 1995).

I believe you would agree that no authority, whether internal, external or international has a right to dictate or even to suggest its will to the Justice. "To call on authorities to withdraw the existing charges" is contrary to basic principles of justice and to international law. Since it is obvious that "the authorities" qualified to bring charges are judiciary authorities and that the "authorities" mentioned in the introductory memorandum are Judiciary instances, I believe that the relevant paragraphs are unjustified and alien to the "rule of law" that the Council of Europe promotes. I cannot understand how this concept of intrusion into the rights of the judiciary is tolerated or even advocated by some of our colleagues with a judiciary or legal background.

3) To assert that "sentencing of Kurdish members of Parliament have deprived the South-Eastern region of the country of two-thirds of its representatives" (paragraph - c) is false, does not fit into the Turkish reality, and it's dangerous as well. The concept of "minority" as defined in paragraph (K) is inadequate. I will try to elaborate:

It is not a "claim"- as stated in the draft memorandum-, but it is a fact that the number of parliamentarians of Kurdish origin is far superior to the percentage of our citizens of Kurdish origin. And, more than half of those parliamentarians have their constituencies in regions other than the South-east. Turkey being a country with millennia of history at the crossroads of civilizations, we are made of several ethnicities and cultures. But, the main point I want to make is different. I do not agree at all with the criteria based on race as a distinctive and major tool for analysis. This criterion is quite a decisive one in Western European tradition, as it is reflected in the work of the Council of Europe and, as I observe, in the draft memorandum. This is not the case in Turkey, where "race" is not and has never been a relevant social or political factor. The historical categorizing had been "Muslim" and "non-Muslim" subjects of the Empire. Among the Muslims, there was no distinction; regardless of their race and origins, they were all equal, both in juridical and practical terms. This is why the relevance of ethnicity based on race in Turkey is radically different than what it is in Central and Western

Europe. As in any democratic country, at the present there is of course no distinction between "Muslim" or "non-Muslim" citizens.

This of course, does not mean that I am not, in fact, that we are not, in favor of freedom of cultural and democratic expression for any citizen who feels this need. Unfortunately, the ongoing terrorist attacks by separatist groups have created an unfavorable atmosphere that I hope, will soon be overcome. It seems that the remainder of "Article 8" that you are referring to in paragraph (D), which sanctions cases of "separatist propaganda", might then be dealt with a new approach.

A last point: Western Europe and organizations like the Council of Europe should be very cautious in dealing with criteria based on race. The over-emphasis on nationalism and ethnic and racial distinctions to dismantle the ex-Yugoslavia has proved to be one of the main factors in the plight of the Balkans in general and in the genocide in Bosnia-Herzegovina, in particular.

4) As a writer and former president of Turkish Journalists Trade Union, I am among those that insistently calls for more press freedom; freedom from the State and from the capital as well. I agree with some general aspects of the assertions in the memorandum (paragraph E), but I believe it's generally exaggerated and contains some factual errors.

Even a single journalist jailed for the expression of his views is too many, but the numbers you have given are a total exaggeration. I wish you had checked it yourself before putting them into the memorandum. The large majority of cases you are referring to are cases, which do not involve journalists. You can send the name-list you have to the International Press Institute, to one of the several Turkish Journalist Associations and check it yourself. Furthermore, majority of the cases you are referring to were not sentenced for the expression of views but for instigation to terror, defamation, etc.

I do not understand how the draft memorandum can state so freely that ...the state broadcasting authority frequently orders televisions and radio stations off the air for "broadcasting reports that embarrass the government". This is one of those assertions that somehow found its way into the memorandum but which harm the overall credibility and reliability of the report. The temporary interdictions to broadcast, were almost all due to offences of denial

106

of the right to reply to individuals and organizations, to pornography and defamation, whereas the memorandum implies that the government, whenever it is "embarrassed" -which is the case most of the time and for most governments- just orders the broadcasters to close-down. Please check the allegations in the draft memorandum. I checked it and found out that only six out of some total 30 temporary interdictions for televisions were of political nature, all six of them referring to the "indivisibility of the country", and none to the government.

After it had a strong negative reaction from public opinion, the tentative "press law" was not even formally introduced. It seems that it is definitely withdrawn.

I will comment on the terminology employed by the draft memorandum to describe the situation in South-Eastern Turkey in a later paragraph.

5) The relevant committee of the Council of Europe continually monitors the situation in the prisons. Much progress seems to have been made.

The approach to "persons disappearing and extra-judiciary killings" should be formulated more cautiously: Of course, your interlocutors are the Turkish Parliament and Turkish authorities, but I wonder on which facts and figures you base your assertion that the PKK "may be" responsible for as many murders, disappearances and atrocities as are the police and security forces. I think that this is an unjustified comparison. You might go through the Reuters and AP reports on the number of teachers (more than a hundred) and civilians murdered in mass executions by the PKK and check the validity of this comparison. Furthermore, South-Eastern Turkey unfortunately has still its traditional feudal set-up; its particular feudal laws and much of the "extra-judiciary killings" are due to feudal murders originating from land disputes, vengeance, quest for clan domination, etc. The ongoing struggle between extremist organizations and between those involved in illegal trafficking is another source of the extra-judiciary killings. And, of course, the PKK "may be" responsible for some...

6) The draft memorandum insistently refers to a "civil war" or to a "serious civil war". This is not correct, neither legally nor objectively. The definition of "civil war" requires the presence of two

"civil" sides fighting each other. This is not the case in Turkey. On the contrary, the total absence of civil involvement (in spite of internal and external provocation) is the main positive characteristic of the unfortunate situation, and a cause for hope. This is partially due to the fact that Turkish citizens, of whatever origin they may be, have historically and traditionally never considered themselves as "minorities". Furthermore, there has never been a "fight" between the people and security forces. The "sides" are the security forces on one hand and a highly organized terrorist group, which receives political support from Western Europe and logistic support from our Eastern / South-Eastern neighbours.

"Civil War" is the correct terminology when applied to a case like "The Spanish Civil War." Actually, it is deliberately promoted to apply to South-Eastern Turkey in order to provide the terrorist movement with additional support. I wish that the Memorandum did not follow this course.

7) Finally, I would like to draw attention to a "general attitude" present in some parts of the draft Memorandum. This attitude bothers me.

First, most of the assessments that the memorandum takes for granted, don't seem to have been checked seriously by our rapporteurs. I pointed out a few examples. It seems that whatever Amnesty International reported, which is based on whatever the Turkish Human Rights Organizations reported, which is based on whatever temporary minor publication in a distant corner in Turkey stated, easily finds its way to the Memorandum. It is authoritatively stated, that ...the 16 lawyers accused of membership to PKK "...spent 7 and 25 days in prison in Diyarbakir, where they were subject to inhuman treatment." (paragraph J). I would wonder on what evidence have our reporters based themselves to put such a clear-cut assessment into the memorandum. I don't mean to say that everything is all right, of course there is lots to be done, but the situation that this memorandum describes in some of its paragraphs is a huge exaggeration and a hasty generalization.

Then, there are references made to "...a Turkish MP imprisoned three times for the articles he had made and found this a normal situation" (paragraph E), or assertions as "...many minorities have disappeared or are disappearing" (paragraph K), which are unbecoming in a serious paper. If I may, I would like to suggest a double-check on some of the allegations in the report.

Finally, I deplore the occasionally sarcastic terminology that is used in some paragraphs. It reflects a subconscious biased approach, creates doubts as to the aims and discredits the memorandum. Paragraph K, for example: *"One may wonder what would have happened if Turkey had applied the provisions of these conventions and of assembly Recommendation 1201 (1993) generously to its provinces in the South-East !"* - The exclamation mark belongs to the original text. -

Dear Mr. Schwimmer, I look forward to your visit to Turkey and I hope that your contacts will provide you with further information.

Ismail Cem, Chairman, Turkish ParliamentaryDelegation to the Council of Europe (Letter to Walter Schwimmer, Rapporteur for the MonitoringProcedure on Turkey, Council of Europe, March 1997 - Excerpts)

* * *

2. An Anti-Islam Crusade?

I have gone through the motion for a resolution, Doc. 7769, 'on the Situation in Turkey' relating to domestic unrest, the protection of human rights and democratic freedoms', signed by you and by some of our colleagues.

I would like to share with you some of my views and concerns:

a) The motion for a resolution, along with some true assessments and sincere suggestions, incorporates mainly unfounded allegations. I hope that you will personally check the validity of these claims. Generally, some obscure news from a doubtful source is picked up by a local 'human rights' organization, which does not bother to investigate and to confirm. Then, its 'assertions' are in turn picked up by an international 'human rights' group, which, without checking and double-checking, brings it to international attention.

b) Once those erroneous allegations are matured for international consumption, they are then channeled to parliamentarians and to press, which, in turn, present them to national and international fora. Sometimes, with good will and sincerity and sometimes as a deliberate political tool, to achieve certain political aims, devoid of any concern for truth and justice.

109

(I am sending you, annexed, a copy of a recent letter that I had addressed to some of our colleagues in view of the Introductory Draft Memorandum on the Monitoring of Turkey, which is broadly related to some of the concerns in the Motion for a Resolution, Doc. 7769.)

c) What is 'original' in the Motion for a Resolution Doc. 7769, signed by you and your colleagues, is that it takes up the argument, the strategy and the cause of PKK, the terrorist / separatist movement, with an unparalleled fidelity. This motion represents the highest level of escalation that the terrorist / separatist cause have reached through the collaboration of Western European parliamentarians. This, after all, is your concern and depends on your political will.

d) My real concern and what I want to share with you is of another nature:

I am afraid that the anti-Turkish (with strong connotations of anti-Islam) discourse in Western Europe, of which your "Motion for a Resolution" is a striking example, seems to be laying grounds for dangerous outcomes, both in Turkey and in Western Europe.

The idea that the Western Europe is initiating a new anti-Islam crusade in the form of an anti-Turkish crusade is gaining ground with Turkish populations both in Turkey and in Western Europe. I might not put it in such words, but I have to say that I sometimes share their impressions. Furthermore, the ethnic cleansing of Bosnian Muslims by the Bosnian Orthodox and the long-lasting passive approach of Western Europe vis-à-vis the massacres in Bosnia has contributed to a common anxiety in Muslim populations. All through the world and especially in Turkey and in Western Europe, where people of Muslim and especially Turkish origin consider themselves as the main targets of a new escalation, mistrust, fears and sometimes-exaggerated reactions are on the rise. Recent negative attitudes of the German and French governments towards their "guest workers", mainly of Muslim faith, have further contributed to these concerns.

Initiatives as this "Motion for a Resolution", in political terms, represents a parallelism between some West-European parliamentarians and a terrorist / separatist organization. They both aim to discredit and, if it is possible, to paralyse Turkey's resolve to fight terrorism. Initiatives as such do nothing but support the concern and the fears of those who feel themselves as the targets of the new

110

crusade. The psychological environment that some of our colleagues seem to be willingly or unwillingly contributing to aggravate, can trigger nothing but trouble in Western Europe, which hosts around ten million Muslim workers, and among which about four million are Turkish citizens.

Dear Colleague, I hope you do not consider my concerns as an intrusion to your political judgments. My concerns are sincere and I believe they are justified. I would like to ask you, if I may, to reconsider your commitment to this "Motion for a Resolution".

Ismail Cem, Chairman, Turkish Delegation to the Parliamentary Assembly of the Council of Europe (Letter to Italian Parliamentarians of The Council of Europe whoparticipated in a joint draft-resolution on Turkey, March 1997)

* * *

3. To End the Illegal Immigration

Western Europe is understandably concerned about illegal immigration. The interesting aspect is that while encouraging that kind of immigration on one hand, on the other, they sometimes tend to put the responsibility to countries, which do their best to prevent such immigration. When Turkey is concerned, they tend as well to romanticize "...those who flee from oppression", etc. In my response to a letter by my colleague and friend Lamberto Dini, I had tried to clarify the causes of such immigration and Turkey's position.

I have received your letter of 30 December 1997 and given careful consideration to its content. We have been following the repercussions of the attempted illegal immigration to Italy. We understand your concerns and we sympathize with them. To be helpful, I would like to convey our views on the points that you raise and on some others, which I consider as essential.

1- I do not agree with the repeated allegory made to "exodus" in your text. If the analysis of the recent events is based on wrong presumptions it will be difficult to reach genuine solutions.

I am sensitive on this terminology for Turkey has both historically and contemporarily constituted a safe heaven, a country that sheltered the peoples who were forced to an "exodus".

111

Let me recall that in 1988 and in 1991, more than half a million refugees from Northern Iraq have found shelter and assistance in Turkey. Iranian masses fleeing the newly founded radical regime, Bulgarian Turks and Bosnians were welcomed in our country, as this was the case in our history, when tens of thousands of persecuted Jews from Spain, Portugal and Germany found tolerance and a home in Turkey.

2- The current problem is a blatant case of illegal trafficking in human beings, an extremely serious form of organized crime. This criminal activity is based on the exploitation of the understandable desire to have a better life. To present this basic cause as a romanticized human rights problem deviates from reality, encourages those who organize illegal immigration and serves their interest. It provides the traffickers with a moral justification. Furthermore, official and ministerial statements reported by the Italian press and which are perceived as promises to grant political asylum to illegal immigrants would probably encourage and initiate new waves of migration.

3- Illegal immigration has always been a source of concern for Turkey. We have consistently sought multilateral cooperation against all forms of organized crime and international terrorism. We have drawn attention to their interrelation, to the funding of terrorism by organized crime -like the organization of illegal migrations- and to networks of crime established in Western Europe under various guises.

4- Our efforts to devise and implement common measures against organized crime including illegal immigration have so far remained inconclusive. This is largely due to false analyses or to miscalculations prevailing in some Western European countries. Their policies meant in practice a tolerance for terror related activities. These acts were, in principle, aimed to Turkey and not considered as a danger to the host country. In fact, they are: The recent samples of illegal immigration is just one of the offshoots of the complaisant attitude effective in most Western Europe. The Italian cases are the logical follow up of some 90,000 such illegal immigrations to Germany in recent years, organized by similar networks and encouraged by similar attitudes (Paul Geitner, "Illegal Migrants Turn to Smugglers", Associated Press, 19/04/1997).

112

We hope that the host countries will be more receptive to our persistent calls for combating international terrorism and organized crime.

5- The illegal trafficking of human beings has been a subject of consideration between Italy and Turkey and it has recently been agreed to make use of and develop the provisions of the existing agreements. We remain committed to such cooperation with Italy and to work for its refinement.

(a) Following our meeting with Deputy Minister Fassino, last November, the Italian Undersecretary for the Interior Ministry had contacts in Ankara. My staff had relevant interviews with your Ambassador in Ankara.

(b) In these contacts, we have proposed the reunion of the Turkish-Italian Joint Committee to look for enhanced partnership against organized crime and to search for joint initiatives. It seems that the Italian side has not yet responded to this proposal. We are ready to cooperate with our Italian counterparts on all possible joint efforts.

(c) We are taking all appropriate measures needed to contain illegal immigration as an organized crime, through or from Turkey. But I would underline as well the need for dealing effectively with its connections in the favorable environment that it generally finds in its host West-European countries.

(Letter to U.Dini, Foreign Minister of Italy, January 1998)

* * *

4. Terror and Assassination are not "Democratic Rights"

The following interviews to two French publications -Le Monde and l'Express- deal extensively with issues of democracy and the impact of terrorism on this development. It further analyses in depth the "minority issue", and the "South-Eastern Issue". These are of particular interest for some Western colleagues. Some of the analyses I developed in these interviews were repeated in further works. In fact, they had a receptive approach from several of my EU colleagues and had a positive impact in EU's future policies.

<u>113</u>

*** *How would you define the "Kurdish problem"? In which context do you place it?*

I believe certain sectors of West European public opinion have insufficient knowledge of Turkish history and apply the wrong instruments and pre-conceived schemes to realities of a different nature. I shall try to elaborate on this point since I deem it important: In analyzing and understanding the ethnic realities of Turkey, criteria based on "race" as a major distinctive tool is erroneous and have sometimes led to a tolerance for terror or to its encouragement. This criterion is quite a significant one in West European tradition, as reflected in its gloomy historical record. It also reflected in its current moral and political problems, such as the increase in racism and the rise of racist political parties.

The racial origin of our citizens is not a relevant factor in Turkey. I hope that we do not lose this feature under the influence of some Western influences. Being a country with millenniums of history and being located at the crossroads of civilizations, we come from several ethnicities and cultures. For example, if we were to conduct a study on our parliamentarians, we might end up with a vast proportion of parliamentarians claiming a Balkan, Caucasian and Kurdish origin. I regret to observe how keen most Western European approaches are on defining our people, in one way or another, by the criteria of race. As I said earlier, this is typically a West European attitude and it is alien to our realities and perceptions.

The concept of race as a distinctive factor and as the main attribute of "minorities" is specific to West European culture and history. In Turkey, where the Ottoman interpretation and implementation of Islam is one of the main components of cultural identity, and where the State had to keep together a multitude of ethnicity for centuries long, "race" simply did not exist as a social or a political category. The main distinctive factor had been religious, and "minorities" were always conceived in religious terms (i.e., Muslim and non-Muslim). There was a degree of tolerance, which for centuries long, constituted a yardstick for entire Europe. When some of our West European colleagues apply their version of social analyses based on their particular socio-cultural experience to a country like Turkey, they are misled. They end up with an overemphasis on race as a social factor and with a misguided concept

114

of minorities. This is probably why these analyses bring up wrong the conclusions and why Muslim Turks, whether of Kurdish, Caucasian, Balkan or any other racial origin, are irritated when they discover that they are suddenly defined as "minorities" by West European discourse.

*** *What is the crux of the problem? Terrorism? Separatism? Aspiration for recognition of the cultural identity?*

Misconception by certain West Europeans, from time to time, leads them to show some sort of understanding for a 14 year-long terror campaign directed against Turkey. This leads them to share an indirect responsibility for the murder of thousands of innocent men, women and children; and of 112 primary-school teachers executed and later photographed for their unique "crime" of teaching Turkish. It must be understood that separatism and terror are methods appropriated by only an extremely small proportion of Turkey's citizens of Kurdish origin. If you add them all up, you would only be looking at about 4-5 thousand terrorists and separatists. What is more, the majority is from northern Iraq, Syria and Iran as opposed to being Turkish nationals.

On the other hand, the link between separatist terror and the backward feudal structures present in South-East Turkey should be taken into consideration. Separatist terror draws its strength mainly from feudal landlords of Kurdish origin. At first glance, this may seem as a contradiction. One might wonder what these extremely wealthy feudal landlords who own tens of villages and exploit landless peasants have in common with separatists and terrorists. However, sharing the same values and concepts, the feudal system and the separatist terror organization have become de facto allies. In order to maintain their existence, both have to protect, preserve and promote feudal values such as "race", "kinship" and "tribal links". In essence, the terrorist movement is based on the principle of race. It is a racist movement; racist, just like the feudal system, like the guardians, beneficiaries of this system.

For feudal landlords, whose social system, power structure and prerogatives are based on race and kinship, to be insensitive towards separatist-terrorists, who as well derive their identity from the same sources, is unimaginable. This would endanger the feudal setup in its totality. In the world of feudal values, this would be an unforgivable act for the landlords. Therefore, separatist terror finds itself in a natural and inevitable social-practical alliance with the feudal landlords of the South-East. The two complement each other, as witnessed during the last decade.

As the world moved away from bi-polarity, and as the Soviet Empire was dismantled, people's interest in their ethnic characteristics grew. Concepts and understandings such as "cultural identity", "sub-culture", "multiculture" and "minority" gained impetus. One must recognize this as a reality of our times. However, as the French President Chirac said for France in his speech in Rennes, dated 4th of December, 1998, one must also "...transform cultural diversity into a factor of unity..."

You mention "separatism". Any approach which connotates a change in the borders of a country, is to be addressed very carefully. This is the substance of international law, the UN and all OSCE agreements. Concepts such as "autonomy" and "self-determination" are concepts with clear-cut definitions and preconditions that are determined by the United Nations. As the most important precondition, a category of citizens, due to their race and/or religion, has to be deprived of holding office in State functions. Therefore, to envisage concepts such as "autonomy" and "self-determination" for a country like Turkey, where people from all ethnic groups hold office at the highest levels of State, would contradict the legal bases and justification for such concepts.

Referring to "freedoms which need improvement", the subject narrows down to "freedom of expression" and "linguistic freedoms". These are thoroughly discussed in our public opinion. As I have pointed out, progress in freedoms, like in any country in the world, is affected by the prevailing conditions. It is difficult to reach a societal consensus in an environment where thousands have been massacred by separatist-terrorists. We have certain shortcomings, but these surely cannot justify the murders of a terrorist organization. They can neither justify the tolerance, sometimes encouragement provided to terrorism by some West European circles. Besides, the current situation in Turkey is not as bad as it is generally reflected. There are over a dozen newspapers and magazines; there are radio stations as well which are published or broadcasted in the two Kurdish dialects, Zaza and Kirmanci. Though it is not legal, there are some television stations that broadcast in those dialects as well.

There is another issue that I would like to point out. Turkey, as it is the case in France, has adopted the principle of a "unitary state". Therefore, there is no room in our system for definitions of minorities that are based on race. Let me give another reference from France. As Term President of the Council of Europe, Committee of Minister, the Minister of State in the current French Government, Mr. Moskovici explains on 23rd of September, 1997, why France is not to be a party to "Framework Convention for the Protection of National Minorities" and the "European Charter for Regional or Minority Languages" as follows:

"...The concept of minorities is alien to principles of law that form the basis of the Republic of France. As a result of our revolutionary tradition and heritage, we have appropriated rights guaranteed to each citizen (individual), as opposed to collective rights for minorities; we prefer the concept of sovereignty to regional autonomy. We are not a federative nation."

*** Besides the fight against the violent acts of the PKK... there is also pressure directed against "pro-ethnicity" politics...

I am against politics based on religion and race. Politics as such is a disgrace for human history, and the fact that it still finds support is a disgrace for our times.

The representatives in Turkey of, in your words, "pro-ethnicity" politics have found the tolerence expected of a democratic society. What cannot be found is the opportunity to cooperate with the terrorist organization and to provoke a certain race to hatred and violence against another. And this is not a limitation found only in Turkey. It is in the legal framework of several West European states, including France. The fact that certain political parties or members of parliament have been found guilty by the judiciary is a result, either of their connection with the terrorist organization, or of their campaigns of racial division or violence. In addition, Turkish law, in conformity with the framework and relevant articles of the European Convention on Human Rights, does not permit the promotion of the idea of "dismantling the territorial integrity". That is, in Turkey, propaganda for the separation of parts of the country is illegal. There may be countries that permit such propaganda. However, within the context of the realities of the Middle East, and of present-day Turkey, which has so much suffered from separatist-terrorist assaults, we

117

maintain our position, which is in line with international law. Legal difficulties on the freedom of expression exist. In a society where thousands have lost their lives because of terror, defining the line between the peaceful assertion of ideas and the encouragement of resorting to violence is sometimes problematic. This subject is intensively debated in our public opinion. I consider these problems as the characteristics of a period that we are leaving behind. As we overcome terror, problems as such will belong to the past.

***What is the policy of the Government with regard to these problems?

Our primary concern is the neutralization of foreign support for terror. The agreement that has been reached with Syria on combating terror, in particular, has dealt a major blow to the primary logistic support for the terrorist organization. There has been some progress in cutting off their support from Western Europe and especially from Greece. We have the advantage now of having brought the reality of the terrorist organization and its supporters in front of the eyes of West European public. Now they finally see in concrete terms what this public opinion has "tolerated" and what some of its politicians supported for years. In order to alleviate the adverse economic conditions that the separatist- terrorist organization was able to exploit, we are actually implementing a special economic plan directed at regions which were hurt the most by terrorism.

With years of work and sacrifice, the activities within our borders of the terrorist movement have at last been contained and, to a large degree annihilated. A new and more optimistic environment emerging, the government has made serious progress on certain issues to make up for some delays in our democratic process. These developments give hope for the future.

*** What do you think of the European reaction to the Ocalan case?

There are varying reactions. In general terms, the following can be said: Certain West European circles have gone as far as supporting the terrorist organization and its chieftain. It seems as if this support comes, at least for the time being, primarily from Greece. There are continuing efforts to politicize what is clearly a matter of terror.

The scope of terrorist attacks that Turkey faced during the last decade has been decreasing constantly. The agreement reached between Syria and Turkey to combat terrorism seems to be decisive in bringing terrorism to the verge of extinction. The era of great losses is now coming to an end. But justice will not prevail unless the main perpetrator of these ominous crimes stands trial in the country of his victims. We do not want a legal case of murderous crimes to be affected by political concerns or scenarios. We expect all involved countries to abide by international law.

Europe should not be a safe haven for fugitives from justice. West European countries should be loyal to their own principles and unite their forces to suppress terrorism and to promote the rule of law.

With respect to public opinion in Western Europe, we observe an interesting development: Since the issue has acquired publicity, there is now an unprecedented level of public interest. Public interest, attracted information. And, a public opinion that is now better informed, has attained a certain degree of objectivity. This is a welcome development. For example, the terrorist organization is finally being seen, as it is, an organization of terror. Along with the usual biased rhetoric, several objective reports were made in recent weeks. This is a very positive change.

Drug trafficking by the terrorist organization, its substantial role in the poisoning of West European youth, and its place on Interpol documents have finally made it into newspapers. France has started inquiring into money collected from people through threats and use of force. Sweden has a new interest in finding realities on the abduction of children to be educated as terrorists. An article on the children in Germany that have been torn apart from their families and raised as terrorists have been recently published in the Frankfurter Allgemaine. I suggest you read it. To sum up, Western European media, which in the past had the practice of wrong assessments, is now reflecting realities as well, in an unprecedented fashion.

We have a saying in Turkish, "...out of each evil, something positive emerges". I hope that the capture of the chieftain of the terrorist organization will present the opportunity for West European public opinion to distance itself from her usual biased approaches.

(Interview given to Le Monde, Paris, December 1998)

"SPILL-OVER" EFFECTS OF OUR 40 YEARS OF "OUTPOST" MISSION: When we talk about "reforms", we mean changes that affect all our citizens of whatever ethnic background. It is true that there is a delay on some points, mainly because of the internal anti-democratic spillover effects of our 40 years as an "outpost of the West" facing the Soviets. Some realities specific to this "mission" had a negative effect on our democratic and institutional development. And, in the recent past, the terrorist-separatist attacks encouraged or assisted by neighbouring geographies. Now, we are in a phase where we are almost overcoming this terrorism. As stated by Prime Minister Ecevit, the more terrorism fades out, the further our process of dealing with delays will develop. This is what is taking actually place. As for your reference to human rights record, I think this record should not be kept solely in regard to a period of terrorist threat. It should be assessed as well on a comparative basis and in regards to years where millions in Europe were exterminated because of their race; in regards to Centuries where some 90,000 people - around 60,000 being women - were burned at stake because of their beliefs or dissent.

Our understanding of "ethnic minorities" has some connotations with that of France and Greece: "Concept of rights based on individual freedoms of citizens, the exclusion of ethnic definitions and collective ethnic rights" in France; "religious criteria for the definition of minorities" in Greece.

(Interview given to M. Howard and published by "Odyssey", Athens, March - April 2000, Excerpts)

* * *

5. Democracy, Lingustic Freedoms and the National Security Council

***Impact of terrorism on Turkey's development ?*
-I- Turkey is currently implementing democratic reforms to enhance the supremacy of law and human rights. The statute of candidate to the UE, recently recognized at the Summit of Helsinki, encouraged Turkey to follow her path. Nevertheless, the motivation, which is behind this process, is the consciousness that our people deserve a better future.

Turkey ratified the majority of the International Conventions which safeguard the humans right and fundamental freedoms. The engagements that these conventions bring about often go beyond the criteria of Copenhagen. The threat of a terrorism encouraged and assisted from abroad blocked till recently the realization of democratic projects. The success obtained in the combat against terrorism gave an impetuous to the work carried out in this domain. In fact, our government has carried out important reforms and will continue to carry them further.

As for the terrorist chief, Turkey is among the founding members of the Council of Europe and she recognized the binding jurisdiction of the European Court of Human Rights in 1987. It is not therefore relevant to link the statute of official candidate to EU with legal obligations, which are already assumed due to Turkey's membership to the Council of Europe.

Turkey having suffered so much from terrorism, the abolition of capital punishment does not find yet an appropriate political environment. It is to note though that no execution took place in Turkey since 1984.

***Democracy, Kurdish "minority" and linguistic freedoms?*

-II- The democratic reform process in Turkey was delayed for obvious reasons. It is reinitiated last May (1999) and will continue. Turkey is one of the rare countries that simultaneously fought terrorism and took steps in the right direction.

Turkey is a democratic country, a secular Republic, a Member State of the Council of Europe and candidate to the European Union. Located at the crossroads of civilizations, having millennia of history, a cultural wealth supported by her particular historic development, experience, cultural and religious diversity. You mention " Kurdish " minority in your question. I would like to briefly recall the historical, conceptual and constitutional framework of our understanding:

a) The historical / cultural heritage of our people;

b) The constitutional principles of Turkey;

c) The secular basis of the Republic;

d) The Treaty of Lausanne (1923) which provided the international basis for the new Republic; stipulate clearly that no distinction is made among the Muslim subjects of Turkey, that there exists no majority-minority relationship among them, and that the "minorities" in Turkey are only the Non-Moslem religious minorities.

Turkey is a unitary State, like France. The official language of the Republic is Turkish. Turkey does not represent the unique example of a country solely with one official language. Within this context, all Turkish citizens are free to use the language they choose.

Our citizens of Kurdish extraction as well can freely speak their language, diffuse programs in Kurdish on radios and publish books, magazines and newspapers in whatever language they prefer. This is realized in various Kurdish dialects, primarily Kirmanci or Zaza, which are almost two different languages. It should be noted though that TV broadcasting - and only TV broadcasting - in these two languages is not legalized, though through private stations they exist to a certain extent.

Most of the criticisms formulated about the use of languages other than Turkish are generally exaggerated and sometimes deprived of objectivity. The enlargement of the scope of personal freedoms is widely discussed. The reform process will continue. Of course, there are problems to be solved. But those problems in no case can provide pretexts to justify or to tolerate terrorism.

***The role of the "National Security Council" in a democracy ?*

-III- Turkish army, through its long history, has traditionally been an agent of progress and modernity. "The National Security Council", has a function parallel to bodies as such in the United States or in Europe. It provides a forum for top civilian and military personalities to share views and to make recommendations to the government on national security issues.

Taking into consideration the terrorist assaults that we have lived through during the last decade, it is understandable that the role of the National Security Council has acquired more relevance. Given the sensitivity of the situation and the scope of the murders terrorism brought about, it is again understandable - though not desirable - that on some points there might have been the possible trespassing of the functional definition of the Council. This is still a subject for debate in the public opinion. Turkey having almost overcome terrorism, having minimized separatist threats to her national security, the role of the NSC is returning to that of normalcy.

122

Furthermore, I want to underline once more that Turkey is not in dire need for "reforming" her democracy or her institutions. The image sometimes created in Western Europe and the U.S. is generally exaggerated and erroneous. What is to be achieved, is to overcome delays in our democratic development. I object firmly any rhetoric, which leads to false comparisons with situations totally alien to Turkey.

(Interview given to l'Express, Paris, May 2000 - Excerpts)

IS THE MILITARY GOING OVER ITS ROLE? *** *But Turkey will never be accepted into the European Union while for example bodies such as the "National Security Council - (NSC)" which comprises both generals and civilians remains as it is today. Turkey must convince Europe that its military is fully under civilian control.*

I don't agree with that analysis; it contains a lot of scenarios that are based on exaggerations. This is one point in which I have a strong belief and I will discuss that with my EU counterparts.

I have been a member of the NSC for three years. I've attended all the meetings. I see and know how it functions. And this is not true. First, it is not a place, which is dominated by the military. I sometimes feel myself as a conservative on some issues we discuss. Second, this is a consultative body. It is for the government to decide whether to go along with the proposals of the NSC or not.

Furthermore, what we discuss really are security issues. In a country like Turkey - which has faced in its recent past several vital security issues, both internal and external - it is normal that such a body is more functional than in some other countries. But hopefully, as we are doing better in matters of internal security, and external as well, so the level or role of the NSC will be more in parallel with some institutions that exist in other western countries. The military here is under the control of the Prime Minister and the government. So there haven't been any recent case, which could be interpreted as the military going over its role.

(Interview given to M. Howard and published by "Odyssey", Athens, March - April 2000)

* * *

6. A Choice to Make Between Terrorists and Their Victims

This interview is one of my major public statements following the appearance in Europe of the terrorist chief after he was forced to leave Damascus, where he and his organization were based for more than a decade. He had found a new refuge in Rome. His presence in Italy was a legal issue and we wanted it to be dealt as such. I further answered questions on the relationship between democratic rights and the encouragement that terrorists had from various circles in Western Europe.

(...) We expect the Italian Government (a) to fulfill its obligations as to the two Council of Europe Conventions that it has adhered, and that (b) it extradites to Turkey the main actor of terrorist assaults *(the terrorist leader who at that time had found refuge in Italy)*. Legally, it is a case of mass-murder, homicide, sabotage, which should be treated as such. As it would be treated by Italian courts if it were realized in Italy. Basically, it is a choice, that Italian justice and Italian administration will make between terrorism and its victims.

(...) We have not asked the diplomatic support of any country. It is not appropriate in a legal case, which we hope will be fair.

(...) It will be completely misleading to establish a link between the cultural demands of some of our citizens of Kurdish origin and those who are terrorists. Terrorism is a crime against humanity. Any social or political demand or the presumed lack of certain freedoms cannot justify the murder and the massacre of thousands. Terror cannot be justified under any circumstances.

(...) The demand that we have made to various West European countries: Not to encourage terrorist groups or their affiliated organizations. Not to be complaisant towards terrorism and not to tolerate those that create religious or / and racial hatred towards certain nations. Some have taken these concerns seriously. Some stayed indifferent. And a few, like Greece, have provided the terrorist groups with all its good offices.

It is also to note that those countries which encourage terrorism elsewhere have now began to suffer themselves in the hands of the evil they have nurtured.

(...) I believe some members of the Italian Parliament are mislead and misinformed by the terrorist propaganda and that they have insufficient knowledge of history and they use the wrong optics and pre-conceived schemes to realities of a different nature.

This misconception by some West Europeans sometimes leads them to show understanding for the terrorist campaign directed against Turkey. This leads to an indirect responsibility for the murders of thousands of innocent people, of women, of children; of 112 primary school teachers executed and photographed in front of a wall, for their unique "crime" of teaching Turkish.

(...) Xenophobic trends in some societies towards their foreign residents mainly of Muslim faith, have further contributed to negative developments. The recent attitudes in some political circles in Italy does nothing but support the concern and the fears of those who feel themselves as the targets of a new wave of hostilities. The last incident is the recent assault on Turkish journalists in Rome. I firmly believe that the xenophobic trend that some Italian colleagues seem to be promoting, can only bring further concerns, fears and trouble to Turkey, and, to Western Europe, which hosts around ten million Muslims, and among which about four million are Turkish citizens.

(...) The illegal trafficking of immigrants was initially misrepresented and misconceived in Italy. Its true nature, which consists of a criminal act to make money by illegal gangs, which exploit the aspirations for a better life of innocents, was quick to surface. Furthermore, it was well understood by the Italian public as well that the boats leave almost predominantly by coasts other than that of Turkey and transports people from countries other than Turkey.

(...) Turkey's presence at the Custom's Union as the "16th Country" already makes it as part of the EU Sphere. As to the integration process, there still is a discrimination, which should be dealt with at the highest level of EU. There has been progress; we hope that this continues and finalizes in the near future.

(Interview given to R. Orizio and published by Corriera della Serra , Rome, November 1998)

* * *

125

7.   Those Who Encourage Terrorism

With the capture of the terrorist chief, who has had extensive support from Greece and later took refuge at the Greek Embassy in Nairobi, Kenya, the scope of Greek participation to the responsibility of thousands of innocents killed by the terrorist organization became more evident than ever. My following statement is probably the one, which is the most strongly worded among all my press conferences. I thought it was well deserved by our neighbour. This was March 1999. Looking back and observing our relations with Greece now, in October 2000, one realizes the huge distance on a peaceful path we were able to cover with Greece.

(*Kayseri, A.A.*) Foreign Minister Ismail Cem pointed out Greece's extended support to terrorism and claimed "Greece has become a terrorist state." In a press conference in Kayseri, Cem called on the West European politicians who tolerate, finance, sympathize and encourage terror to take a look at the recent terrorist violence and reconsider their share of responsibility. Cem said: "The sufferance of our people as targets for terrorism is partly due to these irresponsible politicians." Cem, saying that the scope of terrorism added a new parameter to Turkey's foreign policy, continued as follows:

"I want to make it clear: Turkey is not a friend, she will not be a friend of those who are the friends of a terror organization. Foreign politicians must renounce this dangerous game, this inauspicious mission. Especially Greece must be careful. Owing to her unbelievable irresponsibility in giving a hand to terrorism, Greece has become a terrorist country. The definition of "terrorist country" has its international legal framework. If rulers of a country, its officials, consistently and deliberately support terrorism in view of harming another country, than, according to international law, their state is defined as a 'Terrorist State'. As far as international law is concerned, Greece has become a terrorist state, one that harbours, supports, finances terror and provides in her embassies shelter to fugitive terrorists.

Unless Greece cleans herself of her new definition of a flagrant terrorist state, we do not take her as an interlocutor, for any relevant issue.

We demand from this country (I do not mean entire Greece, entire Greek people, but a substantial part of Greek politicians) to put an end to the support it extends to terrorism and cut off its close links with terrorist organizations."
(Press Conference, reported by the Anatolian Agency foreign languages service, March 1999)

* * *

8.   An Appeal of a Different Kind

This is genuinely "of a different kind..." for I refrain from bringing emotions into political work. Nevertheless, I was so angry at the biased approaches of some West European politicians and media who displayed double standards at racist levels, that I simply could not avoid the emotional touch.

If a well-known terrorist, who devoted his life to organizing terrorist assaults to American cities and who was convicted by German justice for masterminding 25 arson attacks on American businessmen living in Germany, were accorded political asylum in Germany, would that look right?

Or, elaborating on our scenario, if another of the kind were to visit Athens and proclaim before the Greek press that his comrades' next move would certainly be to expand their war inside Switzerland and to target Bern, Zurich and Lausanne? Would that be considered as 'normal'?

Or, if a certain TV station, broadcasting from London and through the benevolence of the British would constantly incite Corsicans to take up their arms and murder the French? Would that appear as making use of a democratic right?

Or, if an Italian government were to make a mockery of its own judiciary system and its international commitments to assist a terrorist responsible for the murder of thousands of Austrians, -and of a major drug-dealing network- to escape trial and to flee Italy?

Would all these deeds be considered as tolerable, understandable and justifiable?

Unfortunately, these are not excerpts from a surrealist tall-tale. Each scenario refers to reality and in each case, the "subject", i.e., Germany, Greece, U.K. and Italy are authentic.

As for the "targets and victims", they are imaginary: It is obvious that they are not American businessmen, Frenchmen, American cities, Switzerland; and the thousands murdered are not Austrians. I hope that they will never be. But if they were, it would have been an entirely different story.

This is the point I want to raise: When it is Turkish businessmen living in Germany who are subject to arson attacks, when the so called "war" is to be expanded within Turkey, when Istanbul, Ankara and Izmir are cited by a terrorist as "potential targets" for terrorist attacks; when it is the Turkish people for whom the incitement to murder is committed and broadcasted; when the terrorist enjoying the good-offices of the "host country" has murdered thousands of Turkish people, then, it all becomes "understandable", "tolerable", and, sometimes, "deserves support".

I am not referring to these realities to draw attention from involved governments. By ourselves, we have managed to bring down the terrorist assaults, which have cost us so many lives. I just want to point out that no society can go on with such a hypocrisy displayed by so many of their politicians. And that complaisance by their leadership will sooner or later make those societies targets of their own encouraged terrorists.

If it's an appeal that I am making, it certainly is not to some governments. It's to the people.

(Press Conference, December 1998)

***

128

CHAPTER IV :
"If the Balkans Had Not Existed..."

1. "...The West Would Surely Have Created One..."

-I- A diplomat once said, "...if the Balkans had not existed, the West would surely have created one..."

In fact, "Balkans", a political terminology originating early 19th century, is more than a geographic definition. It is one, which brings a multitude of connotations. One, which reflects rooted prejudices as well. In fact, some argue that it replaced the centuries old scapegoat for Western Europe, which used to be the East, or Islam. Balkans emerged as "The Other", "The Outsider". In fact, throughout the 20th Century, the Balkans provided Western Europe the "negative model" which, as a yardstick for comparison, helped Western Europe to feel more confident of her material superiority and to provide "morality" to her claims.

It is to note that the Balkan peoples have been made so conscious of their Balkan origins, of negative terminologies like "Balkanization", that they now try to redefine their region not as "Balkans" any more, but as "South-East Europe..." These attempts witness that in the Balkans, there is not only a problem of "destiny", but also a problem of "identity".

Some of our Balkan Colleagues promote in their terminology "Southeast Europe". It seems that they believe the region will be considered more of a "European" one, if they leave behind the negative connotations of "Balkans". In Turkey, we continue to use these two terms interchangeably. For we believe that a new identity cannot be invented by ignoring the past, but rather by reconciling with the past. In fact, the future of the Balkans will, to a large extent, depend on strengthening common elements, which are the produce of a "shared history", belonging to all peoples of the region.

-II- Contrary to some general misperceptions, the Balkans historically had been a peaceful and relatively well-off region of Europe. From the 15th to the late 18th Centuries, this geography was immune to racial / religious oppressions and persecutions which were witnessed in other parts of Europe. Throughout the Ottoman Period in the Balkans, tolerance, coupled with a relatively egalitarian system, which reduced the prerogatives of feudal lords and secured the welfare of the masses, was established.

It is partially due to the liberty of movement and to the tolerance, which prevailed throughout the 15th to the 18th Centuries, that many ethnic groups were able to move freely from one corner to the other in the Balkans. They settled even in remote areas where they found favorable economic opportunities. The mobility of peoples was the most invigorating input to this geography.

The multi-ethnic, multi-cultural and multi-lingual characteristic of the Balkans was preserved and respected under great empires as the Habsburgs and Ottomans.

With the advent of the ethnic nationalism in 19th century, the chemistry of the region changed. The drive to draw political borders along ethnic lines replaced the climate of peaceful co-existence. In this context, the past mobility of peoples turned into an explosive factor in the Balkans: In fact, almost every nation in the Balkans currently has some of her people as "minorities" in another Balkan country; and each nation has others' "minorities" in her own territory.

-III- The root causes of the modern ordeal in the Balkans have sometimes been wrongly attributed to the Ottoman legacy. The reality is that the main factor behind Balkan conflicts is the drive to identify political borders with ethnic lines. This is the result of the ideology of aggressive nationalism, which was introduced into the region in late 18th and 19th centuries. The Ottoman era precedes the period of nationalism, therefore, it is an era where ethnically motivated claims were insignificant.

It is with the advent of nationalism that the inter-ethnic violence has become common place in the region. However, this is not something specific to the Balkans. In this regard, other regions of Europe have gone through even more devastating cycles of inter-ethnic and inter-religious conflicts and wars. Balkans has mimed the other regions only belatedly. Therefore, it is absolutely wrong, prejudicial to point at the Balkans as a region different by its nature from the rest of Europe.

Of course, the clock cannot be set back. No more empires. No more domination by others. The Balkans is a community of independent and equal nation-states. However, in the territory of each nation state lives more than one ethnicity, more than one religious group. There is no mono-ethnic state in the Balkans.

The survival of a nation depends on its internal coherence and strength of its social fabric. This can only be achieved through inter-ethnic tolerance, which is indeed the ancient Balkan tradition. It is due to the climate of mutual tolerance, which prevailed in Ottoman Centuries, that peoples of the Balkans have preserved their specific identities. It is high time to revive this tradition. Indeed, this is what we are all striving for. The recent thaw between Greece and Turkey has revealed that hostile feelings between two neighbourly peoples may be more imaginary than real.

-IV- Each and every Balkan country finds as citizens, people of diverse ethnic origin and faith. This has been a source of richness in the past and a long-standing Balkan tradition of tolerance. The future depends not on the negation, but on the affirmation of these values. The peoples of South-Eastern Europe should benefit from the positive legacy of a shared history, in building their future.

And, in our present day, whenever there is an attempt to draw or redraw borders along ethnic lines, or to ethnically cleanse a geography, then, we find ourselves in trouble.

The wars in the Balkans following the disintegration of Yugoslavia constituted the greatest challenge to European security since World War II. Besides the human tragedies they caused, they had spill over effects, which still threaten South-eastern Europe. Bosnia and Kosovo need no further explanation. These unfortunate developments caused the re-emergence of the Balkans image as the ghetto of Europe.

We have lived through the past decade with all of its human suffering, pain and agony. I will not dwell upon the tragedies we witnessed. Suffice it to say that whatever happened in Bosnia or Kosovo could and should have been prevented in an era marked by the ascent of such values as freedom, human rights, the rule of law and democracy.

131

Now, we seem to be in a new stage, more conscious of the Balkans, more realistic and more responsible. The Balkans is no longer seen as remote or alien outreaches of the European Continent. In fact, centuries-old discriminatory approaches are being replaced by integrationist policies. It is fair to say that the approach of the international community towards the Balkans has radically changed. The views and interests of all major actors seem to converge and the Balkans is considered as an integral part of Europe. In the Balkans, we have come a long way in solving conflicts. But we are still away from the point where we can look to the future with confidence.

(Speech at East-West Institute's Seminar, May 2000, New York)

LET US SET AND ACHIEVE OUR OWN GOALS: *Turkish Minister of Foreign Affairs Ismail Cem has told the " Nasa Borba"* that "...for the next century, Turkey sees her role as a pivotal state between Europe and Asia". Turkey is hosting the ministerial conference of Balkan states, to take place end of this week (May 1998)." Minister Cem said, "...maybe we are still not ready to have common Balkan institutions, but we can create common structures. This will prove both to others and to ourselves that we can act together.

In last year's Crete Summit, major Balkan problems were not solved. However, there was a dialogue between Yugoslav and Albanian colleagues, between Prime Ministers Simitis and Yilmaz. Though by itself it does not solve problems, dialogue and discussion are essential in foreign policy. To bring together parties with a problem is already a positive start. The Balkans is still a discriminatory reference in Western Europe. While preparing this Conference, we aimed at a setup, which promotes consultation and cooperation.

We are considering a project to define a common organization and, later, institution. We'll pave the way for the next Summit in Romania to be more substantial."

*** *Turkey is one of the biggest winners of the Cold War. Can you see a new international role of Turkey in the changing environment?*

132

Turkey is not one of the major winners of the Cold War. On the contrary, she is a loser. Our strategic value during the Cold War was derived from our particularity of a rampart at the outskirts of Europe, blocking the way of the so-called "evil force..." What this mission provided Turkey is arguable. Anyway, once that role was over, the strategic relevance of Turkey was lost. This was a trauma for Turkey. For we had got used to living in Cold War conditions. Our institutions, our mission, our self-esteem our identity were all defined by Cold War concepts and realities.

The spectacular economic growth Turkey realized in the 1980's and 1990's, plus the drastic changes in former Soviet geography provided a new, challenging mission. To be an assertive country cooperating with a multitude of newborn or reconfirmed independent states with which we share centuries old political and cultural affinities.

Turkey is not a winner of the Cold War but a country which is becoming strategically important in the 1990's, not on the basis of her military alliance, but for economic, historical and practical assets.

*** *What would be your message to the participants of the Balkan Conference in Istanbul? Do you consider Kosovo to be an obstacle in your good relations with Yougoslavia?*

I would most gladly say: Balkan peoples, unite! But this seems to be in distant horizons... For the moment, it might be: "Let us get together, discuss and reach conclusions."

As regards the relations with Yugoslavia, it is obvious that we are going through difficult times. First, Bosnia and now Kosovo. I hope that the question of Kosovo will be resolved through dialogue.

Yugoslavia is one of the most experienced and best-organized countries in the Balkans. In the past, she was among our major partners. She has a firm tradition in politics, industry, science, art and literature. With such a tradition, Yugoslavia is in a position to contribute a lot to the development of the Balkans."

(Interview given to "Borba", Belgrade, May 1998)

* * *

2. Balkans of Euro-Atlantic and Euro-Asian Dimensions

Our meeting takes place in the context of a historical renewal we witness in Europe. This is a time of change and hope. The former bounds and limits of the Cold War, which hindered progress in several of our countries, seem to belong to a distant past. Dividing lines based on military and ideological camps are gone. Democracy, freedom and development are at the forefront of our shared values. We communicate with each other with the unifying language of cooperation.

Several among our nations are in a process of political and economic rebirth. We believe that the dynamism of our region and the traditional wisdom of our peoples will contribute to a rejuvenated Europe. It is clear to us and it should be clear for others that peace in Europe can only be achieved if all nations of the continent are fully integrated into a unified and prosperous European entity. The challenge we face is to construct the Europe of the next millennium, with its Euro-Atlantic and Euro-Asian dimensions, capable of providing its peoples and those of other geographies with achievements in freedom and progress.

Our recent past in South-East Europe has witnessed substantial development. It has produced as well drawbacks, and even one great tragedy, which contradicted with the overall optimistic mood of the post-cold war era. I hope and I presume that we all drew the appropriate lessons from the tragedy of Bosnia and Herzegovina to prevent the recurrence of such a catastrophe. By "we", I don't mean solely the South East European countries, but all countries of Europe. They all shared a direct or indirect responsibility. What can be done now is to give all our support for the full implementation of the Dayton Peace Agreement. It is the major means to attain durable peace and stability in this part of our region.

The inevitable turmoil of a period of change has caused some of us to be delayed in joining the upward mobility that our continent is experiencing. The gap should be closed in a realistically short term. Cooperation and integration seem to be the major means. The positive aspects of globalization and the interdependency of all, provide new opportunities.

(Welcoming speech at the Istanbul meeting of the Ministers of Foreign Affairs of South East European Cooperation, May 1998)

134

BOMBING MILOSEVIC? ***Mr. Cem, Turkey of course is a member of NATO. Is it time (September 1998) to plan to bomb Mr. Milosevic?*

I believe that we should all calculate very carefully whether it's time to take such a strong action. But I think we did a timely job by being ready for such a probability.

*****But what we know from Mr. Milosevic is that threats don't do it, only action seems to work.*

We are ready, we have the political will to move forward, if necessary.

**** What would it take for NATO to decide to push the button? We have tens of thousands of Kosovars who have lost their homes, being bombed.*

Yes, we now. We are trying to provide efficient assistance in Kosovo. Bombing a country is not that easy to decide. So we want to make sure that we have done everything possible before deploying such means.

*****So what message would you be sending Mr. Milosovic?*

To take the latest UN resolution on Kosovo and NATO's determination very seriously. If it becomes an absolute necessity, NATO will strike.

*****Which could mean, would prove necessary could mean in the winter we might see some action?*

Well if it proves necessary, it can be anytime.

*****Ismail Cem, Foreign Minister of Turkey, thanks for joining us from New York.*

(Interview given to CNN, September 1998)

* * *

3. Balkan Countries Should Have More Say on Balkan Matters

*** Mr. Minister, in the initial stages of the Kosovo crisis, Turkey was experiencing some serious problems. Indeed, you were complaining to the country's allies that had they listened to Turkey's suggestions, most of the difficulties encountered would not have come into being. But nowadays, we see that there are some very important* *developments. For example, the UN Secretary General has established a "Friends of Kosovo" group to serve as an advisory body regarding the interim administration of Kosovo, and Turkey has been invited to join this group. How do you evaluate these developments?*

Turkey was deeply involved in the joint military efforts to end the ethnic cleansing; deeply involved in the humanitarian dimension as well. After the war, we established two bureaus for coordination and assistance to Kosovo, in Pristina and Prizren. Turkey was the first country to take such an initiative. We have centuries of shared history with the Kosovars; we have a strong Turkish community in Kosovo.

As for the diplomatic and political handling of the issue, both in pre-war (Rambouillet) and post-war phases, I would simply say that they were and they still are inadequate.

NATO in a way was kept out of the political process. The "Contact Group" composed of certain countries handled it. From time to time, both the European Union and NATO played efficient roles, but in reality, the political process was handled by a few "prominent" countries; the "self-appointed" Contact Group, some "leading members" of EU, etc.

Right from the very early stages, I underlined both on NATO and EU fora, at meetings with regional countries, that this decision-making set-up was a mistake. I stated that in this arrangement, there was no Balkan experience. I kept on raising this point at every opportunity, and what I said made a modest impact in the shaping of some new approaches.

Now that the bombing is over and the military aspect of the problem is somewhat eased there is room to be self-critical. Most recently, at the last NATO meeting in Brussels, I said that if countries with insight into the Balkans or Balkan countries themselves had been involved in the political decision-making process, some of the mistakes would not have been committed. Some of the grievances would not have come about. If they had been involved right from the very beginning, the scope of the conflict would not have expanded so far. I was having a private discussion with three or four Foreign Ministers at this NATO Conference where I had criticized the way decisions were devised for Kosovo. Minister Papandreou remarked: "I can sign all that Mr. Cem has said."

I think these criticisms have also played a modest role, and as you have pointed out, Turkey and Greece are now invited to participate at the meeting in New York. The interim administration of Kosovo is entrusted with the UN Secretary-General. The Secretary-General has established this group to serve as a team that he can constantly consult with in implementing Security Council resolutions on Kosovo and in the conduct of the interim administration of Kosovo. This group consists of the G-7 countries and Russia, China -I think they included China because it is a member of the Security Council- the Netherlands, Turkey and Greece. In a way, a small correction...

***Yes, but despite Papandreou's support to Turkish criticisms, Greece continues to constitute a problem. For example, it refused permission for Turkish troops to go through Greece on way to Kosovo, and Turkey is now trying to send its troops through Bulgaria. What are your views on this?*

I consider this as wrong. It was not Turkish troops alone; for a long time Greece did not allow American troops as well, to use her territory for transit. Greece tried to explain this attitude with the sensitive nature of her domestic politics. However, one should not use such pretext for acts that have international relevance.

Unfortunately, interests have a stronger say. Military wise, Greece, indeed, played a dissenting role in regards to Kosovo. They have their own reasoning, such as Orthodox brotherhood, traditional friendship with the Serbs and political affinity for Serbia. For all these concerns, the Greek public was very much against NATO operations. The Greek Government was at a constant attempt to please NATO on the one hand and Serbs on the other. It was obvious that, as a NATO partner, Greece was not reliable. I mock at the "positive" comments made by some foreign observers. "Double standards", one might say...

***But Mr. Minister, is that not often the case in international politics?*

Unfortunately... We have experienced this in NATO, as well. When issues are addressed with member-countries' internal considerations, everyone speaks in line with his political equilibrium back home and acts accordingly. But we should hope that in the long run, when issues are evaluated within a long-term perspective, every country is put in the proper place it deserves.

137

***Mr. Minister, there is also the situation of the Turkish minority in Kosovo. There are reports that this minority is not getting along very well with ethnic Albanians. Indeed, there are some claims that ethnic Turks did not put up enough resistance against the Serbians and, indeed, sometimes took a pro-Serbian position, which irritated the Albanians. There are claims that there exists some uneasiness between the Albanians and the Turks...

I have no information on some of the claims you mentioned. There are two important points: The first and the most fundamental one is that we are not making any discrimination between ethnic Turks and ethnic Albanians in Kosovo. For 500 years we shared a common history, a common state and a common destiny as equal citizens of the Ottoman Empire. No one was a second-class citizen. No one was privileged with respect to others. In a way, we consider them historically as our people, all of them, all Kosovars, without any distinction.

The second aspect is a by-product of the complete disruption of balances in Kosovo. Under current circumstances, we believe that issues related to the Turks of Kosovo need to be handled with more delicacy and more sensitivity. That is why I was personally and so frequently involved with that issue at NATO. It sounds awkward, but in NATO, I had to insist strongly in order to have our troops deployed close to Prizren, where most Turks live. They had proposed a region as if they wanted explicitly to position our troops away from the Kosovar Turks. In the end I succeeded.

There is no such problem (between Turkish and Albanian Kosovars). But one has to be realistic. Population wise, Turks were the smallest among the three Kosovar communities defined by the Kosovo constitution as those with "national" rights. Their sources of power were their intellectual and professional assets. The Turks have always been the most well educated, the most progressive people of Kosovo.

Traditionally, the Turks had managed to constitute some sort of a balancing factor, and maintained their well-being and their rights. After the Kosovo War that brought down all existing balances, the Turkish community's position degraded. . The Serbian element left Kosovo in huge numbers and, given the political realities, lost all their previous political significance. Turks no longer enjoyed the

138

privilege of being the small but sometimes decisive factor. Politically, they turned into the sole "minority" in a society with an overwhelming Albanian majority. Politically speaking, they now face a dominant majority, which is free from indigenous constraints to its power. That's the delicacy of the situation. That's why we are trying to handle it with care.

At the time when the non-agreed Rambouillet draft was being prepared, there was no reference in the text to the Turkish population. It only mentioned the Serbs and the Albanians. We objected to the wording of that draft. I remember writing letters to all members of the Contact Group and reminding that the Turkish community should be given its due place in the agreement, as well as in the new Constitution. Although some of our requests were incorporated to the Rambouillet document, the document itself could not be brought to life and remained, it still remains, a "draft", with no juridical significance.

We have close relations with Albania and the Albanians. We have millions of Turkish citizens with Albanian background. Almost one-and-a-half year ago, I was the first Foreign Minister from an Islamic society to visit the refugees who had fled from Kosovo to Albania. I flew by helicopter from Tirana to the bordering region that hosted the refugee camp. The situation was terrible. The refugees were in a desperate situation. They were in tears describing how the Serbs killed their beloved ones mercilessly.

(Interview given to I. Cevik and Y. Kanli, "Turkish Daily News" Ankara, June 1999 - Excerpts)

* * *

4.   Economic Perspectives for the Balkans

Economy is a key factor to redress the situation in the Balkans. It does not solve as such the political deadlocks, but it facilitates solutions. To be fair with ourselves, both as individual countries and as international organizations, so far we are doing our part quite all right. I do not speak of great accomplishments, but rather of positive initiatives. The prompt reaction by EU and US to contribute to the   Balkan reconstruction, the initiatives that my country has taken

139

within the South East European Cooperation, various proposals that we mutually developed, were all positive steps. These were finalized in the "South East European Stability Pact".

One of the most pressing issues on the international agenda is the integration of Balkans into European mainstream. To this end, we need to establish political stability and launch sustained economic growth in the region. It goes without saying that political and economic factors are interdependent in this context. Economic development requires investment, which would, in turn, need safe and secure climate. However, investment, in particular from developed countries, would not flow into the region unless it is secure and politically stable.

"Balkans", is more than a geographical definition. It is a centuries old political term. It has several connotations including, unfortunately, some deep-rooted prejudices. Discussing the economic opportunities in the Balkans, obviously presupposes a thorough analysis of political realities. Political and economic factors are interdependent. Economic development requires investment; investment looks for politically stable and secure environments. Ironically, the current economic initiatives that we are taking are more promising than the political developments.

It is to note that both as individual countries and as international organizations, so far we have been doing a fairly good job. I do not speak of accomplishments, but rather of positive initiatives. The creation of the *South East European Cooperation Process* (SEECP) which comprises all Balkan countries and which constitutes the first political agreement in the region since 1930; the prompt reaction by the EU and the US to contribute to the Balkan reconstruction, have all been positive steps which led to the "South East European Stability Pact". This Pact, with its" three dimensions" has made a promising debut. I want to pay tribute to its Coordinator, Mr. Hombach, for his relentless efforts.

As for Turkish initiatives, I would like to underline some salient points. Turkey has shared more than five Centuries of history with Balkan countries. Actually, she is very active in the economic and political development of the region: Several independent States and those that re-confirmed their independence emerged in the Post Cold-War era. Among them, seven are situated in South-East Europe.

Several are those with whom Turkey shared centuries of common history, cultural ties and a common state. This background provides for strong economic relationships and a unique platform for political cooperation. Furthermore, these new nation-states have quickly embarked upon the task of rebuilding their economies as well as opening them to foreign investment and competition. Actually, Turkish private investment in the region is about $1.2 billion. By the end of 2000, this total is expected to reach $1.5 billion. Taking into account the joint ventures that are actually being implemented by Turkish and Greek companies, the total Turkish investments to the Balkans will be close to the level of $2 billion by the end of this year. The trade volume between Turkey and the Balkan countries -except Greece- is about $1.5 billion. The trade with Greece was $700 million in 1999; Turkish private sector estimates that it might reach $4 billion in 2005. There are 10 Turkish banks with about 40 branches, which operate in the Balkans. Turkish Eximbank credits to the region total of $200 million. Turkish construction firms, which have a worldwide operational range, are very active all over the Balkans. Hundreds of Turkish companies, most of them small and medium sized are implanted in the region.

If I may add, the recent political developments between Greece and Turkey seem to be contributing strongly to the creation of a more secure investment climate. Having moved politically from confrontation to cooperation, we now provide for ourselves and for the entire Balkans immense economic opportunities. This should be our goal.

Another new dimension that sustains economic cooperation is the growing consciousness about the role of civil society and of sub-regional cooperation. I may cite the "bordering countries initiative" we took with my Bulgarian and Greek colleagues. Last March, we came together and on the same day we visited three bordering cities in each country. This initiative provided for numerous activities among civil society organizations, which are producing economic results for the bordering regions. Another positive development that affects the investment climate is the umbrella provided by the Southeast European Military Taskforce. Six regional countries are cooperating in this endeavor, which has its headquarters in Plovdiv.

Regarding the economic dimension of Balkan perspectives, we can be cautiously optimistic. We might not be doing enough, but we are definitely doing better. Before concluding, I would like to make a final assessment: We should not view "economic investment" as a separate ingredient to be activated once a secure investment climate is assured. Instead, we should consider investment as a main factor to bring about a secure climate. In other words, we should not wait for a climate of security to be fully realized in order to invest. We should invest, knowing that this is the most effective way to bring about that secure environment.

(Speech at East-West Institute's Seminar, May 2000, New York)

CHAPTER V :
Greece & Cyprus

Greece and Cyprus are two recurring themes in our foreign policy. In regards to Greece, there has been substantial progress. Much has been achieved in a year following our initial agreement with Minister Papandreou, Spring 1999. As for Cyprus, in spite of the "proximity talks" that has been going on under the auspices of UN Secretary General, I am not optimistic. For one simple reason: The Greek Cypriots are quite satisfied with the status quo. They are encouraged by the European Union, which admitted them as a "candidate" for accession. They think that sooner or later, they will become a member and have the advantage of making integral part to a powerful union. Then, they figure, they will be in a much stronger position to dictate their will to Turkish Cypriots. Therefore, they do not want any change, they are not after a mutually acceptable solution, and they just want the time to run by. This negative policy was obvious throughout the proximity talks, where they did everything to hinder any progress.

1. To be Fair in Cyprus

This letter was written in 1996, within the existing parameters of the time. The Turkish policy having changed radically due to EU's acceptance of the Greek administration as "candidate", some of the ideas put forward in 1996 and early 1997 are not relevant to the present situation. However, it is interesting to note the changes occurred because of the E.U. decision.

I would like to share with you my personal evaluation of the "Draft Report on the Situation in Cyprus", prepared by our dear colleague the late Lord Finsberg. I will begin by paying tribute to Lord Finsberg who, in his last work at the Council of Europe, has combined an objective and positive approach with his ever-present good will.

The slight uneasiness I have in commenting this report is due to the fact that I feel as I am speaking instead of those who are the genuine representatives of the Turkish Cypriots, but cannot take up their cause themselves at the Council of Europe.

"Recent Political Developments"
a) I agree that the Confidence Building Measures (CBM) proposed by the UN Secretary General could -and should- facilitate an overall settlement. I go even further, it seems that they constitute the starting point for a peace process. If a "solution" were to be reached, the CBM's, which were alternately -but never conjointly- accepted by both sides, would provide the catalyst. The "Set of Ideas" proposed by the UN General Secretary might contribute to the framework for a solution as well. Out of the 100 "Ideas" proposed, the Turkish Cypriots accepted 91, and declared ready to discuss the remaining ones.

b) I agree as well that a direct dialogue between the leaders of the two communities should begin at once. I do not claim to be a totally "objective" observer in the Cyprus conflict, but in this particular aspect the credit goes to President Denktash who for the last two years have made a demand for "dialogue" but was constantly refused by President Clerides. Our report, I hope, brings an additional incentive for dialogue.

Furthermore, a suggestion brought up by Ms. Madeleine Albright, during her visit to Cyprus, then U.S. Ambassador to the UN, which proposed the establishment of a "military dialogue" between the two sides, seems to me as positive and might be mentioned in the Report.

c) The proliferation of "special representatives for Cyprus" of various national and international instances does not seem to help the case. Lord Finsberg names three (UN, EU, Great Britain); two USA special representatives (one for the State Department and one for President Clinton respectively) should be added to the list. Others like Russia and Finland have their representatives as well. With so many "special representatives" involved, differences or nuances of expectancies among them do not facilitate the quest for a solution.It seems that pretty soon there will be a need to appoint a

"Coordinator of Special Representatives for Cyprus..." I would think that the difficult mission of resuming the negotiation process in Cyprus should be left to the UN and to the two communities and that all other interested parties should confine themselves to contributing to UN's task.

"The Security Situation"

a) I share with late Lord Finsberg his condemnation of the murders of two Greek Cypriots.

Unfortunately, some new paragraphs have to be added, the main one condemning the unprovoked, cold-blooded murder of a Turkish Cypriot guard, a murder claimed in the statement issued by a group calling itself "Greek Elites Brigades" and "performed by selected Greek Commandos", as reported in the Greek weekly newspaper "Stohos", 17/9/1996.

b) The security issues of Cyprus are so complex and intricate that it is not surprising for a condensed report like ours to deal with these aspects partially. The military presence in the island will hopefully decrease in the context of a political settlement. In the meantime, this "military presence" ironically provides for the security of both communities. Given the facts, it is not realistic or justified to put the two communities in risk of mutual bloodshed for the sake of rhetoric and fantasies. The "international community" should have learned from the lessons of Bosnia. Both communities should reject any suggestion that brings into perspective risks of Bosnia-like massacres.

c) The concept of "international force" is not realistic. Cyprus is not a laboratory experiment; Cypriot communities are not there "to test" new formulae on them. In spite of all negative aspects of the situation, of the explosive nature of the Cypriot reality, violent clashes and loss of human lives have been almost non-existent or minimal in the past two decades. Any risk factor to be introduced to the present Cypriot scene would be irrational. The massacre of the Bosnian Muslims in spite of the presence of such "international forces" is still fresh in memories, as is the experience of the 1963 - 1974 period in Cyprus itself, during which an "international force", UNFICYP, was nothing but a passive observer to the bloodshed.

"Human Rights Issues"

There has been much progress on the Karpass issue. As far as I know, there is not much left which is unsettled. As for the 'missing persons' the report says almost all that can be said on this unfortunate issue.

"The European Union"

Most of the assessments in these paragraphs are valid but I disagree with the inadmissible neglect of international treaties. I would also like to discuss if the "probable accession of Cyprus to EU" can or cannot inspire "optimism".

a) The Report refers to "...the vetoing by Turkey of accession of Cyprus to EU" which "the Greek Cypriot side stressed that Turkey should not be allowed". Furthermore, it is also stated that "(...) if the Turkish community is being unreasonable (in the negotiations to re-unite the island and establish the Federal bi-zonal, bi-communal State) "...EU may well invite Cyprus to join and will not permit a Turkish communal veto to prevent membership."

The "veto" which is being discussed here is not of the kind "to be allowed" by third parties. It is not a kind of "veto" void of legal substance, which would make it easy to override. It is a guarantee provided for the communities and contracting parties by the 1960 treaties that constituted the "bi-communal" Republic of Cyprus. Those treaties make it clear that the accession of the Republic of Cyprus to any international organization within which both Greece and Turkey are not members requires the consent of both communities. This is put forward both by the treaties and by the binding legal engagements related to the treaties. Furthermore, the U.K., Greece and Turkey guarantee the fulfillment of the agreements.

It is obvious that unless the legal base and the legal consent exist, the Republic of Cyprus cannot, legally and ethically, access to EU (provided that both Greece and Turkey are not members). It is the legal and ethical obligation of the U.K., Greece and Turkey not to let such a process to take place. It is also obvious that the mutual consent will not come into being unless an overall peaceful solution is reached in Cyprus.

If an accession to EU overriding the constituent legal basis created by the 1960 treaties of the Republic of Cyprus seems to be in perspective as a "fait accomplis", it is certain that the division of the island will become permanent. The Turkish Cypriots have made it clear that the integration of northern Cyprus into Turkey will become inevitable and will be realized. There should be no doubt about that point.

This would bring about difficulties for all concerned. I would therefore suggest that the legal aspect of the whole matter is underlined in the Report; that we refrain from providing an "understanding", an indirect "acceptance" for the probable violation of binding international treaties.

b) I do not believe that the beginning of negotiations between EU and the Cyprus Republic would "hold the key for progress". In fact, though it is an important element in the problem, the accession to EU -as long as it is perceived in violation of the constituent agreements- is not a main concern for the Turkish Cypriot side. For it is a process, taking place outside the Turkish Cypriot community; this community is not associated with this process in which it has no say. Its only relevance to the Cyprus question is that its development will trigger the permanent division of the island and the integration of northern Cyprus into Turkey.

"Conclusions"

a) It does not seem likely that a change in the representation of Cyprus at the Council of Europe helps in any way the quest for a solution. On the contrary, it will only aggravate the resentment of the Turkish Cypriot side; which is excluded from participation. I do not see any imminent need for such a change, which will cause a new round of tensions in a moment where we should avoid all causes of tension.

b) The reference made to the Turkish Cypriot community as a "Turkish Cypriot Minority" (paragraph 35) is a factual error. In all legal documents, the constituent treaties, UN resolutions and UN terminology, there is no mention of "minority"; The Turkish Community is always described as a "community", on equal footing with the other "community" (UNSC Resolutions: s/5575 - 4/3/1964; 353 - 20/7/1974; 367 - 1975: "...representatives of the two communities on equal footing", etc.)

The opening statement of the Secretary General of UN at the intercommunal talks (New York, 26/2/1990 - UN Document no. S/21183, p.7) is explicit in many ways:

147

> *"...Cyprus is the common home of the Greek Cypriot community and of the Turkish Cypriot community. Their relationship is not one of majority and minority, but one of two communities in the state of Cyprus. The mandate given to me by the Security Council makes it clear that my mission of good offices is with the two communities. My mandate is also explicit that the participation of the two communities in this process is on equal footing. (...) The political equality of the two communities and the bi-communal nature of the federation need to be acknowledged."*

MY CONCLUSION

Well, after all these explications, I want to underline that I still want to be an optimist. But, optimism is not enough; both Greek and Turkish Cypriots should be good-willed, sincere and cautious if they really aspire for a common solution.

For example, this rhetoric about "Occupied part of the Island", "Occupational forces", etc. does not serve any one: First, one should remember that the Turkish intervention did not come out of nowhere. It was the direct result of the fascist coup-d'Etat of Sampson and of the Greek Colonels, destroying the constitutional set-up and murdering hundreds of Turks as well as Greeks.

What is termed as "occupation" is, for one-fourth of Cypriot population, "liberation"; the "occupying forces", are, "liberating forces". Insisting on harsh terminology does not contribute to the quest for a solution.

I believe that a solution is possible. But, security should be the primary concern, the main parameter. Neither Turkey nor Greece can afford the probability of reappearance of violence on the island, which would oblige both of them to confrontation. "The Solution" should be carefully planned and applied in phases; after the compilation of each phase; a thorough evaluation must be made before deciding to proceed to the next phase. The process should be gradual and prudent.

A final comment: "The Annex 2" has no place in this report. I do not discuss its substance; of course it is partial but that is not the point. What is important is that if such a view is to be annexed, the opposite view should have been demanded and included as Annex 3. As it stands, it reflects a double standard and a definite partiality. The correct attitude is not to have annexes of this sort.

148

At the Council of Europe, the Cyprus question has almost always been dealt with as if it were the subject for a "political rally". The main goal of many of our colleagues being the defamation of Turkey and the condemnation of Cypriot Turks. It was a matter of "home consumption" exploited in view of constituencies back home.

It seems as if the majority did not care much about a solution or about lives of the Cypriots, especially of Turkish Cypriots lives:

Our 59 colleagues rightfully condemning the murder of two Greek Cypriots in "Declaration No. 250" of 15 October 1996, did not even bother to mention the murder of the Turkish Cypriot, which had taken place at 8 September 1996, weeks before the presentation of their "declaration".

This is not correct. It is not ethical either.

I hope that on the occasion of Lord Finsberg's Report, instead of the usual follow-up of mainstream prejudices, emphasis is put to contributing to a solution in Cyprus.

Lord Finsberg's memory deserves such respect.

Ismail CEM, Chairman, Turkish Delegation to the Parliamentary Assembly of Council of Europe (Letter to Mr. Barsony, Chairman of the Political Committee of the Parliamentary Assembly of Council of Europe, December 1996 - Excerpts)

* * *

2. Another Missed Opportunity

I would like to present to you the views of the Turkish Delegation on the Resolution on Cyprus that is adopted by the Parliamentary Assembly of the Council of Europe.

1) We regret that the adopted resolution represents an opportunity that the Council of Europe has missed in regards to her contribution to a consensual solution in Cyprus towards the establishment of a bi-communal bi-zonal federation of two politically equal communities as defined by the UN. As it stands, the Resolution unfortunately has underlined the improbability of a "unified" Cyprus and the incapacity of the Assembly of the Council of Europe to have a unifying mission in Cyprus. On the contrary, with the enhancements this resolution brings to the partiality and bias faced by Turkish Cypriots, the Council of Europe has created a new momentum towards the permanent division of the island.

2) The way in which the Resolution handles "the accession of Cyprus to the EU" is of great concern: If an accession to EU gets into perspective as a "fait accomplish", overriding the constituent legal basis of Cyprus established by the 1960 treaties, the division of the island will become permanent. The accession to the EU -as long as it is perceived in violation of the constituent treaties- is a process taking place outside the Turkish Cypriot community. The Turkish Cypriot community is not associated with this process in which it has no say. Its only relevance to the Cyprus question is that its development will trigger the integration of northern Cyprus into Turkey.

3) We deplore the lack of understanding and of wisdom in most of the debates. We deplore the inadequacies in the final resolution. As members of the Turkish delegation, we had hoped that The Council of Europe would have a positive role in a consensual solution as defined by the UN This solution now seems to be as remote as it can be and the role of The Parliamentary Assembly in such a solution seems to be lost forever.

This Resolution turned out to be a usual follow-up of mainstream prejudices. It's only result and effect being a new share of responsibility for the Parliamentary Assembly of the Council of Europe in the build-up for a permanently divided Cyprus. For its part, the Resolution of the Council of Europe has come as an urge to the Turkish Cypriots to realize that it is only by them that they can create their future.

(Press Conference at the Council of Europe, January 1997)

* * *

3.   An Act of Self-Defence by Turkish Cypriots

Thank you very much for your e-mail of August 1; for your congratulations on my appointment and for your suggestions. I hope my ministry will be a positive factor for peace and understanding in the region and in the world.

The accession talks between Cyprus Cypriots and EU don't have to be a "threat", but the way they are perceived and conducted by the Greek Cypriot Administration and EU are unfortunately leading to a point, which constitutes a threat for all interested parties:

Besides the obvious infringements of the accession process to the constituent treaties of 1960, the Turkish Cypriots have found themselves in an awkward situation which leads them into a decisive setup without their consent and contrary to their will. They -and their government- have made it clear that they do not and will not accept a "fait accomplis" which turns them into a submissive minority in a hostile environment. I believe that for the accession talks to achieve positive ends, they should be preceded by a mutual consent of both sides as to the modalities and objectives of the process. Otherwise, the reaction of the Turkish Cypriots and their proposed partial integration to Turkey (integration in economic and social matters and partnership in defense and foreign policy) would constitute a legitimate act of self-defense of those that do not agree with a statute that is forced upon them. Nevertheless, I am not a pessimist and I believe that there is still hope for a solution, which is mutually acceptable for Turkish and Greek Cypriots, for Greece and Turkey.

As for "...Turkey to get its foot in the door of EU" that you mention, I certainly approach the problem of Turkish accession in a different manner. My government does not aspire for a foot in the door. The accession to full membership in EU is a major goal for our government, it is not an obsession.

I have always considered the West European interest "...in the Kurdish issue and in human rights" as one with contradicting dynamics. Of course, several media and policy circles are genuinely interested in the human rights aspect, but quite a number pursue a policy of supporting or endorsing terrorism in view of their political / economical interests. We should not overlook the goodwill existing in some concerns but we should not be naive as well.

(Letter to L. Mortimer, writer, Financial Times, London, August 1997 - Excerpts)

* * *

4.   Q & A on Turkey, Greece and Cyprus

***Hello everyone, welcome to our interactive forum questions and answers, "Q&A", at CNN. Plans are on the way for some fairly high-level talks between Turkish Government and Greek Government leaders over Cyprus. Greek Cypriots in the South and*

Turkish Cypriots in the North run the Mediterranean Island. Given by the conflict on the island is well over two decades old that must be settled down to improve relations. We'll ask our guest; Ismail Cem is the Turkish Foreign Minister. He is in New York for the 52nd Annual UN General Assembly and later today he'll meet with his Greek Counterpart Theodoros Pangalos for private talks. We'll ask him about that meeting and about plans on Friday for UN mediated security talks in Nicosia between the Turkish Cypriot leader Rauf Denktash and the Greek Cypriot leader Glafkos Clerides. For his part, our guest has been also actively involved in discussions over Cyprus's possible entry to the European Union. Turkey also wants to be a fully-fledged member of the EU, but so far remains only a member of the Customs Union of the EU, which may or may not lead to full membership. Greece, which is a member of the EU, recently offered some incursion weds to Turkey and its EU efforts. Foreign Minister Pangalos was quoted to saying "Turkey of course belongs to Europe." Tensions are building over the Greek Cypriot leader's decision to buy anti-aircraft missiles which Turkey claims threaten its security. Turkish Prime Minister Mesut Yilmaz reportedly wowed that Turkey would take action to prevent that deployment. The United States criticize Mr. Yilmaz for his rhetoric, but also remain depose to the purchase and deployment of the Russian S-300 missile systems. For his part, Greek Cypriot leader Clerides has offered to cancel the deal if Turkey would accept proposals for the demilitarization of the island. During Monday's O&A program, we asked Britain's Foreign Secretary Robin Cook to assess the Cyprus situation. Here is what he has told us:

"We made a commitment that we believe the Cyprus should have the opportunity to join the EU and that should not be dependent on resolving the division of the island, of course we must better, it's better if we could resolve the division of the island and I have had a number of conversations both in Cyprus and in New York just support the process of trying to bring the two sides together."

Let's hear what our guest has to say; we welcome Ismail Cem to the program.

Mr. Cem; let's, begin with your meeting later with Greek Foreign Minister Pangalos. How well do you know him and what do you plan to discuss with him?

Well, on a personal basis I know him for quite a time, for many years we were both active members of the European Council's Parliamentary Assembly. It is now interesting to have Mr. Pangalos as my counterpart and try to see what we can do on certain issues. We made a rather positive beginning in Madrid, but somehow we didn't achieve what was expected of the understanding that was reached. Therefore, I would probably ask him what we can do in order do reactivate the Madrid declaration which is supposedly a first full step to improve Turkish - Greek relationships.

***Now, how severe is this issue of Cyprus on trying to improve that relationship?

What was decided in Madrid was to avoid any conditions or preconditions for the initiatives to improve relations. That was a genuine point in the Madrid understanding. I believe that at least the first steps should not be linked to concerns other than those strictly of bilateral nature.

*** Our first call is on the line Mr. Cem, it's Greg in Denmark I think. Greg, go ahead.

- Q - Hi, how are you, Minister, the same question I gave to Mr. Cook yesterday, I am going to give again to Minister here. What is the Turkish Government doing with regard to Cyprus issue, and how high is the tension between Greeks and Turks? I am half Greek anyway.

What we are trying to do is to convince all parties concerned in Cyprus and out of Cyprus. There are two separate entities, two peoples in the island. And each has her own legitimate rights. A solution can be derived from the acceptance that they are politically equal, that they have their own sovereignty. Neither one of the parties would accept a situation, which might endanger the future of its children.

***Mr. Cem, this e-mail question came from Sydney/Australia over the Internet. It says: "Please explain why Turkey is opposed to the purchase by Cyprus of a Russian anti-aircraft missile system." And now, what I should do is to explain to you that it is the Russian S-300 missile system, which Turkey is after, and Greek Cypriots are after as well.

153

Maybe I misunderstood your question but Turkey is not after buying those missiles. It's the Greek Cypriots who are in the process of purchasing them. We are strongly against their deployment in Cyprus for we don't want to turn the Eastern Mediterranean into a new arsenal of sophisticated Russian military equipment. Furthermore, those missiles will bring a threat to Turkey. It is to note that that Russian S-300's are becoming a kind of a fashion in our part of the world. We hear that Syrians are going to purchase some S-300's. The Israelis as well are concerned. We believe that this latest fashion, this process of deployment, should be cancelled.

***Does Turkey have any S-300's?*

No we don't have S-300's.

****I understood that perhaps Turkey was talking to Russia about buying some of these.*

No, that's not the case at all. We are very much opposed to having that kind of missiles around the Mediterranean. Though we have good relations with Russia, we do not want, we are not very happy to have Russian military finally involved and present in Eastern Mediterranean.

****Let me ask you about the range of these missiles. Because I know Turkey is very worried of the Greek Cypriot having them because of the threat to Turkey as you say. Yet even the Russians say the range is about 150 km., no more than that.*

Those sophisticated missiles can become much more efficient through some modifications; they can have multiple use. Plus, it is not only the range of the missile; it is the weapon, the warhead that the missile carries which is crucial. And those missiles can carry highly destructive chemical weapons, in fact all sorts of weapons, up to 250 km, which is quite a distance.

****Greek Cypriots would have one of these missiles, because they feel threatened. This fax from Nicosia asks what gestures has Turkey made to the Cypriots that the acquisition of weapon is unnecessary and there is no threat of Turkish aggression.*

In spite of some problems, some tensions between the two communities, actually neither one is under the threat of the other. There is no threat originating from Turkey, as well. This is a blunt pretext for the prospective build-up of missiles in the Greek part of Cyprus. In fact, in 1964 - 1974, there were incidents where Turks were massacred.

The fascist coup d'etat by the Greek Cypriot Sampson killed more than a thousand Greek Cypriots, and, of course Turkish Cypriots. We had those difficult times in Cyprus but since around 1974, (the liberation of Turkish Cypriots by Turkish armed forces) the two communities leave in peace and by themselves. There is a balance, a stability, which is not based solely on weapons, but on Turkey's and Greece's a mutual obligations, mutual presence. So there is security, covering at least the basics of human needs. Well, with the presumed deployment of S-300's by the Greek Cypriots, the whole picture changes. A missile is a very symbolic weapon, a very dangerous weapon, and I don't believe the Greeks will ever be able to install it. That might well create another Bosnia. And we are to give nothing in return to the cancellation of the S-300 project. It is initiated by the Greeks, they are the ones to cancel it, by themselves.

*** *All right Mr. Cem, don't go away. We have to take a short break at this stage. Ismail Cem is our guest, he welcomes your questions and comments now by telephone, fax or e-mail. By the way, we asked the representative of the Greek Government to join us, but so for we had no response, certainly Cyprus is an issue, don't go away, we plan to bring you the Greek viewpoint out in the future date.*

*** *Welcome back to the program, we are discussing Turkish politics today in particular the dispute in the island of Cyprus. Leaving as the United Nations General Assembly session is on the way, New York talks over Cyprus with a UN maintained buffer zone a schedule to take place. Our guest will be meeting with his counterpart Theodore Pangalos later on today. Ismail Cem is the Turkish foreign minister. He joins us from New York ready to answer your questions and comments. Let's get our call from Turkey on the line straight away, go ahead your question.*

- Q - Mr. Cem, hello, I'm calling from Ankara, Turkey. I would like to ask you, why instead of arguing on a lot of easy questions, why don't we just ask the main one: what is the reason for bringing those missiles into Cyprus?

We have asked this question, we have tried to talk with all parties interested and we are telling them that it is senseless to have an arsenal of missiles build up in a tiny island. This will only provoke other kinds of arms build-up around Cyprus. Therefore, we are asking that question, we hope that others are doing the same, as they should.

155

***We have that e-mail from Japan. He says that Turkey recently forged new ties with Israel. How does this affect regional security?

We should continue with our policies of positive relations with the Arab countries as well as with Israel. I believe that Turkey is a stabilizing factor in the Middle East, by having a dialogue and sometimes cooperation both with Israel and with Arab Nations.

***Let's hear what our caller in Turkey has to ask to Mr. Cem. Go ahead caller.

- Q - How will be Turkey's position when the European Union will begin negotiations with the Southern part of Cyprus?

Turkish Cypriots believe that they are drifted into a process where they have no say, where Greek part of Cyprus is unduly considered to be the representative of the entire island. This process, if it ends as the Greeks anticipate, will create conditions where the Greek majority will dominate the Turks, who will constitute a helpless minority in a hostile environment. This, of course, is not a feasible scenario. As I was referring a minute earlier, the Bosnian syndrome is important. Throughout the world, Muslim populations facing hostile majorities feel themselves in danger. This is true with Turkish Cypriots as well; they don't want to live through a new Bosnian tragedy. We will not let anything as such to happen.

***I try to touch a little bit on the Turkish situation with the EU in a moment. Let's go to our caller on the line from Greece for a question. Go ahead.

- Q - Hello, yes, I would like to ask how could you expect the Greek Cypriots to negotiations with Turkey since they are still threatened and killed by occupying Turkish troops in the Northern part of the island.

No one is threatened or killed in Northern Cyprus; the Turkish armed forces are not occupying troops, they are liberating armies who liberated Turkish Cypriots from the massacres of the fascist Greek-Cypriot bands. And, Turkey does not negotiate with Greek Cypriots, whose interlocutors are the Turkish Republic of Northern Cyprus .

***Now back to Turkey's Foreign Minister, Ismail Cem who is fielding your questions. He is joining us from New York. We have an e-mail question for you Mr. Cem. It says Does Mr. Denktash, referring

the Turkish Cypriot leader, negotiate for the well being of Turkish Cypriots or does he strictly follow Turkey's interests?

Denktash naturally consults with us. But, basically he makes his own policies; he negotiates for the Turkish Cypriots and he does it independently.

****We have a call on the line; I think it is from Turkey. Go ahead.***

- Q - Yes, hello. I would like to ask to the Turkish Foreign Minister please, Greeks have militarized the Greek islands around Turkey. Now, it seems to be the turn of Cyprus. How long is it going to go on like this, and what is the policy of the Turkish Government on the islands that have been militarized, although, through existing agreements, they are not supposed to?

You are referring to the Lausanne agreement and to the 1947 Paris agreement. Those islands, unfortunately, are armed against Turkey in spite of the treaties, which stipulate that they shouldn't be armed. Well, we have always rejected the fait accompli that the Greeks brought about. But frankly, we do not want to create further problems. You're right in saying that we cannot afford to have those Russian S-300's in Cyprus, and we shall prevent their deployment.

****Another caller in Turkey, a brief question please. We are almost ahead of time.***

- Q - Hello. Do you think Greeks and the Greek Cypriots could ever be a threat to Turkey? Why don't you divert that money instead of military purchases to more real important issues in Turkey rather than to that bluff going on in the Mediterranean?

I agree that Greece and Southern Cyprus are not major threats and we can surely deal with them. But when you have missiles around you, you have to be careful, you have to think about your people's security. And I hope one day not only Turkey, not only Greece, but all countries in the world will spend their money not for rearmament, but for the good of their peoples.

****Ismail Cem, thank you very much for being with us on Q&A. Q&A with Riz Khan, CNN, September 1997*

* * *

5.   Realities of Cyprus

-I- The Cyprus issue has been on the agenda of the Security Council for almost 34 years. This roughly corresponds to UNFICYP's presence in the island. It may be high time for this Organization to find a real answer to why a solution has eluded us all this time in spite of the dramatic changes that have occurred both on the international scene and in Cyprus and despite all the commendable efforts of the successive UN Secretaries-General.

After so many years it would be wrong, I believe, to continue to link a 34-year-old failure to the lack of political will or to the intransigence of one side or the other. We should ask ourselves where we failed, why the mistrust is still so deep in the island and whether we have made the right diagnosis to the problem.

There are two distinct peoples, two separate administrations and two democracies on the island. Along with these realities, bi-communality, bi-zonality, the maintenance of 1960 system of guarantees should be considered as incontestable foundations of a settlement.

It is obvious that reluctance to recognize the realities in the island and the tendency to apply pressure to one side alone have not led us to a negotiated solution. The last two rounds of talks in Troutbeck and Glion have solidified this perception.

We do believe that the lessons of the past and the current developments on the international scene should compel us to adopt a realistic approach to the Cyprus issue. The establishment of equilibrium between the legal and political status of the two sides to the dispute could be a starting point of a rethinking process.

Time is pressing to initiate such a process since one can foresee that in late 1997 a chain of events might cripple efforts to find a negotiated settlement and further increase the tension both on the island and in the region. (EU Summit next December, 1997, which might decide Greek Cypriot's "candidacy" to the Union).

As witnessed in the recent face-to-face talks, the pursuit of EU membership by the Greek Cypriot side has become the main impediment to progress. It renders the negotiating process increasingly meaningless and an agreed settlement even more elusive. Turkey and the Turkish Cypriot side firmly believe that efforts to carry forward this membership process will cast a dark shadow on the talks and can destroy the very foundation of the negotiating process. On various occasions, we made our position clear on the issue of EU membership of Cyprus. The 1959 and 1960 Treaties on Cyprus established an internal institutional balance between the two communities of Cyprus and simultaneously, an external balance of interests between Turkey and Greece in their relationship with Cyprus. These treaties unequivocally preclude the membership of Cyprus in any international organization, political and economic union in which both Turkey and Greece are not members. Therefore, from a legal point of view, Cyprus can only join EU after a solution and simultaneously with Turkey. From a political point of view, it also appears to be the only viable outcome. We continue to entertain the hope that those who are concerned will act in the awareness of their historic responsibility as time approaches toward a decision on an issue, which will have a determining effect on the future course of events in Cyprus.

The deployment of S-300 missiles to Southern Cyprus is an other gloomy prospect. Coupled with ambitious rearmament efforts that the Greek Cypriot side has embarked upon, the purchase of highly sophisticated missiles aims at jeopardizing the security of the Turkish Cypriot people and of Turkey. We sincerely hope that at the end wisdom will prevail and this project, which may seriously affect peace and stability in the entire region, will be discontinued.

Speech at the U.N. General Assembly, September 1997 - Excerpts

*** Obviously a longstanding dispute between your country and Greece and the Greek Cypriots. We just heard that in the last hour with the Greek Cypriot president Glafcos Clerides saying that they do not like your suggestion of a confederacy. Can you explain to us what your plan is?

Well, I think this is a hasty response. For we believe that throughout those many years since the 1960's there is nothing done in order to find a mutually accepted solution in Cyprus. Therefore, if we are looking for one, we have to be realistic, we have to be energetic, we have to be imaginative and we have to have the final settlement in view. After all, what the UN wants is a unified Cyprus. President Denktash has proposed the confederation. He suggests

159

a unified Cyprus of two sovereign, equal, confederated entities. I hope that the Greek Cypriots and the Greeks will be realistic and have a constructive approach.

(Interview given to CNN, September 1998)

* * *

6.   Russian S-300 Missiles: Latest "Fashion" in East Mediterranean

"S-300's ARE THEIR PROBLEM..."***: *The United Nations is now making a new attempt to solve the Cypriot issue. The U.N. officials will have separate talks with both Turkish and Greek Cypriot leaders. Do you expect anything from this initiative?*

I do see probable success in these efforts if the focus is on issues as the water-distribution in Nicosia, or on lost properties, on technical topics. But if the meetings are steered towards political disputes, I can't predict success.

****As far as we know, the deployment of Russian-made anti-air-craft missiles on southern Cyprus has been postponed due to these talks. Where do you think the current (deployement) process will lead?*

If you allow me, I'd like to say 'No comment.' I made very solid commitments earlier. I see as well that my anticipations are being justified. From the very beginning, I said that the S-300 missiles would create embarrassment and trouble for both Greece and the Greek Cypriots. Now they themselves are postponing the deployment, for they fear the outcome if they pursue their original timetable and accomplish this project. I don't really know how long they will continue to postpone it. This is their own problem. We have told them what we will do if the missiles are brought to the island. Turkey has already calculated all consequences of her planned actions. We know what we will do. This is now the Greeks and Greek Cypriots problem.

(August 1998)

160

DEPLOYMENT OF S-300s: A CRIME ON THE HORIZON:

1. I would like to warn all countries concerned that the deployment of Russian-made S-300 missiles in South Cyprus, within the framework of a Greek and Greek Cypriot scheme, is announced to be in its final phase.

2. These missiles not only threaten Turkey, the Turkish Republic of Northern Cyprus and the Eastern Mediterranean, but also affect NATO's defense mechanism throughout a wide region.

3. The powerful radars of the S-300 control systems are to be operated jointly by the Russian military personnel and the Greek Cypriot soldiers. This is planned for an "extended period." They have a wide coverage encompassing the Incirlik Airbase. By means of this radar system, which has the Eastern Mediterranean within its scope, information on Turkey's and NATO's military activities in the region will be directly available to the Russia and the Greek Cypriot Administration, who are not members of NATO. And this will happen via the contribution of another NATO member, that is, Greece. Besides the threat they impose on the region, the S-300 missiles will greatly damage NATO's South East defense mechanism because of their above-mentioned features of surveillance. Their supporters in the Middle East could also share the vital information, which would be available to the Russia and the Greek Cypriot Administration.

4. This dangerous play is staged by the unskilled directors in Greece and performed by the unskilled players of the Greek Cypriot Administration. We have persistently explained the facts to all interested nations and institutions, and enabled them to see beyond the smoke screen. The intentions, plans and their false propaganda of the Greek side have been thoroughly exposed by our efforts. All interested parties now acknowledge the irresponsibility of the Greek government in regards to the S-300 missiles. The Greek government is criticized by NATO, EU and the US and heads for an isolation within the international community.

5. Perplexed by the strong reactions that her missiles deployment plan drew, the Greek government is now accusing U.S. as well for their "Cyprus Policy". Alleging that Clinton had "lied" to

Greece before the elections, the Greek government has threateningly declared that the Greek community living in the United States of America will no longer contribute to the election expenses of candidates for U.S. presidency. As for the statement by Greece suggesting that Greek Americans divert their contributions from presidential candidates to Greek Armed Forces, this is a farce.

6. Not daring - so far - to finalize the deployment of S-300s in Southern Cyprus, in spite of the declared time-table, Greece now tries to discredit the "Peace Water" project which entails water to be transported via pipelines from sources around Antalya to the Turkish Republic of Northern Cyprus. The water coming to TRNC from Turkey has changed the political geography of Cyprus to the advantage of the Turkish party. Due to this project, the TRNC will become a "center for distribution of water" in the Eastern Mediterranean.

7. The international community has been able to observe the difference: The Greek party who tries to deploy the S-300 missiles on the island, that is to say, to bring death to Cyprus and the Eastern Mediterranean; and Turkey who brings water to Cyprus, in other words, life.

8. Turkey's policies vis-à-vis Eastern Mediterranean and Cyprus are clear: Those who imagined that they could use the S-300 missiles as a leverage to obtain concessions from Turkey have been totally mistaken. The intended deployment of S-300 missiles is a problem for Greece and the Greek administration of southern Cyprus, it's not problem for Turkey. We do not give anything in exchange for the Greek party to come back on their decisions. They have to face the humiliation, which was generated by their eagerness to wage missiles' terror in the Mediterranean. In the case of an effective deployment of S-300s in Cyprus, let there be no doubt: The balances in the island will be radically changed by Turkey and new structures will emerge, in line with the vested interests of the Turkish Cypriots.

(Press Conference, Ankara, July 1998)

S-300s THREATEN THE WHOLE REGION: Ismail Cem, the Turkish Minister of Foreign Affairs, said that the recent purchase of Russian S-300 missiles by Greek Cypriots initiates a new "fashion" in Eastern Mediterranean. Cem was referring to recent rumors that Syria as well got in line to add this deadly Soviet weapon to its arsenal. "...The Russian company is even trying to market them in Turkey", Cem said.

The Turkish Minister of Foreign Affairs, in a statement he made to A.P. in New York, said "...I tried to convey to all Ministers of Foreign Affairs I talked the extreme danger that this missiles build-up represents for peace in the Mediterranean and in Middle East". Cem was referring to his interviews with Secretary of State Albright, with UK's Cook and with his counterparts from Europe and Middle East.

Actually attending the opening session of UN, Cem's statement is as follows:

"The recent purchase of Russian S-300 missiles by Greek Cypriots initiates a new 'fashion' in Eastern Mediterranean. Recent rumors points that Syria as well got in line to add this deadly Soviet weapon to its arsenal. The Russian company is even trying to market them to Turkey...

I tried to convey to all Ministers of Foreign Affairs I talked with in UN, the extreme danger that this missiles build-up represents for peace in the Mediterranean and in Middle East: To Secretary of State Albright, to UK's Robin Cook, who represent a guarantor country for Cyprus and to all my counterparts from Europe and Middle East. The decision by Greek Cypriots, clearly violating UN Security Council resolutions on Cyprus, creates a fatal threat to Turkey and to neighboring countries. We strongly urge the international community to stop the Greek Cypriots in their military build-up.

It is preoccupying to see Greece, the greatest supporter of the S-300 deployment, aggravates the Greek Cypriot provocation through its Foreign Minister: Mr. Pangalos, first insulted Turkish leaders as "...murderers and bandits" with whom its not possible to have a dialogue (Interview to Mega TV, Sept 24; Eleftherotipia Sept 25; Adesmeftos Tipos, Sept 25). Then, in a second interview, he repeated the same remarks in stronger words and claimed that he would not dialogue with "a murderer".

I deplore this attitude; this is not the way a civilized person would conduct a discussion. It seems that Mr. Pangalos tries to escape from Greece's 27 April 1997 commitment to mutually create

163

a wise-men's council with Turkey which would examine all problems between the two countries and put forward appropriate proposals. And he tries to block the process of dialogue to which Greece committed itself in the July 15th 1997 Madrid agreement.

We bring these words of the Minister of Foreign Affairs of Greece as well as his pretexts to shy away from Greece's commitments, to the attention of all the countries interested in the Turkish - Greek relations."

(Interview given to A.P., New York, September 1998)

GREEK DREAM OF S-300s IS OVER... Greece and the Greek administration of Southern Cyprus have officially declared that they are burying their plans to deploy S-300's in southern Cyprus. This is good for them. They have taken back all their assertive discourse; they have acknowledged their humiliation. We can now proceed with an analysis of this aborted Greek initiative.

First thing that draws attention is the following: Within the framework of their so-called joint defence doctrine, which is in fact a "joint attack doctrine", the Greek-Greek Cypriot duo wanted to establish a threat against Turkey and the Turkish Republic of Northern Cyprus. Thus, these infamous missiles were ordered from Russia at a cost of approximately 500 million dollars.

The first objective is to deploy in South Cyprus weapons with a range that covers the entire territory of Turkey. The second objective is to force Turkey to yield to a Greek / Greek Cypriot blackmail: "...If Turkey and TRNC make concessions, if, for example, Turkish airplanes refrain from flying over Cyprus, than, the S-300 project might be abandoned." We had parallel messages from various friendly countries.

We responded by stating that we would not fall into the trap of political trade-offs, bargains or blackmails. Turkey never discussed the issue, let alone bargain. We pointed out that these weapons were a misfortunate product of the Greek - Greek Cypriot cooperation and that it was up to them to clean their mess, or face the consequences. We made it clear to everyone that nothing should be expected from us "in return"; no changes in our policies or attitudes in regards to Cyprus.

Our government made it clear that "...if the Greek-Greek Cypriot side deploys these missiles in South Cyprus, Turkey will do whatever that is necessary, both in political and military terms." We conveyed our determination to Greece and to all interested parties.

Through their official declaration, the Greek side made public yesterday that the project of S-300 deployment in Cyprus is canceled. Thus, the end of a tragicomedy. It is far beyond anybody's limits to threaten Turkey with missiles deployed in South Cyprus. This last episode displays clearly that any such attempt will face serious consequences.

On the other hand, the Greek Cypriot Administration's defeat in the S-300 project by no means puts an end to its efforts to purchase sophisticated weapons. These are still a nuisance for Turkey and the TRNC. Recent developments, such as the construction of a military airbase in Baf, a naval base in Terazi for Greek assault boats and the Greek-Greek Cypriot endeavor to purchase new Russian weapons, testify that the they continue to pursue their hostile ends. We are carefully watching these developments, and taking all necessary measures. Nobody should expect us to be a mere bystander to the rapid armament of the Greek-Greek Cypriot side that has been ongoing within the framework of their joint attack doctrine.

We are as well keeping a close watch on the illegal arming by Greece of some Aegean islands. This takes place in flagrant violation of the letter and the spirit of international agreements (Lausanne and Paris Treaties). This issue has been brought to attention at international fora.

I would also like to indicate that Greece -at least a certain group of Greek politicians- have been encouraging terrorists to perpetuate their killings in Turkey. I would like to state once again that in Europe, Greece is the main base, protector and supporter of terrorism. Greeks still have their dream of destabilizing Turkey. With Greece's para-military camps which train terrorists, with terror bands who freely roam the country, with her "November" terrorist organization which killed scores of foreigners in Greece -and, somehow, not had one member apprehended by Greek police- Greece appears determined more than ever to pursue its ambitions even if the price to pay is a pact with the devil. We have disclosed and displayed in all platforms the close connection between terrorism and Greece.

165

The last indication came about during the expulsion of terrorist chief from Syria: As he was on his way to Rome, the Greek government did not hesitate to declare her support for the terrorist and his band.

Another impediment to international norms by Greece is her treatment of the Turkish minority in Western Thrace. Violating the rules laid down by the Lausanne Treaty, Greece denies fundamental religious freedoms to Muslims of Western Thrace. In line with a dismal human rights record, Greece has repeatedly charged a 70-year-old mufti of being "illegally elected" by the Muslim community. As a measure of intimidation, Greek justice forced him to rush from one court to another and sentenced him to short prison terms, some of which were than converted to monetary sanctions. We observe as well the oppressive policies traditionally imposed by Greece on all her minorities, Muslim minorities of Turkish, Macedonian, Albanian origin, and the Vlach minority.

To conclude, it can be stated that Turkish government has brought down this plot of S-300s, which the Greeks and Greek Cypriots devised. I want to make it clear as well that Turkey does not have the slightest intention to assume a hostile policy towards Greece. The establishment of good relations, mutual understanding and cooperation between the two countries will be to the benefit of Turkey, as well as of Greece. In fact, we had proposed to Greece a plan of reconciliation, based on five points (February 1998). The basic idea was that Turkey and Greece, by way of dialogue and agreement should solve any existing bilateral issue. Our proposal found encouragement and support from E.U. countries and U.S., but was flatly rejected by the Greek government. I renew my invitation: Let us put on the table every bilateral controversy and search together for solution.

***How do you see the international evaluation of Greece's decision to drop the S-300 project ? Do you foresee a reduction of troops in Cyprus ?*

I believe that many countries must have realized by now that Turkey does not change its policies in case of such oppression or threat.

Given the actual conditions, suggestions such as the reduction in troops or weapons are not realistic. This is an issue that can be taken up if an atmosphere of peace and mutual understanding is established and modalities for a final settlement are agreed. I would also like to add that foreign policy is a realm in which one has to be realistic. Two recent developments: Last night, the Greek Cypriots have fired at the Turkish positions along the Green Line. This is the third of such cases. Furthermore, additional Russian weapons - I do not refer to the S-300 missiles, but other land-based conventional weapons bearing highly technological features, which have been purchased by the Greek side.

***There is news claiming that the Russians have also sold S-300 missiles to Armenia. The Azerbaijani authorities have stated that this would constitute a serious threat against Turkey. They said as well that these weapons could even be handed over to PKK. Do you ever see the signs of a similar escalation in the Caucasus concerning the S-300 missiles?*

I will not comment on hypothesis such as the presumed handing-over of weapons. Nevertheless, as you have also pointed out, it is a fact that Russia has been already selling and donating Armenia a great number of weapons, though these might not include S-300's. Azerbaijan is highly concerned. We watch over the developments, ready to assist the Azeris, if there is a need.

***You stated, "Greece is the primary harbor, protector and supporter of terrorism and that Italy is following suit." The presence of the terrorist chief in Rome is affecting the Turkish-Italian relations in a negative way. Now, there is a new development: The transfer of Hakan Sukur, a Galatasaray footballer, to Italy, at a surprisingly high price. This has led way to certain questions, which implied that "Italy was trying to look sympathetic to Turkey and hence wished to use the above-mentioned Hakan for public relations." How would you comment on this transfer case?*

I do not agree with the above-mentioned comment, because it is merely owing to Hakan's high quality as a player that Italian clubs seeks him. Any need for any additional justification, is groundless. Though I might feel sad as a Galatasaray supporter, I am pleased as the minister of foreign affairs when a great Turkish player as Hakan makes part of one of the most powerful teams of the world.

167

***Will Turkey try to hit the S-300's if they are deployed in Crete as Turkey threatened to do so when the now aborted plans to deploy them in Cyprus were imminent ?

I don't really like to speak on "ifs" and presumptions. It is obvious though that in Crete or elsewhere if there is a threat directed to Turkey, we will do the necessary assessment and we will respond by appropriate political and military means, in measure with the nature, relevance and scope of the threat.

(December 1998)

THE ACKNOWLEDGEMENT OF TRNC'S SOVEREIGNTY:
***Mr. Minister, The G-8, or as you prefer to call it, the G-7 and Russia, made a call for the resumption of the peace talks on Cyprus, and the UN Secretary-General has disclosed his intention to invite President Rauf Denktash and Greek Cypriot leader Glafcos Clerides to talks this fall. Although the Turkish Republic of Northern Cyprus (TRNC) and Turkey have been annoyed by this initiative, Clerides has not yet clarified his position, and Athens seems quite pleased. How do you evaluate these developments?

The G-7 and Russia have their views on Cyprus. We have ours.

There are two States on the island. They both have a democratic set-up. One of the two, the Turkish Cypriot State, is treated unjustly. She is under an economic embargo. Despite this, the per capita income in the TRNC is considerably higher than the per capita income in Turkey. The TRNC citizens are content with their lives, and we are doing our best to be supportive. In fact, both peoples live in security; there has not been a major inter-communal incident since 25 years. In the past, clashes used to be a daily reality, with the Turks almost always having the victims part.

The issue today is, whether a model, which brings the two States together, might be developed. This presupposes a solution acceptable by the two parties and the reconciliation between the two peoples. There are efforts, initiatives to that end. We definitely support a joint solution. But we believe that it is primarily for the two parties to forge a common solution; based on the realities on the island; not one some theoretical and, in most cases, biased rhetoric.

External pressures and impositions on the Turkish party, which has developed into a "fashion" by the Security Council and some West European countries, render a settlement more difficult.

As the Foreign Minister of Turkey, I am at ease regarding Cyprus, due to two factors: The first and foremost is the "Denktash factor". We have full confidence in President Denktash. We trust him and he has our full support. Some foreign observers misjudge Denktash, they consider him as an "obstacle" to a mutual solution. On the contrary, he is the best interlocutor for a mutually acceptable solution.

Than, on the issue of Cyprus, the Turkish Foreign Ministry has traditionally been quite successful. I am not speaking solely of my own term as Foreign Minister. Over the past decades, the Foreign Ministry has consistently positive results in regards to making others understand the realties of Cyprus and the aspirations of Turkish Cypriots. Though we still have a long way to go, this has become a constant trend. This was mainly due to our efforts to match our proposals with the dynamic realities in and around Cyprus. To give an example, in the not so distant past, we were proposing a federal settlement and (Greek Cypriots and Greece) were raising hell on our suggestion. They were saying that Turkish Cypriots could not be given federal rights, by no means... Now they are fully supportive of a federal settlement. But again, they are out of synch with realities, which by their nature are dynamic: Given the acceptance of "Cyprus" as a candidate to EU (1997), which is a flagrant impediment of the constituent treaties on Cyprus of 1959 - 1960, and given the declared intentions of the Greek party "...to turn the Turks of Cyprus into a minority with a large degree of autonomy" (FM Pangalos of Greece), Turkish Republic of Northern Cyprus put forward the "Confederation" as the only means for a mutually acceptable solution.

External pressures will not trigger anything positive in Cyprus. I met with some representatives of those (G-7) countries and told them that what they were trying to do was wrong, that such attitude would lead nowhere.

Turkey will overcome this problem. Everyone should know this well. Anyhow, they know it.

***Mr. Minister, with regard to these developments, how relevant is the assumption that "being the richest does not necessarily mean that they are the wisest"?*

169

Yes, this is what I have said. But, of course, I did not mean a particular state or person. It should not be assumed that because a country is rich, on all accounts it would make the wisest suggestions and display the wisest behavior. The same is valid for individuals as well.

***In any case, the latest reports indicate that pressure will mount in the days to come to get the talks on Cyprus to resume on or around October 10th. Do you think such a process could start? And, if it were to start, on which parameters should the new process be established so that a result can emerge from it?*

I naturally assume that you are not expecting me to speak on assumptions. Any remark on whether or not a process starts would be an assumption.But since President Denktash made it clear only few days ago, unless the existence of the TRNC is acknowledged; unless the equal existence of the Turkish Cypriot state, the right to sovereignty of the Turkish Cypriot people is acknowledged; unless the Greek Cypriot side abandons its claim of being the representative of the entire island, no solution can emerge from any meeting. If, on the contrary, realities are acknowledged and proper conditions laid down, a settlement could be within reach. Besides, there is the need for preparation before such a meeting takes place. Obviously, this is not the present case.

It will be positive if proper conditions are there and a meeting of the two presidents takes place. If not, it won't be the end of the world. We should not over-exaggerate this issue.

There are certain subjects on which a country has a firm position that is moral and ethical. For us, Cyprus is such an issue. In cases with moral and ethical justification, insistence generally brings results. One might recall the issue of the S-300's (Russian-made missiles) to be deployed by Greek Cypriots in Southern Cyprus. We had stated that we would not permit their deployment. Some friendly countries suggested "trade-offs"; "Turkey to bring adjustments to her position in regards to Cyprus, in return, the Greek Cypriots to refrain from deployment". We flatly said "No". "...No trade-offs, but the missiles not to be deployed in Cyprus". Well, we were morally, ethically justified. And the Greek side had to take back all their previous rhetoric and cancel the deployment of S-300's in Southern Cyprus.

(Interview given to "Turkish Daily News" Ankara, June 1999 - Excerpts)

* * *

7.   What About the Turkish Minority in Greece?

I am writing you, Ms President, to share my deep concern about the Turkish Moslem minority living in Western Thrace, Greece.

It is the fate of this minority to face growing numbers of racially motivated repression or assault whenever animosity escalate between Greece and Turkey, or between Turkish Cypriots and Greek Cypriots. Unfortunately, provocation triggered by Orthodox religious authorities in the region and by para-military Greek organizations sometimes ends up in mass violence.

During the recent incidents that occurred in Komotini, on 16th August 1996, two elderly Turkish women of 60 and 70 years of age were brutally beaten by the mob. Furthermore, 35 shops and offices belonging to the Turkish minority were vandalized. These events reflect the present reality in Western Thrace. The Greek local authorities were reluctant to take any preventive action and were, at best, passive witnesses to the acts of violence in progress. In a way, a re-run of the wide-scale atrocities of 29th January 1990 was staged.

Since the latest incidents of mid-August, the Greek citizens of Turkish Moslem origin living in Western Thrace are under perpetual threat and are subject to discriminations and humiliations. Overall, besides their inhuman characteristics, these attitudes, threats and assaults are in direct contradiction with Greek laws and with the bilateral and multilateral obligations of Greece.

Given the escalation due to the recent cold-blooded murder of a Turkish Cypriot security guard, I am deeply concerned about a new outbreak of atrocities by fanatical Greek organizations in Western Thrace. I would therefore like to appeal to you, Ms. President, to take whatever measure is possible within the framework of the Council of Europe to remind the Greek authorities of their commitments and responsibilities vis-à-vis their citizens of Turkish origin. I would also like to ask you if you could draw the attention of political Groups and relevant Committees of the Council of Europe to this issue.

I am again deeply concerned that unless preventive measures are seriously considered and implemented by the Greek

171

authorities, the Turkish minority in Western Thrace will continue to be the subject of perpetual discriminations and acts of violence.

Ismail Cem, Chairman, Turkish Parliamentary Delegation to the Council of Europe

(Letter to L. Fischer, President, Parliamentary Assembly, Council of Europe, September 1996)

* * *

8.   Problems and Achievements...

-I- In our relations with Greece, our principal objective is to promptly tackle, through a substantive and result-oriented dialogue, the issues, mostly related to the Aegean, that still stand between our two countries. To this end, we have made several appeals to Greece to agree to a dialogue and to begin a process with a view to settling our differences.

We do not rule out any agreed method of peaceful settlement to our bilateral differences. Furthermore, we have implemented unilaterally a number of confidence building measures in the hope that they would be reciprocated. We expect that the Group of "Wise Men", consisting of two non-governmental personalities from Turkey and Greece respectively, will finally be able to meet without further delay. This group has the task of preparing a report to be submitted to both governments with non-binding recommendations for dealing with the issues.

We also eagerly await the translation into concrete deeds of the understanding reached during the NATO Summit in Madrid, last July, for promoting better relations between our two countries.

Delaying these processes by linking them to preconditions or artificial issues will not serve the best interests of either country. Our bilateral problems cannot be resolved by the efforts of Turkey alone, and that a mutual commitment and display of good will by both parties are imperative.

-II- It is mainly due to the Greek veto that there was no improvement at the EU's Cologne Summit. Even back at Cardiff, the EU might have declared Turkey a candidate country, if it were not for the Greek veto. Yes, we have problems with Greece.

172

We have always advocated dialogue and peaceful resolution of problems. The West Europeans finally have a clearer vision of what goes on between Greece and us. In the past, they were totally victims to Greek propaganda that Turkey was against reconciliation. And now, EU and the entire world see that Turkey is seeking reconciliation and peaceful resolution of disputes.

Nowadays, we are expecting a response from Greece to our offer for cooperation in the fight against terrorism. As you know, about a month ago I wrote a letter to Foreign Minister Papandreou and I am waiting for his response. *(The interview with Foreign Minister Cem was conducted on Friday night, a day before the Greek response to Turkey - TDN).*

***Indications are that Greece will say no to Turkey's offer to cooperate in fighting terrorism...*

That's their business. What I did was right, and international public opinion in its entirety has endorsed what we did as right. A response might arrive pretty soon. And when it arrives, we shall not rush a reply. We are not in a hurry. We shall study it; we will then announce the views of our Ministry and Government to the Greek response. If the response is positive, we will not expect that everything will come to a happy ending. If it will be negative, that would be their business. But they should be careful, because Greece was caught red-handed in the case of the terrorist leader *(separatist Kurdistan Workers' Party (PKK) chieftain Ocalan).*

After we forced the terrorist chieftain out of Syria and had Europe closing her doors to his face, Greece assisted, supported and harbored the fugitive terrorist. She did not act as a responsible state. She is now paying the price for the way she handled the whole matter. Greece has lost her ability to deceive the world. Greece has lost her credibility.

Now, we want to be on friendly terms with Greece. That's what befits Turkey. A country of 65 million people cannot and should not have policies of enmity against a neighbor of 10 million. We want friendship and peace. But we cannot sacrifice our vital interests for the sake of friendship and peace.

I hope that Greece will come to the same understanding. If they don't, again, that's their business. They have more to lose then we do.

173

***Before the Helsinki Summit, we spoke with the German Ambassador to Ankara. He had said that Germany saw Turkey as a "problem solving" country and that this was the reason why it was supporting Turkey's EU candidacy. He had stated that Turkey's success in applying pressure on Syria, hence naturally raising the tension, but then quickly restoring normality after seeing Ocalan's expulsion was an example of Turkey's problem solving ability.

-III- Yes. However, we had no such pre-calculated policy of "fighting a little bit, and then forcing an agreement." Taking into account all relevant factors, we acted in determination to go till the end, if necessary.

Another development took place with respect to Greece. We first displayed to the world and made everybody understand the link between terrorism and the former Greek Administration. The assistance they provided for the terrorist organization, the services they rendered, the harboring they offered through their embassies to the fugitive terrorist, etc. Yes, we were tough on Greece in our words and deeds. But with the change of attitudes in Greece and after a certain point, we managed together to reach an understanding.

***Greece's current Foreign Minister George Papandreou can in no way be compared with his predecessor. Do you think Turkish-Greek relations would still be where they are today; had not Greece managed to avoid the mistakes of the Pangalos era [hosting Ocalan at the Greek Ambassador's Residence in Kenya]?

I do not know. But, frankly, we always wanted to pursue peaceful policies towards Greece. We launched a number of initiatives when Minister Pangalos was in office. One of those initiatives came as early as my second week in office. We adopted the "Madrid Declaration" with Minister Pangalos (July 1997). In that document, we engaged our countries to the fundamentals for peace and understanding. The context addressed both parties but in reality it meant specific engagements: Greece engaged herself to refrain from any kind of unilateral act in the Aegean (this is to say, any unilateral act to extend her continental waters) and we engaged ourselves not to make use of force or formulate the threat of using force (presuming that Greece holds her promises and refrains from a unilateral act). "Madrid Declaration" is a trilateral document, initiated and supported by the U.S. Secretary of State Madeleine

Albright. While we expressed our content with "Madrid", the Greek side, immediately after their return to Athens, started to criticize the agreement that they had reached. They tried to downplay their engagement ever since. But, of course, it is there as a binding document. Well, we Aegean are sometimes difficult to understand...

Another initiative was the five-point reconciliation package I offered Pangalos in February 1998. That proposal got a very positive reception in Europe and in the United States, but Greece rejected outright. We have always sought to have closer ties, but previous Greek policies opted for tension and confrontation, rather than conciliation and cooperation. I am now pleased that with Minister Papandreou we use the same language of reconciliation and cooperation. But, I should also make it clear that Papandreou is as keen on Greek interests as Pangalos. The difference is that, contrary to Pangalos, Papandreou sees it in Greece's interest to be on good terms with Turkey.

***Papandreou appears to be more rational.*

Definitely. He is better in both listening and explaining. His coming to office as Greek Foreign Minister was a fortunate development for Turkey as it was for Greece. I believe we will manage to hold on to this current positive state of affairs.

***From a bumpy start -the Ocalan saga- to the current state of affairs, a lot of ground has been covered in Turkish-Greek relations. Although there was much anticipation of a last-minute "Greek surprise" to Turkey's EU candidacy bid, it did not happen. And now, Turkey and Greece are preparing to sign certain documents that have been shaped in talks over the past months -talks held at "senior official level." I believe, there will the signing of an accord to cooperate against terrorism.*

We are very close to reaching an agreement. "Cooperation against terrorism" is a very significant issue. Amongst all the agreements that we will be signing, this will have a very special meaning. The agreement for cooperation on combating terrorism, drug trafficking and the illegal transportation of immigrants, will open new avenues. We shall be signing four or five agreements during Papandreou's visit to Ankara. I will later travel to Athens where the remaining agreements will be finalized.

-IV- ***What do you see as the main goal with respect to Turkish-Greek relations?*

I do not agree with the arguments claiming that we have addressed nothing of substantial nature. It is not true. We have already concluded nine important agreements with Greece, including one on cooperation against terrorism. People now speak of Cyprus. I have never considered Cyprus to be a bilateral issue between Turkey and Greece and I have never taken the subject up during talks with my Greek counterpart. As far as Aegean issues are concerned, we have told EU, NATO and the United Nations that we are ready to discuss all Aegean disputes, within the framework of the relevant article of UN Charter. No one should expect more. Regarding the conclusions of the Helsinki Summit, in regards to Turkey, there is a reference made to paragraph four of the same summit document. It is very clear, any party can ask for any issue it considers as such to be handled through international law. We have stated and re-stated that we are willing to take all disputed Aegean issues - not uniquely the only and one issue the Greeks consider as such- to be solved through all means of peaceful solution -not solely by the one means (ICJ) that Greece insists upon- but through all mechanisms (ICJ included) stipulated by relevant article of UN Charter; and, incidentally, enumerated by the "Agenda 2000" document of EU.

Having commented on those two subjects, obviously, I am quite satisfied on behalf of Turkey and of Greece, with all results achieved in such a short period. Both countries and both peoples have gained immensely through the rapprochement process.

(Speech delivered at the 52nd General Assembly of the United Nations, September 1997 - Excerpts; (Interview given to "Turkish Daily News" Ankara, January 2000 - Excerpts); (Interview given to I. Cevik, broadcasted by "Kanal 7", Istanbul and published by Turkish Daily News, Ankara, August 2000);

* * *

9.   Through "Realism" and "Justice   "

-I- I read the interesting article of my colleague Mr. Papandreou, Minister of Foreign Affairs of Greece, in La Stampa (14 June 2000). Mr. Papandreou develops valuable ideas on the relations between Europe and Cyprus, Turkey and Greece. I would like to contribute as well, through a Turkish optic.

I believe that the sustenance of peace, security and development in Eurasia and Europe necessitate Turkey's active participation. The recent Kosovo crisis and consequent problem of refugees, the economic and democratic development of the Central Asian republics, the security of Georgia, the establishment of stability and cooperation in the Balkans, the efforts for the resolution of Azerbaijani-Armenian conflict and the support to the Middle East Peace Process all point to Turkey's important role in this large geography.

In this context, particularly in the European context, the *rapprochement* between Turkey and Greece that we initiated has already brought about very positive contributions. I would like to cite two examples:

The *rapprochement* between Turkey and Greece and the decision by the Helsinki Summit of the European Union to accept Turkish candidacy for membership (December 1999) paved the way for a fundamental geo-strategic change. Turkey and Greece are no longer bordering countries along a strategic fault-line. "Candidate" Turkey taking her new place in European Union's geographic entity, the political borders of EU are removed from the Aegean and from the Balkans. They are now located further in the East, East of Turkey's Asian borders. EU frontal countries are not facing Turkey anymore. Symbolically and on real terms, Greece and Turkey are no longer facing each other as potentially conflicting parties on the opposite sides of a dividing line, which carries an international significance as well. Today, the two countries are separated by national boundaries only, just like any other two countries. This development I believe, pre-empts the fixation of some circles about the scenarios of "Clash of Civilizations".

"Mutual re-discovery by the peoples of Turkey and Greece of one another and their re-conciliation" had provided the main dynamics of the *rapprochement*. It constitutes now the main result of the same *rapprochement:* Almost on a daily basis, politicians, mayors, businessmen, unionists, artists, writers, sportsmen and student groups visit each other across the Aegean. The trade between the two countries is flourishing. An unprecedented flurry of activity is being observed in the Aegean coasts and Thrace. Bilateral tourism is on the rise; joint investments are being carried out. A Memorandum of Understanding concerning EU-Turkey-Greece joint pipeline project to transport Central Asian and Caucasus energy to Western Europe has been signed.

177

In other words, the peoples of the two countries have not only superseded their politicians but they have raised a most significant barrier: The rapprochement between these two peoples constitute the best guarantee against the inclination displayed by some politicians, once in a while, to return to the confrontational past.

-II- It befalls on all of us to protect, preserve and further develop the Turco-Greek rapprochement, which is already yielding positive results for peace and economic development in Eurasia and Europe. In this context, Turkey's position is clear: Turkey has committed herself to accept and consider in the European and Eurasian family, all nations fighting for democracy within their own boundaries and peaceful cooperation outside them. In Europe, this is the case for both Yugoslavia and Greece.

Turkey believes that the international community has much to gain by hosting a peaceful Greece, on condition that Greece respect fundamental principles that define all modern democracies. Of course, our bilateral problems some of which have to do with centuries old prejudices and misconceptions will not suddenly wither away. But we want to play a constructive role in Greece's quest for a better understanding with Turkey, in supporting her to get rid of her unfounded fears of Turkey and of her old animosities towards Turkey. This requires the firm renouncement by Greece of unilateral acts -as we both have renounced for the Aegean issues through the joint Turkey-Greece-US "Madrid Declaration" of August 1997. We need as well a political will by Greece to submit to international law, as defined by Article 33 of the United Nations Charter (negotiation, mediation, arbitration, International Court of Justice) and as referred to in the Helsinki Summit of EU, all Aegean issues that Turkey and Greece consider appropriate to do so. Turkey has officially informed Greece her readiness to address Aegean issues in this context. This policy has been conveyed to all interested circles, including NATO and the EU. Now we are waiting for Greece to consider herself ready for the implementation of international law. Likewise, we are expecting Greece to respond positively to our nine proposals pertaining to military cooperation and security in the Aegean.

On the other hand, I believe that progress in Greece on certain human rights and democracy issues will further enhance our cooperation. This progress means for some Greek politicians to refrain from the use of unfounded, unethical allegations and clichés. We are very worried about the ongoing oppression of the Turkish people of Western Thrace. Serious initiatives are needed for the protection of their human rights and minority rights. They should be relieved of limitations to their religious rights, which are guaranteed by the Lausanne Treaty. The complaints of Greece's Macedonian, Albanian and Vlach minorities are a source of concern as well. On all these issues, Greece still has to develop norms that conform to European values and standards. I expect Greece to take substantial steps to address these issues and thus contribute to the further development of Turco-Greek relations.

-III- Cyprus is a subject generally defined in a misleading way by the international media. International media generally glosses over the substance and reality of the relevant issues. Instead, it contents itself with the biased inspiration provided by some powerful political center, financial interests or ethnic pressure groups. Public opinion and understanding are thus generally based on misinformation.

To define the division of Cyprus as "...the last wall of Europe" might sound fashionable but the connotations it brings and the parallelism it draws is totally erroneous. First of all, the line defined as a "wall" was drawn by the United Nations Peace Force in 1963, in order to protect the Turkish Cypriots from the assault of the Greek Cypriots. This is the year when the Greek Cypriots illegally usurped the state apparatus and conducted violent assaults against Turkish Cypriots.

1. The present situation in Cyprus came into being after the coup engineered by Greek Cypriot fascists in 1974. The coup toppled the administration of Makarios that was internationally recognized as "legitimate" and forced the Head of State to flee the country. Nikos Sampson, the leader of the Greek Cypriot fascists, who was acting in coordination with the "Colonels' Junta" in Greece, murdered many, even "leftist" Greek Cypriots. They staged the well-know fascist terror, and moved to make the Turkish Cypriots subjects of the "Greek Cyprus" which was to make integral part of "Mainland Greece".

2. Turkey as one of the guarantor powers by virtue of the London and Zurich Agreements intervened to terminate the ongoing massacres and to prevent the perpetration of similar atrocities in the future. Accordingly, Turkey averted an "ethnic cleansing" in the island and precluded the Turkish Cypriots to share the tragic fate of the Muslim Kosovars and Bosnians of the future. Turkish intervention can never be considered as an "occupation" because it symbolizes "liberation" for nearly 200.000 Turkish Cypriots. On the other hand, (for the Turkish Cypriots) it is irrational to describe Turkish presence in their own land as an "occupation". Furthermore, due to Turkish inter vention, not only the fascist coup in Cyprus failed, but also the fascist junta in Greece collapsed.

3. Following the years 1963-1974, during which hundreds of armed clashes took place and human lives were lost, the liberation of Turkish Cypriots brought peace for both parties. For 25 years, tranquility has prevailed in the island. Turkish Cypriots and Greek Cypriots live in the island as two independent states, two functioning democracies and two peoples in security. In spite of a ruthless economic embargo imposed upon them by the Greek Cypriots and implemented by the EU, the Turkish Cypriots made considerable economic progress. What is being sought today is a mutually acceptable solution for two parties who are both relatively well off and whose security is guaranteed.

4. It is stipulated by the United Nations that both parties through separate referenda should approve a comprehensive settlement mutually acceptable by the parties. In case this settlement is rejected by one of the parties in referenda, the proposed solution becomes null and void. It is out of question that an international organization can impose its own solution on the parties. In this framework, the membership of "Cyprus" in the EU, in which Turkey is not full member would be an indirect "enosis" and contrary to the London and Zurich Agreements.

5. If a mutually acceptable settlement is sincerely sought, then the model is quite clear: Based on the realities of Cyprus, a confederation consisting of two States. According to this model, the two independent entities, by virtue of reaching an agreement between themselves, transfer some of their functions to the

confederal bodies. Thus, both the integrity and diversity that emanate from the realities of the island would be preserved. If a confederal model as defined by international law is to be implemented, the realities of Cyprus provide the most appropriate circumstances. A mutually acceptable settlement in Cyprus cannot be reached through romantic descriptions but through the realistic assessment of facts of the island, provided that the Greek Cypriot party has the political will to that end.

The developments in Turco-Greek relations make me conclude as follows: The common fate of problems is to be "solved" when the appropriate time comes. The level, which the Turco-Greek relations have attained in such a short time, inspires cautious optimism. It lays the ground for us to look at the future with more confidence. I hope that this great opportunity will not be undermined and that the level of relations will be continuously upgraded.

(Article published by "La Stampa", Rome, July 2000)

* * *

10. Both Turkey and Greece Have Gained From "Rapprochement"

***One year ago, in the wake of the Ocalan crisis, relations between Greece and Turkey were at a near all-time low. Now they appear to be the best they've been in several decades. To what do you attribute this remarkable turnaround?**

I believe our initiative and the positive response of the Greek government paved the way for developments, which have already proved to be mutually beneficial. I had tried to initiate a somewhat similar process with former Minister [Theodorus] Pangalos (my formal letter of February 12, 1998) but had a negative response. Minister Papandreou's approach was different, inspiring trust and displaying political courage, if I may say so. I am pleased to hear that recent polls in

Greece displays a substantial support of his policies. As to our peoples, they did a wonderful job, though it needed tragedies for them to discover their feelings for each other. This provided a strong encouragement to the ongoing process we had initiated with Minister Papandreou.

***Were the earthquakes the chief catalyst for rapprochemen tbetween the two countries?*

Actually, everything began on May 24, with my letter to Minister Papandreou - so it's way before the earthquakes. This was a short letter, suggesting an agreement on the need to work together to combat terrorism. His response was a very detailed one. Mr. Papandreou mentioned several subjects such as tourism and commerce but he stated that dealing with organized crime and terrorism was a priority for both Greece and Turkey. Then he said the possibility of concluding bilateral or even multilateral agreements on all our differenccs could also be envisaged in the light of our progress in cooperation. So I realized things were possible. We then decided to meet in the margins of the "Friends of Kosovo" meeting with the UN Secretary General in New York. We drafted an outline for our work and made parallel declarations. So everything got on track.

***After Ocalan, when things were very tense, the Kosovo crisis seemed to come just at the right time for Greece and Turkey; they had to cool down whatever was happening in order to play the NATO game on Kosovo.*

Frankly, whenever we discussed Kosovo with Papandreou, I never had in mind the terrorist's case, not at all. Kosovo was an issue where we both were very sensitive, about which we had very strong feelings. It needed a cooperative approach, from the two Balkan NATO countries. So instead of making things more difficult for NATO we looked for coordination, and through this understanding, we had a closer dialogue with Greece. This was helpful.

*** *So the cooperation over Kosovo led on to more trust between the two countries?*

I think that this was felt more strongly in Greece than in Turkey. In Turkey it didn't really have an effect on our evaluation of Greece. We took it natural that as two NATO members we cooperate, as all NATO members did at that time. And as Balkan countries we had more responsibilities. I wanted the Balkan NATO countries to have more responsibility and a larger say on Kosovo. I had strongly advocated this idea in one of the NATO ministerial meetings. And it was supported by Minister Papandreou right away.

***What does Turkey stand to gain from improved relations with Greece?*

The gain is mutual: Tensions are dropping; there is a growing atmosphere of trust; Turkish and Greek civil-society organizations of all kinds meeting almost every other day; nine agreements which already provide substantial results; cooperation within EU; coordination in the Balkans; joint economic ventures already on track; official visits by Greek and Turkish Foreign Ministers, the first of their kind since 20 and 30 years, respectively; Turkish and Greek flags waved together in Concert Halls and Stadiums in both countries. If someone had described this picture some eight months ago, we would all have agreed that he was daydreaming.

*** *Yet there is a lingering degree of suspicion in both countries. In Turkey, some commentators seem to suffer from what is called the Sevres Complex, which refers to the Treaty of Sevres, and makes some Turks think that every diplomatic move from the international community is designed to denude Turkey of territory. For example, do Turks still view the Greeks as being obsessed with the Megali Idea?*

No. Perhaps there are a few (Greeks) who still think about the Megali Idea. I don't believe we should take them seriously. Some writers and some sections of our public opinion do make from time to time references to the Sevres Treaty. I don't think it's a complex, though Sevres has very negative connotations in our memories. But somehow when people in Turkey talk about Sevres, they don't have Greece in mind. What they mean is the major European powers.

****Are there any gestures that Turkey could make to further improve relations? For example, reopening the Halki seminary?*

The phase of gestures seems to be already accomplished, for we are dealing with deeds and realities. We have accomplished in six months more than what had been done in 40 years. Further improvement will stem from concrete developments, of which I am hopeful. As for a setup that would provide further higher education in religion, it is a complicated matter. I am aware of Greek sensitivities.

****Current talks between Greece and Turkey have centered largely on a number of minor confidence-building issues. Of the agreements already signed, which do you see as the most significant?*

I totally disagree. The current talks and the nine agreements signed are substantial. All are of equal relevance; though in our initial proposal we had said that the agreement on fighting terrorism would be essential. If what we have already achieved in six months were "minor confidence-building measures," why then they were not realized in 40 years ?

***Granted. But when do you expect to discuss more substantive issues, such as Cyprus and the Aegean?*

Cyprus is not on the agenda, except that we both support and encourage the proximity talks. We have not discussed this subject. Yes we have referred to it and said we should find some time to exchange informal views. I said I should explain thoroughly our ideas about a confederal set up. But that was all.

As for the Aegean, any time which is convenient for both parties.

***What do you believe was gained from the recent proximity talks on Cyprus at the UN?*

Involved or interested countries are now more aware of positions, proposals and sensitivities of both parties. Furthermore, it seems now that the way for a further round of proximity talks is paved.

*** Do you expect movement on Cyprus issue to be the key to everything between Greece and Turkey?*

No I don't. I think that we are on the right track and that the process of rapprochement between Greece and Turkey will go on. It is a substantial process, with all the economic links we are forging now, and the relationship between our respective civil societies. In Turkey I know that there is a very strong political support for the processes, and no one from the opposition is really objecting. And so it will go on. In talks with Minister Papandreou I have the impression that grounds are being laid for more developments in the Aegean. But I believe we shall achieve more progress after the elections. That is of course if the Greek policies are there. Then I think we will make further progress in our sensitive bilateral issues.

*** Who is calling the shots on Cyprus, Ankara or Mr. Denktash?*

I think we're calling the shots together. We have a great respect for President Denktash. And he is really a politician of very high caliber. And I have told my foreign colleagues interested in Cyprus that they should not consider Denktash as an obstacle to a mutual solution. In fact, he is the greatest asset for a mutually acceptable solution. And it is obvious now that President. Denktash has a positive approach.

If I look back at the two rounds of talks that took place, the proximity talks, the Turkish side has been more forthcoming than the Greek side. Well, that is my perception. And I detect in the Greek Cypriots a kind of reluctance to move as they observe the Turkish side being more forthcoming.

Greek-Cypriot public opinion questions the whole idea of getting together with the Turkish Cypriots. They say "...we [the Greek side] are well off, we have money, we have everything, we have security, we hope to be part of the EU. So why should we create a new situation that might bring a lot of problems, not only to the Turkish Cypriots but to the Greek Cypriots as well ?"

*** *Could you foresee a situation where Turkey is accepted into the EU without a solution to the Cyprus question?*

I really wouldn't know because it depends on the dynamics of the stage we will be in at that time. We made it very obvious that we don't link the two subjects together. I really, genuinely and personally believe that the confederal set-up is a very good solution.

***Both Greece and Turkey have vociferous nationalist elements on the domestic political scene that may feel uncomfortable with the current rapprochement. After last year's elections in Turkey, many commentators predicted that a government led by Ecevit and the right-wing Nationalist Action Party (MHP) would be unwilling or unable to make any concessions on what are termed "national" issues. How big a factor is this in influencing Turkish foreign policy?*

The Government led by Mr. Ecevit in coalition with the National Action Party and the Motherland party is just as forth coming as the Government led by Mr. Simitis. On the other hand, I have a different perspective: Neither the Turkish or Greek side sees our relationship as one of "concessions," on any "issue." Both governments see it as one, which aims at finding points where national interests meet. So far, they are both successful. With the confidence that success provides, I am cautiously hopeful that in some more intricate issues as well, they will find paths where interests coincide.

*** *Will a change of government in Ankara—of which there have been several in the past few years—mean a change in foreign policy?*

185

I consider a governmental change is unlikely, but after all this is a coalition. As with policies regarding Greece, there is a strong consensus. I will be surprised if that consensus wouldn't be there in case of a new government. Of course, styles might change, and though the personality factor generally is not a decisive one, in foreign policy, it is a factor. This of course helps. I believe that George Papandreou and I are able to understand each other well. And we have parallel understandings in matters other than foreign policy. If there is a political change in Greece, I hope the actual consensus will remain and the policies that we are pursuing persist.

***To what extent are economic reform and democratization linked in Turkey? Will there be one without the other?*

As linked or de-linked in any country.

(Interview given to M. Howard and published by "Odyssey", Athens, March - April 2000, Excerpts)

* * *

11. From Negative Anticipations to Positive Expectations...

I am honored to receive the East-West Institute's "The Statesman of the Year" Award for , together with my colleague Minister Papandreou. As representatives of Turkey and Greece, Yorgo and I are standing before you today for one simple reason: We have faithfully translated the feelings of the Turkish and Greek peoples into policies and acts.

Back in June 1999, we had already initiated, as two Ministers, a process of consultation and joint work on our bilateral issues. This was later expedited by the immense solidarity between our two peoples during the tragic earthquakes of last summer. On both shores of the Aegean, Greeks and Turks discovered that they care for each other much more than what was generally presumed.

In the past, whenever Turkey and Greece were mentioned together, whether on world news or in diplomatic circles, the context would be one of anxiety, of confrontation, or simply, of bad news. Well, that is what we have started to change. We are working on transforming negative anticipations into positive ones. Now, when

186

the names of our countries appear side by side, the expectations that follow are of "cooperation" and "friendship".

Lasting peace and understanding among nations is built on carefully crafted agreements, which reflect an equitable balance of interests, as well as on good will and positive sentiments. We have thus far concluded nine agreements. They all pertain to important areas of joint work. However, this is not enough. We should expand our cooperation to other bilateral issues. We still have a difficult task ahead. Mutual confidence and caution is still essential for further progress.

As the spirit of community and of civil society is an emerging factor in both domestic and international spheres, I believe we have a most receptive environment. We have ended our own Cold War and initiated an atmosphere of Détente. Now it is time to create our own Peace. A peace and cooperation to last for generations to come.

Like all peoples around the world, Greeks and Turks also aspire for peace, security and economic development. What we accomplished demonstrates that if two countries in dispute can talk with each other, respect each other's sensitivities and explore the future together, then, they can create the right environment for progress. The point of departure for our efforts to reconcile was to take full stock of the realities on the ground. I am convinced that this is the only viable way to proceed. This should be an inspiration for all others in the region, who are faced with the task of seeking realistic and mutually acceptable solutions for the disputes between them.

Well, I know that scores of men and women around the globe work everyday to build lasting peace and understanding among nations. I would like to pay tribute to all those whose names we may never know, but who - like Yorgo and myself - endeavor to do their best. They all have a share in this award that you so kindly bestowed upon us. An award, which we receive with the hope that it contributes to a world, we will be proud to leave to our children.

(Speech on the occasion of reception of "The Statesman of the Year Award" granted by the "East-West Institute", May 2000, New York)

* * *

CHAPTER VI :
The European Union

***Four months after I had taken office as Foreign Minister, we were to have the Luxembourg Summit of EU. I believe I defined the "problematique" for EU correctly in my article published simultaneously by several European and US newspapers, November 1997: Admitting or rejecting Turkey's candidature (and, eventually, her membership) is a strategic choice for EU; which, either way, defines the civilizational characteristic of EU, its mission, its conceptual and geographic boundaries.

Ever since, I am deeply involved with our EU relations. Helsinki, December 1999, was a success for those who made a clear choice for EU's future, a success for Turkey as well.

I do not think feasible for any party to retreat from her 1999 decision. As Alain Duhamel wrote, having accepted Turkey's candidature, which will sooner or later lead to her membership, EU will never again be the EU that we all used to know. Duhamel was not very happy about it. Well, I believe EU changed positively.***

1.   For EU, an Issue of Identity and Vision

Will the future of the European Union be limited by religious and racial connotations or will it be one that reaches out and boldly contributes to the diversity and unity of a much larger geography?

The EU is now deciding on its enlargement process. One important decision is what role to offer Turkey, which provides Western Europe's main historical, cultural and economic link to Eastern horizons. The choice that EU makes will either provide the EU with a crucial bridge of conciliation with civilizations of other characteristics, or will be discriminatory and have no effect or even negative effects on the persisting dichotomies.

This seems to be the choice, which EU will make on the 12th of December, by the Luxembourg Summit.

We consider ourselves both European and Asian, and view this duality to be an asset. Therefore we are disturbed when the European trait in our identity is questioned: If being European is a "historical" or "geographical" definition, we live and we have lived 700 years of our history in Europe, and as a European power. Our history was molded as much in Istanbul, Edirne, Tetova and Sarajevo as it was in Bursa, Kayseri and Diyarbakir.

If being European is a "cultural" definition, things get a bit more complicated: If "European" is defined by a religious criteria, if the EU is a "Christian Club" then the setting is not appropriate. But if "European Culture" is defined as the EU officially claims, that is, by factors such as "democracy", "human rights", "rule of law", "gender equality", "secularism", etc., then, in spite of needs for further progress on some issues, we have shared and contributed to this contemporary "European culture" for 75 years.

Then, we ask ourselves, where is the "real problem"? What is it, which justifies the negation of declared EU commitments made to Turkey over a period of three decades? What is it, which causes the reluctance to call a country that has an association agreement with EU since 1963, a country that is part of the EU Customs Union, a "candidate"? Why is there such a discrimination against a NATO member who has contributed extensively to the defense of Europe? Against one of the most dynamic economies of Europe, a country which will bring a lot in term of markets and growth to the whole of Europe?

My counterparts from EU name three sets of "reasons" or "conditions": Greece, Cyprus and Human Rights. In the four months our government has been in office, progress was achieved in all three issues. Furthermore, I have been able to discuss several issues with my counterparts and -hopefully- convinced them on some aspects.

Concerning relations with Greece, a member country, conventional criticism is generally unfounded. First, we need two sides to solve a bilateral problem; one of the sides cannot be held responsible when both parties must contribute for a solution. Second, though I cannot claim to be an "objective observer" I can sincerely state that at least in my time in office Turkey has done a lot to improve relations. The third parties involved in negotiations to promote a better understanding between the two neighbors can bear witness to our efforts. The parallel declaration of goodwill by Prime Ministers Yilmaz and Simitis in Crete is a cautiously promising start.

As for the Cyprus issue, there has to be a positive approach from four sides, even five, when we include the U.K., the other guarantor country. Again, Turkey cannot be held as the only responsible actor when there is many involved. The Greek Cypriot side, at the eve of elections, is far from the compromises and concessions needed for a process of conciliation. The Turkish Cypriot side insists on equal recognition. This position seems to draw some positive attention now, especially from the U.S. special representative Richard Holbrooke. Furthermore, the recent statements by President Denktash on the probability of forming a "joint government" in Cyprus to tackle problems of Cyprus and of the EU, give some cautious but hopeful signals. I have to note, though, that the announced deployment of S-300 missiles by the Greek Cypriots has further aggravated an already sensitive situation.

In my recent talks with my EU counterparts, I have thoroughly addressed the "human rights and democracy" problems. I stated that I agree with most of the well-intentioned criticism but reject politically motivated and exaggerated claims. I have to add that during my government's time in office, there has been considerable progress. Some positive legal acts concerning prison sentences were realized. With the separatist terrorism within Turkey declining, three out of the nine provinces that have been under a state of emergency for ten years have been returned to full democracy. Several others are expected to follow. This might have already happened if the U.S. and Iraq had not come so close to a military confrontation and stimulated fears of a new wave of Iraqi refugees flooding into those provinces.

Yes, we have our specific issues that need further improvement, like any other country. But after all, Turkey and the EU are not talking about immediate membership. Rather, we are referring to a long accession process, which would also aid in the elimination of some of the above-mentioned problems.

If the "three sets of conditions" -generally referred to as obstacles- are either dealt with positively by the current Turkish government and / or they are out of the unilateral reach of Turkey, then what is the cause of this negative approach by the EU? On the eve of the new millennium, is the undeclared cause for discrimination, as Mr. Jacques Attali recently stated, the fact that Turkey is a Moslem country?

It seems to me that EU still cannot decide whether it can face the challenges of an emerging new world; whether it is capable of seizing the vast opportunities of encompassing new economic, historical and cultural dimensions; whether it can contribute to the harmonization of civilizations rather than to the professed "clash" of civilizations; whether it will enclose itself within a confined strategic vision and continue to call for a problem-solver from another continent to resolve European problems like Bosnia or Cyprus; whether it exists as an introvert organization or emerge as one which takes responsibility to create a better world for itself and for all. The EU should realize that Turkey contributes to all these causes positively, perhaps decisively.

I hope the EU makes the right decision.

As for Turkey, I hope as well that the EU does not discriminate against us; that it does not act unjustly by excluding Turkey's candidacy from its present enlargement process and pre-accession strategy; that it does not cause further resentment in Turkey; that it does not deflate Turkey's enthusiasm and momentum; that it does not take a course which would damage its relationships with Turkey; that it does not stimulate in Turkey new questions on what our country really means for Western Europe.

I have repeated several times that the EU is not an obsession for Turkey. A discriminatory decision by the EU will not mean the end of our country's horizons, which reach far beyond the EU.

But as the Turkish Foreign Minister, I sincerely hope that a positive result comes out of the Luxembourg Summit.

The opposite will be insensible. It will be unfair. It will also limit EU's own horizons.

It is still not too late.

(This article was published in "International Herald Tribune", "Le Monde", "La Nouvelle Belgique" and several other West European newspapers, in November 1997)

* * *

2.   Scenarios for EU's Luxembourg Summit

Dear Colleague,

I wanted to convey to you, informally, some of my observations and suggestions regarding Turkey's outlook, prior to EU Council of Ministers' informal meeting.

I have been in office for over three months and had the honor and pleasure of meeting almost all my colleagues representing EU member countries.

I want to thank you all: Of course, we did not necessarily concur on all issues. But I had a positive approach from my colleagues as to Turkey's concerns and suggestions. It seems to me that we established a personal contact with all my counterparts. In fact, the subject of Turkey's accession, which seemed to be "a closed file" when I took office, has resurfaced, at least to be evaluated once more.

From my point of view, this development is an occasion for a new assessment. I would therefore like to present my interpretation of the future of Turkey's relationship with the EU.

1) There seems to be three probable scenarios:

a -The twelve candidates, Turkey included, start negotiations for membership on equal terms, each making progress as to its capabilities.

b -The twelve candidates, Turkey included, are placed on equal footing in a "Conference", which has substance and presents economic / financial support commitments. With some candidates, the negotiation for membership starts after the Conference is convened. Turkey is not included among the early negotiators, but is supported by a pre-accession strategy and has the right to start negotiations when it fulfills objective criteria.

c- Turkey is not named among the candidates for full accession; or, is placed in a Conference devoid of substance; or, is offered some kind of a "plus" statute which, in fact, leaves it out, alienating her from the "normal" candidates.

2) As for the "Three Sets of Conditions" generally referred to by my colleagues, I have the following comments on some of their aspects:

a- On "relations with Greece", a member country, I believe that the conventional criticism is generally unfounded: First, we need two sides to resolve a bilateral issue; one side cannot be held responsible for finding a solution. Second, though I cannot claim to be an "objective observer", I sincerely can state that during my time in office, we took significant initiatives to improve relations, but were rejected in these attempts. Occasionally, we even had to bear accusations such as "...murderers, thieves and rapists". Others, who were involved in negotiations to promote a better understanding among Turkey and Greece, can bear witness to such attempts that our Ministry has undertaken. Nonetheless, I believe that there still is a chance for a constructive relationship. The "Wise Men's Council" proposed by EU Presidency, accepted by both parties but somehow hindered by Greece still offers an important means.

b- As for the Cyprus issue, there has to be a positive approach from four sides, maybe five, when we include the UK, the other guarantor country. Again, Turkey cannot be viewed as the only responsible actor to provide a solution, when there are so many involved. I am not optimistic for the short term: Being assured by EU of due membership process, the Greek Cypriot side have no incentives to pursue substantial negotiations; at the eve of elections, it is not eager to make the compromises and concessions needed for a process of reconciliation. The Turkish Cypriot side insists for equal recognition as the vital first step, a condition rejected by the Greek Cypriots. Furthermore, US policy initiatives to be formulated by Ambassador Holbrooke have still not been declared. In addition, the announced deployment of S-300 missiles by the Greek Cypriots further aggravates the delicate situation: Bearing a direct military threat to Turkey, it necessitates counter-measures by Turkey. The Russian military personnel accompanying the S-300 missiles, brings additional military presence to Cyprus which, in the worst scenario, might even lead to multi-sided confrontations, involving several or all of the actors: Greece, Turkey, Greek Cypriots, Turkish Cypriots, Russia, and, eventually, the EU.

c- In my recent discussions with my EU counterparts, I have addressed thoroughly Turkey's "human rights, democracy and South Eastern problems". I stated my agreement with most of the constructive criticism; but rejected the politically motivated and exaggerated claims. I also tried to clarify that I would of course discuss such matters -unfortunately present in all our countries to some degree- within the scope of our bilateral relations with member countries; but that I would not review them within the framework of the EU, if, after the 12th of December, Turkey

194

is not recognized officially among the "candidates" for EU accession. It will then be appropriate to discuss solely economic issues related to the Customs Union, not political issues which are proper to the European Union. Since we took office, there has been significant progress. Some positive legal changes concerning journalists were realized. The separatist terrorism within Turkey declining, three out of the nine provinces that were under a state-of-emergency for ten years, returned to full democracy. Several others are expected to follow this course by the end of the year. It is quite probable that progress continues.

3) As to my conclusions:

a- Given Turkey's economic strength -the EU presidency has declared that the Turkish economy is stronger than that of any other candidate's economy-, I suppose that Turkey might begin the process of accession to EU, in spite of some political difficulties: Yes, there is a need for further improvement in various fields. But, after all, what we are talking about is a "process", which would take years; it is not an immediate membership to be realized tomorrow. Furthermore, such a process would inevitably have positive impacts on several of Turkey's problems, on the further improvement in some fields and especially on issues related to Greece. I imagine that between a member state and one that is in the process of becoming a member, disputes would not have as much significance and will disappear when both are members in due time. I do not want to be misleading, and I have to say that the Cyprus issue will not be solved promptly when Turkey starts negotiations for EU membership. The Cypriot situation incorporates its own particularities; its difficulties and its fears. Nevertheless, the outcome of 12th of December is likely to have some positive -or negative- impacts on all issues.

b- I believe that the worst possible outcome of 12th December would be one of ambiguity. I strongly support a clear-cut definition of Turkey's role envisaged by the EU, even if it will be of the worst kind, i.e., one of a "distinct" partner, of a suigeneris associate, of a "plus" type relative, etc. The ambiguity that currently prevails is hurting our relations within the Customs Union and our economy. Since Turkey's economic prospects are based mainly on her membership to E.U., Turkey's potential for attracting long term

195

foreign investment is significantly hindered due to the uncertainty of her accession process.

c- For the new government, the EU is an objective, it is not an obsession. If Turkey were to be "left out" of the integration process, this would affect our economic choices and priorities. But it would limit our political horizons; it would not hinder our strong economic prospects, neither would it reduce EU to an insignificant role in our commercial relations. If things stay where they currently are, it would mean a huge opportunity lost for Turkey, and, I believe, for EU as well. I very much hope that the path for Turkey's full membership does not remain blocked. In the coming weeks, I shall be meeting with several colleagues. In this on-going process, I am sure we shall be working with the good will we have mutually nurtured and that we shall further contribute to a better understanding. And, hopefully, we shall welcome to Western Europe new economic, cultural and historical dimensions.

(Letter written to EU Foreign Ministers, October 1997 - Excerpts)

* * *

3.   European Security, WEU and EU

A new Europe is emerging. This is a Europe based on common value and envisaging a common future. Being familiar with the work of this body, I know that the WEU's Parliamentary Assembly is playing an important role in this evolution, particularly in the field of security architecture.

-I- Ensuring the future of our continent is the priority task in the making of a new Europe. This objective can only be attained if security is understood as a concept embracing the whole of the continent, taking into account the security needs of all countries, taking care not to create new divisions, or zones of influence, or gray areas.

Based on this approach, Europe's new security architecture should be built on the pillars of:

- A transformed Atlantic Alliance together with the new consultative partnership forum of the Euro-Atlantic Partnership Council,

- A robust transatlantic partnership,
- New fora of cooperation and consultation with Russia and Ukraine,
- A deepening and enlarging European integration process,
- The Council of Europe and the OSCE as overarching roofs with their new institutions and cooperative mechanisms,
- And finally regional groupings, from the Baltic Council to the Black Sea Cooperation, from the Balkan initiatives to Economic Cooperation Organization.

As regards regional schemes, Turkey has recently taken an initiative for the creation of the Multinational Peace Force Southeastern Europe. By signing the agreement to this end on 26 September 1998, in Skopje, seven countries in the region have taken an important step towards turning this initiative into reality. By virtue of the principle of rotation, the headquarters of the force will first be located in Plovdiv (Bulgaria) for four years and then transferred to Constansa (Romania), Edirne (Turkey) and Kilkis (Greece) respectively.

As a matter of fact, a re-designed Europe and Euro-Atlantic community with interlocking systems and agencies is gradually taking shape. But more needs to be done. The key concept in building a new Europe should be "integration". This is also the underpinning concept of the enlargement processes pursued by European institutions, namely EU, WEU and NATO.

Turkey is in favor of an effective interaction between the WEU, EU and NATO in which the WEU will play an important role. This scheme will help to create a stronger European political apparatus that will be supported by wider political consultations and operational capabilities. We firmly believe that such a mechanism can function harmoniously when and if all of the countries involved are able to contribute to each and every stage of preparation and implementation of eventual European operations.

-II- When discussing European integration, I should underline that my country's outstanding objective is to become a full member of both the EU and the WEU.

Turkey signed the Accession Agreement with the EU as early as in 1963. Turkey became the first and so far the only non-member country to enter into a Customs Union with the EU in 1995. Thus, we have already become an integral part of the economic Europe. Full

197

membership to the EU would only be a natural outcome of this process. We are aware that EU membership requires fulfillment of the Copenhagen Criteria. We stand ready to work with the EU to this end. However, with the decisions of the Luxembourg Summit, the EU has adopted a discriminatory attitude towards Turkey in the application of the Copenhagen Criteria. For 11 countries, these criteria were set as conditions to be fulfilled for" being a member", whereas for Turkey, the same criteria have been imposed for granting only the status of a "candidate". It goes without saying that such discrimination was unacceptable for my Government. The Cardiff Decisions remedied this situation to a certain extent. The problem is not yet solved. All we want from the EU is to be treated on an equal footing with the other candidates. Some improvements have recently been made in this regard through the Progress Report of the Commission where Turkey is perceived as one of the 12 candidates. We expect the position of the Commission to be endorsed at the political level. Such a decision would pave the way for further strengthening of Turkish-EU links.

On the other hand, we have continuously advocated that the rigid linkage between WEU and EU membership should be abandoned. Thus, the perspective of full membership in the WEU for all European allies will be opened.

In that regard, I would like to underline that we have highly appreciated Mr. Anteater's report and the ensuing recommendation on security in a wider Europe. On the other hand, Mr. De Puig's visit to Turkey in July was also a very positive step in Turkey's relations with the WEU.

-III- The European Security and Defense Identity (ESDI) is a concept that Turkey has supported since its initiation.

However, the decisions taken to build the ESDI can only become a political and a military reality if there is consensus that it is to be achieved by common European will. This will should be expressed through WEU, where all European allies have become full members.

In this perspective, we are satisfied with the harmonious work underway in the WEU and NATO for reinforcing the transparency, cooperation and complementarities between the two organizations. We will continue to support the efforts aiming at putting all the essential elements of the ESDI in place within the Alliance by the Washington Summit. This presupposes proper mechanisms, which will satisfy all the countries concerned. In this regard, Turkey attaches particular importance in preserving NATO as the basis for collective defense under the Washington Treaty.

-IV- Having discussed briefly how to ensure the security of our continent, I will address an issue of equal relevance: How to ensure the security of the citizen.

Our societies still continue to face important challenges such as drug smuggling, illegal trafficking in human beings, child kidnapping and terrorism. These scourges threaten the fabric of our societies and the well being of our citizens. In order to build a better future for our children, we have to contain and eventually bring an end to these socio-political deviations.

During its term, my Government has given priority to the fight against organized crime and terrorism. We have made important headway on both tracks. Mafia-like organizations have been dismantled and their leaders are now behind the bars.

Our Government has achieved particularly important success in fighting terrorism. A terror campaign that has been in full swing for more than a decade is finally thwarted.

For the last 15 years, Turkey has suffered a lot from organized acts of terror, launched mainly from the territories of some neighboring countries. More than 5000 civilians, mostly of Kurdish origin have been massacred by the terrorists There can be no justification for terrorist violence. Killing masses of innocent people, of women, children, elderly people and teachers is nothing else but murder. Furthermore, the same organization is responsible for a large part of narcotics smuggled into Europe as well as for abduction of children and extortion of money in Western European countries.

(Speech at the Parliamentary Assembly of Western European Union, November 1998)

* * *

4. Turkey and Europe: Looking to the Future From a Historical Perspective

As several of my EU counterparts have later confirmed, it seems that the speech I made to EU Foreign Ministers in September 1999 had a role in convincing them to decide for Turkey's candidature in Helsinki, December 1999. I had prepared that text very carefully. I sincerely believe in each and every one of the analyses I was presenting. In fact, these reflected thoughts that I had developed through the years, in my books and articles.

-I- I will try to address the relationship between Turkey and the European Union, against the background of history.

In fact, our long history has been molded through an ongoing process of interaction with the West and with the East. As a country and people, we have been situated at the crossroads of civilizations. Historically, we lived in a very large geography, which provided for the main trade routes and for the dissemination of ideas and religions. Therefore, the external environment, external dynamics, and the interaction with Europe, confrontational and harmonious at times were among the decisive factors in our historical development. Thus, the Turkish / Ottoman presence in Europe during the 15th, 16th and 17th centuries brought forward new ideals and new patterns of social relationships. Given the realities of an era when feudalism, lack of tolerance and exploitation of masses prevailed, humane values and a highly egalitarian, efficient and sophisticated organization were introduced.

This new civilization and its moral values contributed to the evolution of Middle Ages into modern times. It turned Turkey into the safe-haven of the persecuted ethnic and religious masses in the 16th century and onwards, a role, which Turkey had to resume through the II. World War.

As modern times approached, the historical interaction with the West contributed the external dynamics, mainly positive, for the institutional reformation of Turkey in the 19th and 20th centuries.

It is interesting to note that the founding-leaders of the Turkish Republic in the early 1920's, coming out of battlefields where they faced the Western invasion forces, were mainly inspired by Western models to create a democratic society and a secular Republic. This bears witness to our pragmatic sense, but also to Turkey's ability to overlook past grievances and to create the future.

-II- The historical development of Turkey, its cosmopolitan characteristics, its civilization that comprises western as well as eastern values, a multitude of beliefs and ethnicities, bestowed upon Turkey a unique identity:

We consider ourselves both European and Asian, and view this plurality to be an asset.

Our history was molded as much in Istanbul, Edirne, Tetova, Kosovo and Sarajevo as it was in Bursa, Kayseri, Diyarbakir and Damascus.

If "European Culture" is defined, as it is by EU, that is, mainly by factors such as "democracy", "human rights", "rule of law", "gender equality", and "secularism", then, in spite of the need for further progress on some points, we have shared and contributed to this contemporary "European Culture" for 75 years.

I want to elaborate on a few elements of "European Culture", for it seems that sometimes there is a need to contribute mutually to a better understanding:

I have always said, as a writer, politician, and as a Minister as well, that there are some delays in certain points in our democratic development. This, in spite of the fact that Turkey is among the front-runners in Europe in some fields of democracy as gender equality, women's votes, secularism, upward mobility, etc. I have as well stated that in some of the criticism formulated, the departing points might generally be justified. But, the overall conclusions, as well as the distorted and inflated image, which sometimes comes about, are unjustified.

It is not an excuse or a pretext, but it is obvious that the difficulties we faced in developing certain points of our democracy is mainly due to the horrible terrorist campaign which we faced. During the last 15 years, the terrorists have killed thousands of civilians. There were cases like that of the 128 primary-school teachers who were executed in groups.

As our Prime Minister Mr. Ecevit has explained, the more we free ourselves from the constraints of terrorism, the greater will be the momentum of democratic reforms. Actually, we are in the process of overcoming terrorism. Some positive changes are already taking place:

It is interesting to note that, during the last three months, the Parliament, through a record-breaking performance, has enacted two major constitutional changes and 62 laws, including several legislative reforms. Several were of the nature of a democratic reform. Frankly, I do not think these would have been possible about a year ago, when terrorism was not as limited in its scope as it is today.

I would also like to underline that the conceptual and legislative changes that are taking place represent an ongoing trend; a trend which is initiated by Turkey's internal dynamics.

-III- One of the causes of some misunderstandings is the difference of perceptions, which are based on different historical experiences.

In analyzing and understanding the social fabric of Turkey, criteria based on race, as a distinctive and major tool leads to wrong assumptions.

We do not conceive of the racial origin of our citizens as a relevant factor in Turkey. No one really cares about the race of anyone. Ottoman and Republican Turkey, being a geography with millennia of history, we are composed of numerous ethnic backgrounds and cultures.

The concept of race as a distinctive factor and as the main attribute of "minorities" does not fit in our realities and perceptions. In Turkey, where the Ottoman interpretation and implementation of Islam is one of the main components of cultural identity and where for centuries the state had to keep united a multitude of ethnicities, "race" did not exist as a social and political category. The main distinctive factor had been religion, implemented with great tolerance, and the difference was always conceived in religious concepts, i.e., the Muslims and the non-Muslims. On the other hand, "Muslim Ottoman Subjects", whether in Sarajevo, Kosovo, Istanbul, Kayseri, Cairo, Aleppo or elsewhere, and of whatever ethnic origin, were totally equal in their status.

This is the background of our present perceptions. Contemporary Turkey based itself on this heritage of non-discrimination; and developed it through its modernization process. When some West European Scholars apply their version of social analysis based on their particular socio-cultural experience to a country like Turkey, they are misled. They end up with an overemphasis on race as a social factor. This is probably why these analyses bring up wrong conclusions and why Muslim Turks whether of Balkan, Kurdish, Caucasian, or of whatever origin are somewhat irritated when they discover that they are considered as "minorities" by the West European discourse.

One last point on the subject, a political one: I have to state that I am strongly against policies and parties based on ethnicity. Underlining and promoting racial differences in a country generally lead to disastrous results. I believe that this approach should be left to the past, where ethnic cleansing has recently cost 200.000 lives in Bosnia and Kosovo, and, in the not so distant past, caused the loss of 7 million European lives.

This, of course, does not mean that I am not, in fact, that we are not, in favor of freedom of cultural and democratic expression for any citizen who feels the need.

-IV- Considering Turkey's candidacy and membership, I always ask myself, what is it that Turkey will contribute to the European Union; what will be its genuine input; what will be the enhancement that Turkey will bring to the European Union? And, what will be the advantages that Turkey will have by being part of the European Union?

As for advantages, I believe that being part of EU will provide Turkey with a challenge and with a wider opportunity to attain a higher rationale in all aspects of its organizational, political, social, democratic and economic life. The historical, cultural and geographic settings of Turkey, which provide for ample interaction with our international environment, enhance the contribution of positive external dynamics.

I can refer to the positive aspects of our already existing partnership in the Customs Union: It was a huge challenge, it is only 4 years old, but this union has motivated Turkey to reach an economic competitiveness and an industrial infrastructure and skill comparable to that of EU.

On the other hand, I do not overlook the limitations and burdens that this partnership has caused. The yearly trade deficit Turkey has with EU countries is around 10 billion dollars. We have concerns and proposals that need to be further discussed.

But, we are already integrated to the economic dimension of EU. This challenge and this participation have facilitated for us to build the most dynamic and the most competitive economy in a large geography, stretching from Central Europe to Central Asia and to the Middle East. And I have to add that we have achieved this end without any considerable economic assistance from EU.

I believe that initiating the process of being part of the political dimension of EU will bring about parallel results in reaching higher levels of a new rationale. I anticipate a positive interaction.

Furthermore, we are now in a better position to take advantage of this process, for we actually benefit from having a strong government and a sound majority in the parliament - a privilege we have not had in Turkey for the last five years.

-V- What Turkey can contribute to EU is a historical experience of a different kind; a dimension that only a country that for centuries was the representative of a huge geography and a genuine culture can provide. And which, actually represents the assertiveness of its republican and democratic evolution, and its unique role as a "model": Being the only country with a predominantly Muslim population which has the ideals and practices of a pluralist democracy, secularism, rule of law, human rights, gender equality, Turkey enjoys the privilege of constituting a paradigm of modernization. It is a center of attraction for huge masses of people, all over the world, who aspire to democracy and modernization.

Furthermore, the Post Cold-War political framework witnessed the appearance or the confirmation of several independent states. Out of the multitude of those "new" states, almost all - in the Balkans, in the Caucasus or in Central Asia - are those with whom Turkey shares a common history or a common language and cultural affinity. This provides Turkey with a new international environment of historical and cultural dimensions. Turkey, as a long-standing actor in these geographies, has become a vital partner in their economic restructuring. Turkey, thus provides a political and economic center for the emerging Eurasian reality and constitutes Western Europe's major historical, cultural and economic opening to Eastern horizons.

Nevertheless, it seems to me that EU has not yet firmly decided on its policies vis-à-vis the challenges of emerging new geographies; whether it is interested in the vast opportunities of encompassing new economic, historical and cultural dimensions; whether it can contribute more to the harmonization of civilizations in a world endangered by the much discussed "clash" of civilizations; whether it will assume a larger responsibility to create a better world for all.

Turkey contributes to all these causes positively, to some, perhaps, decisively.

-VI- In order to further develop our relations, the confrontational approach that has sometimes been displayed should mutually be put aside. Generally, problems are solved more efficiently if the other party's sensitivities, concerns and constraints are taken into consideration.

Western Europe, for a long period of history, considered Turkey as "The Other", to put it in Edward Said's terms. Turkey was the anti-thesis, the outsider, and the different. Now there is growing evidence that this unfortunate categorizing is withering away. It is a mutual responsibility to assure that this positive trend further develops.

Finally, I expect that a just and clear decision be reached in Helsinki Summit of December 1999. I believe that Turkey should be declared an official candidate for accession to EU.

Human values are universal. "The Copenhagen Criteria" are values that are not particular to EU; they are values, which are shared by millions inside and outside Europe. They are values that we share, which we develop, and will continue to develop, whether we are a candidate, a member, or not.

I believe in a future, which is brighter for Europe. I believe in Turkey's contribution to this future.

(Speech at the luncheon offered by the Foreign Ministers of EU, September 1999, Brussels)

TURKEY AND THE EUROPEAN UNION: ***What is the current state of affairs in Turkey-EU relations?*

Turkey's relations with the EU have two dimensions. Economic and political. Several points in our Customs-Union Agreement need to be revised. But I should add that we do not have major complaints regarding our trade relations with the EU. I may say that particularly in 1998, which were an economically difficult year for the whole world, our exports to EU countries, increased by 8 %. The EU market is becoming a reliable market for us. This is important. With respect to our imports, which are mostly investment goods, EU is a high-quality trading partner.

The Customs Union with EU provides a support to our quest for new markets in different geographies. Latin America might provide for an example: I am trying to strengthen the political infrastructure of our relations with Latin American countries. Economic relations will be easier to develop on firm bases. When, in two or three years' time EU and Latin America will probably have a kind of Customs Agreement or a Free Trade Agreement, Turkey, through her Customs-Union with EU, will be able to penetrate the Latin American markets on equal grounds with EU countries. That would be a substantial opportunity

On the political front, we have a definitive, clear stand. We told EU that until they officially accept and declare Turkey as a candidate for accession, we would   not discuss with them our sensitive issues. This is a matter of principle. In our relationship with individual EU countries, either party may raise any issue on a bilateral basis. But within the EU framework, unlike previous Turkish Governments, we do not take up sensitive subjects. It's not appropriate to elaborate on such issues with an organization, which does not consider you even as a candidate.

I should add though that some development was witnessed at the last EU Summit in Cologne. For the first time, Germany, which is quite influential in EU, has adopted a policy inline with Turkey's expectations and waged a battle over it. Although we didn't share some elements, some wording of the German position, this is a significant development. We expect the Finnish Presidency to follow the same track.

(Interview given to "Turkish Daily News" Ankara, June 1999)

* * *

5.   EU's Conceptual and Political Horizons

As the 20th century draws to an end, Europe is finally putting the memories of two devastating wars and a long and bitter Cold War behind it.

The last decade of the century was aimed at rectifying some historical errors and misfortunes, which have affected the lives of millions of Europeans. Indeed, Europe is nurturing the dynamics of integration. The continent is gradually uniting, from West to East and from North to South, with a view to achieve common goals.

-I- WHERE EUROPE ENDS: DEFINING THE PRIORITIES: The main issue to be addressed, the main decision to be taken, seems to be the following: How will the EU's geography be defined? Which criteria will define this choice? What will be the parameters? What will be the priorities?

It is obvious that the definition of borders will vary according to the sensitivities, concerns, perspectives and goals. For example, lines drawn from a purely economic point of view would differ radically from one, which gives top priority to defense and security. A person imbued by the past might aspire for a monolithic, unidimensional European Union and determine its borders accordingly. A diametrically opposite vision might prevail for someone of a different sensitivity.

Borders are generally drawn in relation to the concerned entity's geo-strategic goals, given that this entity has the means to achieve its goals. Therefore, the decision of EU on its borders, will be defined by the synthesis of the multitude of interests that member countries share or do not share. Drawing the borders of EU will be affected as well by EU's strategic vision; its geo-strategy.

Then, one might venture to ask, what is that strategic vision, geo-strategic perception on which the future of EU will be built?

It seems to me that the EU has not yet firmly decided on its strategy vis- à-vis the challenges of emerging new geographies; whether it is interested in   the vast opportunities of encompassing new economic, historical and cultural dimensions; whether it can contribute more to the harmonization of civilizations in a world endangered by the much discussed "clash" of civilizations; whether it will assume a larger responsibility to create a better world for all.

On the other hand, the perception of EU's geo-strategic mission and EU's definition of its borders is of major consequences for the two Aegean countries, Turkey and Greece.

EU has to decide where the demarcation is: Will it reach the historical boundaries of Europe? Will it include Turkey and thus move the borderline further to the East? Or, will it divide the Aegean into two, having EU's border in the Balkans and in the Aegean, encompassing Greece and standing against Turkey?

The way EU decides will have far reaching consequences. "Historical", one might say:

EU which does not include Turkey, will have its Eastern borders in the Balkans and in the Aegean; all EU frontal countries will be facing Turkey on the other side of the border. It will perpetuate a lingering confrontational situation between Greece and Turkey. Symbolically and on real terms, the two countries will be facing each other as potentially conflicting parties on the opposite sides of a fault-line, with all the symbolic and real-term insecurity that this situation brings about.

This is not an environment, which provides for peaceful and safe relationships. Neither for EU, nor for Greece, nor for Turkey.

Having Turkey in EU would mean that EU's borders do not stand anymore between Greece and Turkey, but stretch to the East. This will enhance the cooperation between the two Aegean neighbors and will provide further stability to the region. In strategic terms, European Union's security zone will thus be extended.

The past bears witness to the fact that enlargement has become imperative for Europe. If peace and prosperity is to take root, then European nations must integrate both in a deeper and a wider manner. It is for the same reasons that Turkey-EU relationship should be addressed with a strategic vision.

-II- REDRESSING THE RELATIONSHIP: Two years after the Luxembourg Summit, the European Commission took a major step forward in its recommendation addressed to the Helsinki European Council on the recognition of Turkey's status as an accession candidate.

By proposing to put an end to the discrimination that Turkey faced since December 1997, the Commission intends to correct the existing injustice. It paves the way for a promising development in

Helsinki. Furthermore, the Commission demonstrates a strategic vision of Europe's role on the eve of its enlargement. The Commission's position points at a Europe that contemporary world needs. This is a Europe of solidarity, which, instead of searching for hegemony, strives for the distribution of values. Values that are European but deeply universal as well. Like the goal of creating a community of nations whose unity and strength lies in its cultural, ethnic and religious diversity. This is indeed the philosophical dimension, which qualifies the European Union to lead a struggle against the threat of intolerance and the clash of civilizations.

The status of candidate will provide Turkey an accession partnership, which will mean a qualitative change in our relations. If Helsinki Summit adopts the proposal of the Commission, a new momentum will emerge. This decision will change the essence and the context of our relations by inserting more coherence, dialogue and confidence. This will bring about a new perspective of strategic nature.

(Article published in EU Quarterly Review, Brussels, October 1999 - Excerpts)

* * *

6. Making Our Position Clear to EU

In politics, whether international, national or "party politics", what I am most afraid of is "misleading" my interlocutors, my constituents or the public opinion. In my dialogue with EU Foreign Ministers, I have always been very caucus not to mislead them in any way, not to provoke false impressions. I prefer saying less rather than saying more. In the course of my relation with EU colleagues, I believe they realized my particular sensitivity. This helped to build a mutual firm trust. Though I wanted Turkey's candidature to be and though I probably worked more than any one to achieve this end, I have been extremely correct in all controversial issues we discussed. I kept up with this tradition when we were just ten days from Helsinki. I thought that I should make a formal declaration on where we stand, including points on which we do not agree and which might hinder our candidature. I put in writing and sent letters to my colleagues, stating our final position. Not to "mislead" anyone, no matter the scope of the prospective achievement...

News items are appearing in the press about Turkey's stance on European Union's Helsinki Summit and on relations with Greece. Some of these not only fail to reflect reality, but are deceptive as well. On the other hand, there are constant requests from the media for information. In order to further clarify certain issues, I am reiterating Turkey's position on key-points:

1) Since 1963, Turkey has been pursuing the aim of developing its relations with the European Union, then the "European Economic Community". For the last 37 years, this determination has been reiterated in all Governmental Programs and approved by the Turkish Grand National Assembly. In all these Programs, it was underlined that Turkey's EU membership is a right derived from the 1963 Ankara Agreement and policies were formulated along these lines. The "Customs Union" established between Turkey and EU in 1996 has been an important step in this ongoing process. Our present government has maintained the same determination for the further development of relations with EU and on Turkey's EU membership.

We consider this common approach of all Turkish Governments as a reflection of Ataturk's ideal of "sharing the contemporary..."

2) EU membership is a top priority for Turkey, but it is not an obsession. In case Turkey's EU vocation is not realized, there will be no setback to our assertiveness, modernism and democracy, since we are already on this track, for a long time and by ourselves. Obviously, we shall keep to it whether we are a candidate to EU or not. EU candidacy and membership will add to this process further impetus and momentum.

3) Turkey-EU relations have entered a turbulent phase when candidate status was denied to Turkey by EU's "Enlargement Summit", December 1997. Turkey expects an end to this discrimination in the forthcoming 1999 Helsinki Summit. Turkey has indeed declared that she accepts the Amsterdam Agreement and Copenhagen Criteria of EU. In this context, Turkey expects equal treatment with other candidate countries. For the sake of being admitted as candidate, Turkey is not to accept additional criteria or additional conditions, any extras that are rot relevant for all candidates.

4) Progress in Turkey's accession to EU membership will considerably contribute to the security, stability and economic

210

welfare of a vast region. EU borders passing through the Balkans and the Aegean -as in the present- created an additional and critical "fault-line" between Turkey and Greece. This inevitably paves the way to extra tensions between the two neighbors, divided now by "international" as well as existing national borders. Whatever their intentions, this is a potential conflict situation for Turkey and Greece. Turkey's EU candidacy and membership will eliminate this negative potential and will guarantee stability and cooperation in the Balkans and the Aegean.

5) There have been significant and positive developments between Turkey and Greece since the "Joint Working Groups" initiative in May 1999. The two countries can solve their bilateral problems and establish a lasting friendship as long as they have the political determination and good will. The achievements realized in the past months have further strengthened this belief. We sincerely hope that the process further develops.

6) Relations in progress since May 1999 have already produced concrete results: Texts agreed upon during Turkish-Greek joint committee meetings are ready to be signed. The issues, which have been discussed are not "secondary", but essential issues. The agreement on "Combating Organized Crime, Drug Trafficking, Illegal Immigration and Terrorism" was considered as top-priority by Turkey; a pre-condition for the development of bilateral relations.

These agreements might be signed in mid-December if present positive trend does not run into obstacles. In this context, inviting the Greek Foreign Minister to Turkey, holding a signing ceremony of the agreements, further development of bilateral relations, cooperation on relevant EU matters and regional issues, are envisaged.

7) Following the initiation of joint committee meetings, relations between the two countries yielded concrete social, economic and political progress. Civil societies of both countries are involved in dialogue, reciprocal visits and joint activities. Joint economic ventures are emerging and trade in bordering regions flourishing. Tensions in the Aegean are decreasing. The two countries are cooperating for stability in the Balkans. It is in the interest of both countries to sustain the momentum.

8) There are problems between Turkey and Greece, which need to be addressed, especially in the Aegean. It is possible that the two neighbouring and allied countries may overcome these problems through mutually acceptable means and transform the Aegean into a sea of friendship. This must be the common goal for both countries. In order to attain this goal, both should refrain from unilateral actions in the Aegean, abstain from provocations and threats, take mutual concerns and interests into account, create an atmosphere of confidence and security, and thus be able to resolve problems through peaceful means. To this end, we are ready to work together. Turkey has no territorial claims. Turkey considers that Agenda 2000 includes appropriate procedures for the resolution of the bilateral problems existing between two countries.

On the other hand, we are of the view that the idea of setting up a "Wise Men Group", which had been put forward by the Netherlands at the time of their EU Presidency in April 1997 and agreed upon by both countries could be reactivated. This initiative, which could go ahead following the Helsinki Summit decision on Turkey's candidacy, will contribute to the quest for peaceful means to solve Aegean problems.

9) Turkey has put the Cyprus issue outside the framework of her relations with EU. Turkey rejects any kind of linkage between her candidacy to EU and the Cyprus issue. We sustain our legal and political objections to the unilateral application of the Greek Administration of Southern Cyprus for EU membership. We believe that at this point in time when UN Secretary General is about to start proximity talks between the two parties in New York, any statement and attitude, which could have a negative impact on this process or on the chances of a comprehensive solution, must be avoided. On the contrary, the parties should be encouraged on an equal basis.

10) With the above in mind, it is considered that the Helsinki Summit constitutes an important opportunity for EU-Turkey relations and for the positive process between Turkey and Greece. We expect that all EU countries will make use of this opportunity to its fullest extent.

(Declaration made on 30 November 1999 and transmitted to E.U. Foreign Ministers, ten days prior the Helsinki Summit)

FM: "TURKEY NOT JUST ANY EU CANDIDATE"
*** *ANKARA, December 13, 1999 - (Reuters) - Foreign Minister Ismail Cem cautioned prospective European Union partners on Monday that Turkey was no ordinary candidate and was determined to join the bloc without sacrificing its unique blend of East and West.*

But Cem said Turkey, at the same time, had to "pull itself together" if it wanted to bring its human rights policies in order and rein the costly state apparatus.

A European Union Summit in Helsinki accepted overwhelmingly Moslem Turkey as a potential member of the 15-nation bloc at the weekend, ending decades of Turkey being kept at arm's length by the wealthy European club.

Turkey now joins another 12 countries scurrying to meet the Copenhagen criteria set by the EU to measure readiness to join.

"Turkey is not just any candidate", Cem told reporters in the Capital Ankara. "Turkey has a different identity and a very different historical experience than to others."

Cem said that Turkey would move rapidly towards membership and bring with it the heritage of a country that has always looked both toward Christian Europe and the Islamic Middle East.

"Turkey's candidacy to EU changes the nature of this organization. We represent the synthesis between West and East. EU will now have an Islamic dimension as well", Cem said in a wide-ranging speech assessing Turkey's future after the Helsinki Summit.

He joined Turkish Prime Minister Bulent Ecevit in saying that Ankara would become a full member sooner rather than later.

"I believe we can bring the economy to a position ready for full membership within two to three years", Ecevit told Turkish State Television late on Sunday night.

Turkish media were equally upbeat on Turkey's chances. "We will enter in 2004,"said a banner headline in the Sabah newspaper on Monday

But Cem said that deep changes were needed if Turkey was to rid it self of human rights abuses and a sprawling inefficient state.

"We need to pull ourselves together and prepare if we want to move to membership as soon as possible", he said. "We will not make it with this disorder, we need to be more disciplined."

But he drew the line at awarding Turkey's estimated 12 million Kurds minority rights. Protection of minorities is a key part of the Copenhagen Criteria. Turkey outlaws Kurdish-language education and broadcasting as potentially divisive measures.

"We are trying to widen individual freedoms as far as possible... But we are not in the business of creating new minorities", Cem said in a speech designed to calm Turkish worries about the implications of EU membership.

He stressed that Turkey would press its case on the divided Island of Cyprus from inside the EU, rather than outside. He also predicted gradual resolution of rows with EU member Greece.

Cem predicted a gradual end to Turkey's huge state subsidies of the agricultural sector.

Turkey's economy has been hampered for the last 20 years by raging inflation and high interest rates. But structural reforms implemented by Ecevit's government have won the backing of international financial institutions and market investors.

(Steve Bryant, Reuters, December 1999 - excerpts)

* * *

7.   An External Dynamic for Further Progres...

***How important was the Helsinki decision for Turkey? Do you fully accept the conditions for Turkish entry into the EU as stipulated at Helsinki? And is there the domestic political will in Turkey to push though the necessary measures?

It provides a positive, effective external dynamic in Turkey's already strong pace to attain a higher rationale in all fields. It enhances as well the geo-strategic position of Turkey which is an Asian as well as a European power and which has historical, cultural, political and economic links in a geography stretching from the Balkans to the Caucasus, Middle East and Central Asia.

In the Helsinki decisions, there is not a special or extra condition particular to Turkey. In fact, this is one point we had made very clear to EU prior to Helsinki: We had said that we would accept, as any other candidate, to fulfill the Copenhagen Criteria in order to become a full member. Nothing less, nothing more. As is the case

214

for all candidates and as it still is with existing members. We know that this is a bumpy road, with ups and downs. Of course, we do have the will.

***Becoming a member of the EU implies a deal of scrutiny of Turkey's inner workings. Is the country ready to accept what some are bound to term outside interference"?*

The modalities of the accession process, as long as they are implemented in line with common, objective practices of EU, the Amsterdam Treaty, the Copenhagen Criteria, and with good will, I do not foresee much difficulty. Where as when there is a feeling that double standards are at play, or when legitimate sensitivities are over-looked, difficulties might occur.

***It has often been the criticism of outside observers of Turkish politics that there are too many different centers of decision-making, and that the Turkish Military call most of the shots. How can you convince the EU that the Turkish Army will come under civilian control?*

This is not a valid analysis. It is based on false presumptions and prejudgments. There are, as it is the case with all pluralist democracies, several "centers of decisions" in Turkey, of which it's not the civilian and military bureaucracies but social organizations (trade-unions, employers organizations,etc.) that are the most effective. It is the parliament and the government who "call the shots." I do not see a need to convince anyone on speculative scenarios and inflated—sometimes politically motivated—allegations.

*** Since the Helsinki accord, you've had several senior European politicians coming to Turkey and lecturing you on human rights, which seems to indicate that Turkey still has a long way to go in this area.*

I don't accept the term lecturing, and I doubt it's still a long way.

The difficulties that we have will probably be over in not so distant future.

*** Is there nervousness on the part of Turkey about EU candidacy? That the Europeans will change their minds. Is there a tendency to see the EU as a "Christian Club?"*

It would be unfair to see EU as such after Helsinki.

Only a few months since our candidacy and we are already feeling the improvements. The political, psychological and physical borders we have to deal with have changed - all for the better.

215

When do you think Turkey will actually become a member of the EU?

An answer would be speculative. It might take less time than many presume.

GREECE, CYPRUS AND EU: The Helsinki Summit posed neither the Cypriot issue nor the Turco-Greek dispute on the Aegean as conditions for the candidature of Turkey to the European Union. On this point, the Helsinki Decisions are very clear.

It is as well to be underlined that Cyprus is not a "bilateral" issue between Turkey and Greece, but it is an issue mainly between the Turkish Cypriots and the Greek Cypriots.

Although no criteria other then those of Copenhagen was en visaged for the preparation of Turkey to accession, Turkey makes her best to bring these issues to a final settlement. With regard to Cyprus, the third round proximity talks will continue under the auspices of the Secretary General of the United Nations. The objective will be to prepare the ground for direct negotiations on Cyprus.

A mutually acceptable solution in Cyprus can only be attained on the basis of reality. For years, the Turkish and Greek Cypriots have carried their lives within the frameworks of their respective States. These two States, on the basis of sovereign equality, can lay the foundations for a final agreement. In this context, the proposal advanced by President Denktash to create a Confederation by the two equal and sovereign States is for us a realistic and viable option.

As for the disagreements between Turkey and Greece, I am of the opinion that the friendly relations and confidence we have initiated last year contribute to the stability of our region and of Europe. The 9 agreements we recently concluded bears witness to the success of the process in progress. I am confident that as two neighbours we have the potentials to solve our bilateral problems.

(Interview given to M. Howard and published by "Odyssey", Athens, March - April 2000, and to l'Express, Paris, May 2000 - Excerpts)

* * *

8.   The Journey to Hope

-I- The recognition of Turkey's candidate status to the European Union has ushered in a new era in Turkey-EU relations. It has been a long time since the Association Agreement was signed in 1963. Since then, "Membership to the European Union" has been a common objective in the programs of all the Turkish Governments. An advanced stage was reached with the completion of the "Customs Union" in 1996. At the Helsinki European Council in 1999, Turkey's candidacy to the European Union was decided.

Now, the Accession Partnership document has to be prepared by the European Commission along with our contributions. Subsequently, the National Program that will this time be prepared by us with the contributions of the European Union and which will take the shape of a very comprehensive plan will have to be materialize.

As the hopeful common journey of Turkey and the European Union is starting, we know that everyone has many things to do. We expect the long and difficult accession process to be completed in the shortest possible time, with the Union and Turkey fulfilling their respective obligations.

With this new era that we have initiated, a new chapter is being opened in the history of both the European Union countries and of Turkey. A strategic transformation is occurring. From now on nothing will be as it used to be...

-II- The frontiers of the entity of countries European Union represents, will no longer pass through the Balkans and the Aegean but will include Turkey and stretch to the east of Turkey. Within this framework, new mutual obligations are emerging. As entities located in this common geography, both EU and Turkey assume the responsibility of protecting each other's welfare, security and integrity.

Turkey's candidacy to the European Union has reinforced its strategic and political status. Turkey's contribution to her own historical geography has now further increased. The improvement of its relations with EU obviously does not bring neglect from the part of Turkey in her relations with non-EU countries. On the contrary, Turkey is now in a more privileged position to expand her overall foreign relations.

The European Union will from now on benefit from the unique historical experience, cultural wealth, contemporary characteristics, young population and dynamic economy that Turkey represents. Turkey will provide the European Union a unique access to new horizons, civilizations, cultures and economies. The new European Union encompassing Turkey as candidate is being truly transformed into a multi-cultural and multi-religious organization.

-III- As Turkey now proceeds towards an enhanced "rationale", sophisticated criteria and advanced objectives, towards a further developed democracy, political, social and individual relationships, she will benefit from the stimulating and facilitating dynamics of her candidate status. She will have the support of the experience and of the good will of the European Union. In her quest for an everlasting progress, Turkey will now have the benefits of catalyzing effects of the European Union.

As I mentioned, a new chapter is being opened in the history of the European Union and of Turkey. Naturally, problems and difficulties exist. Yet, hope exists above all. I wish this emerging environment to be beneficial to Turkey, to the European Union and to countries of the Eurasian geography, which is substantially affected by developments in Turkey. *Speech delivered on the occasion of "The European Union Day" (Ankara, May 2000)*

CHAPTER VII :
Redefining Turkish Foreign Policy

"...*Foreign Minister Ismail Cem said that the decision of the European Union Helsinki Summit to name Turkey as a candidate "...demonstrates that E.U. has decided to change. EU candidacy is a historic decision in regards to Turkey, but it is more of a historic decision for EU herself."*

The Minister noted that "...rather than confining itself to a limited geography as a small, ethnically defined club of rich countries, European Union has taken a bold step by accepting Turkey a candidate for accession". Cem stated that, in doing so, EU now develops into a multi-cultural, multi-religious, multi-ethnic entity. Cem added, "...after Helsinki, EU has new horizons full of new challenges and opportunities..."

Foreign Minister Cem claimed that the "Adana Memorandum" between Turkey and Syria for cooperation in combating terrorism was a major turning point, which triggered positive developments, mainly the diminishing of terrorist assaults to Turkey. This, in turn, facilitated the implementation of democratic changes and paved the way for the Helsinki decision.

Talking on Turkish-Greek relations, Cem disclosed that Greek Foreign Minister George Papandreou would be visiting Turkey on January 21-22. Describing Papandreou as a "rational person," Cem said "...It was as fortunate development for Turkey as it was for Greece that Papandreou became the Greek Foreign Minister". He also said that he believed Turkey and Greece would be able to maintain the prevailing positive approach.

****Mr. Minister, Turkey has had a very remarkable year; perhaps one of the most remarkable years of the last century. Throughout 1999, you have played a key role in all of these significant developments. Turkey lived through a process this year that started with the Abdullah Ocalan escapade and ended with us becoming a candidate for EU membership. What we want is to analyze* *this year with you. Shall we start with Ocalan? The pressures exerted by Turkey on Syria, Damascus denying him of the shelter he had been offered until then, his journey through European airspace, his capture, and the trial... How do you evaluate all these developments? Particularly in regards to EU's Helsinki decision offering Turkey candidacy for accession?*

Positive results were brought about by three main factors: (a) successful governmental policies; (b) favorable strategic conjuncture; (c) our redefinition and reshaping of Turkish foreign policy.

During the last three years in particular, we have managed to introduce a new and different perspective on how we perceive the world and ourselves. In a philosophical, ideological manner, perhaps, my ministry played a pioneering role. New policies were developed along a new vision, on a new foundation. These policies proved to be successful.

I will try to describe some of the attributes of this rather ideological approach: I have always believed and wrote that "history" and "culture" were the two "absentee" in our foreign policy. In spite of the evident reality that, given Turkey's imperial past on three continents, history provides our most important asset. It is to note that while we shared for seven centuries the same state and parallel cultural traits with some of today's twenty-plus independent countries, neither nationalism nor the industrial revolution were in place. Therefore, multitude of nationalities could live in peace under the Turkish realm. During most of this time, Ottomans provided a social and economic system which was much more egalitarian, just and caring than those of feudal lords and rulers of Central and Eastern Europe. The religious tolerance exercised was incomparable with the intolerance that reigned in the West.

One would presume that given this past, contemporary foreign policy would make a large use of this magnificent asset, which is history and culture to promote better foreign relations; to build economic ties on the already existent socio-political infrastructure. Well, Turkey did not.

What my ministry achieved is the insertion of these two valuable factors to our policies. It seems that we have succeeded to a relatively large extent.

Another element in this new approach is a will, an attempt to know ourselves better: Where we come from, where we intend to go, what our mission is? And what we figure our contribution to the long march of humanity might be? In other words, a quest for the role that we have, or we should have.

And, we tried to get rid of some old clichés and complexes, which lingered on our assessments.

Some new analyses and policies emerged:

I stated for the first time on a governmental platform that "...Turkey is an Asian country, as well as European." We developed the concept of our "Historical Geography" and the strategic value that it has in our relations with countries that make part of this geography.

Besides our traditional relations with the West, we confirmed our interest in forging positive links with the countries on our East and on our South. To gain their trust and their friendship became one of our top priorities.

However innocent these policies might seem, they were significant in the particular Turkish environment. To confirm that Turkey is Asian (...as well) was a courageous assessment, given the fact that for decades aspiring or mentioning anything but "Europe" was almost considered as a sacrilege, especially in the "intellectual milieu". On the other hand, anything with an "Eastern or Arab connotation" was, again for decades, synonym for "backward", "unfriendly", "untrustworthy", etc. We liberated our foreign policy from those long-standing misconceptions.

Underlining that history does not bring about frustrations alone, but opportunities as well; we promoted our relations with the East, with the Magreb, with the Middle East and with Africa. We tried to bring a new momentum to our relations with the Balkans and Caucasus, with Central Asia, all these geographies that make part of our historical and cultural heritage. These were not realized at the expense of our relations with the West. On the contrary, our relations with the U.S. and with Western Europe improved constantly. This trend reached a landmark in our candidacy to the European Union. The policy we pursued was never one in quest of "alternatives", one to shift basic choices. On the contrary, I stated on several occasions that the more we make progress in our relation with the West, in regards to EU in particular, the precious we get for the East; and, vice-versa.

221

"...To become European", "to be considered as European", "to be certified as European through the acceptance of candidature to EU" were sentimental exaggerations and, maybe, complexes which I denounced right away.

I declared, again for the first time on a governmental level, that Turkey is "already" European, and for centuries; that she was not in need of a proof or of third parties' credentials. We set a target for Turkey; we said Turkey should become a global state, a power encompassing regions by the early 2000's.

Through assessments as such emerged a new pattern of behavior, a new conceptual framework, and a new set of practices. A new vision: We began observing our environment and ourselves through a new optic, with a newly acquired confidence. We were able to detect new opportunities, new roles and new privileges, which, as a matter of fact, were not new at all. They were always there, historically present, but a new consciousness and confidence was needed for us to realize their being. As this new understanding developed, Turkey became more conscious of her assets. A country which no longer is a naive and mediocre emerged in the international scene as an assertive actor.

In fact, the awareness of our assets, and the new fondation that we provided for Turkey's foreign policy are at the roots of whatever success we may have achieved:

From our resolute stance which made Greece and Greek Cypriots to come back on their decision to deploy S-300's in Cyprus, to our firm position vis-à-vis Syria which led to the agreement "to fight against terrorism". From our growing capability to make the international community better understand our concerns on terrorism, to the growing audience for the "Confederal set-up for a mutually acceptable solution in Cyprus". From the "Southeast Europe Cooperation Initiative" that we developed, to the "Caucasus Stability Pact" that we are forging. From intensifying relations with Arab countries as well as with Israel, to an extended role in Central Asia and to emerging friendship with Sub-Sahara Africa; to our developing relations with Greece, to our policy which convinced NATO (at Washington Summit) to provide the new EU military organization with NATO capabilities only on a "case-by-case" basis and by unanimity decision. And, occurs, our candidature to EU that finally was declared in Helsinki.

222

First, we defined correctly Turkey's EU aspirations; we put it in the appropriate perspective: I stated that "...EU candidacy and membership is a goal for Turkey, not an obsession".

With the then popular terminology, we said "...we would not go knocking on doors to beg for admission".

We underlined that Turkey's foreign policy covers a wide spectrum and that Turkey's EU accession, though essential, represented only one of her two main goals: The other being to assume a central, decisive role in the emerging Eurasian reality. Instead of the traditional rhetoric about "...what we'll get from EU", we initiated a new reflection, on "...what we are to provide EU". We analyzed the strategic interests EU will attain by having Turkey in, and we brought this to the attention European public opinion.

Prior to Luxembourg Summit of December 1997, I had said that if "...discrimination were adopted and Turkish candidacy rejected", we would end our discussions with EU on sensitive issues as "terrorism", "human rights", "Greece", "Cyprus", etc. Not that I refrain from discussing such topics: On the contrary, the more we discussed such issues the better our positions were appreciated. I was able to understand my interlocutors better. Therefore, I continued to discuss with some EU countries our sensitive issues as well as their sensitive issues, on a bilateral basis. But, I had stated, it is senseless to discuss such topics with an organization that does not even consider Turkey as a "candidate". My interlocutors, it seems, had not taken this seriously at the time. It is exactly this firm position that we took after Luxembourg.

TRIGGERING POSITIVE CHANGES: A decisive development is the "Adana Memorandum" (Fall 1998) agreed upon by Turkey and Syria. I believe that this event has played a key role and paved the way for crucial developments, which facilitated Turkey's candidature for EU membership.

In October 1998, we made it very clear to Syria that we were fed up with the logistic support that they were providing for terrorists. This was going on for twelve years. We asked them to stop immediately harbouring and supporting the terrorist organization. We said that we were going to take whatever measure to achieve this end, by ourselves, if necessary.

Syria did cooperate. The "Adana Memorandum" was signed, Syria began dismantling terrorist mechanisms established in her geography, the terrorist leader had to leave Syria.

From that moment onwards, it was not important whether or not Turkey managed to capture the terrorist chieftain, main responsible for the murder of thousands of innocent people. The crucial change was the isolation of terrorists from their main logistical base. I had said during my first days in office that one of my aims and a mission for my ministry was to deal with the exterior dynamics of terrorism. The Eastern dynamics of terrorism were finally contained, through the cooperation we established with Syria. We were to deal later and quite successfully with the "Western" dynamics of terrorism, which have hurt Turkey so much, and for such a long time.

Following these achievements, the relevant Turkish ministries estimated that bringing the terrorist leader to trial was just a matter of time. He first embarked upon a European adventure. At that time, a sudden, strong gust of anti-Turkish sentiment started to sweep across Europe. These sentiments, however, lasted only about two weeks. Within those weeks, Turkey managed to convey to European public the realities of the matter. We took advantage of the burst of interest in the European public opinion and presented our views, which were finally drawing attention and consideration. I had to travel to Rome (where the terrorist leader was sheltered) for a NATO meeting and held a press conference which was intensively reported all over the world. I explained Turkey's sensitivities to the international media. We succeeded in getting our views across and displayed how wrong some European perceptions were. I believe our efforts proved to be effective and successful, to a certain extent.

All these developments were instrumental in paving the road, which lead to Turkey's candidacy. Turkey being relatively relieved of terror assaults was able to move on with several democratic changes and legal adjustments. These developments provided a positive atmosphere for Helsinki.

***Helsinki definitely opened up a new era. Turks have now received a morale boost. However, serious discussions are also taking place. What is our current position ? What is the homework that Turkey has to do before accession ? What steps do you think Turkey will have to take in the months ahead in order to fulfill the Copenhagen criteria ?

Turkey must avoid mistakes at the philosophical, ideological and political levels. This is absolutely critical. It would be wrong to get over-excited. We have to approach the issue in a rational, composed and planned manner. We should proceed with a plan and we should not lose the existing momentum. If we set off with over-enthusiasm, it will soon die out.

We must realise that Turkey is not an ordinary candidate. Without exaggerations, we should be conscious of the fact that with our strategic assets, economic might and cultural singularities, we are - as a "candidate" - probably contributing to EU more than some others might as "members". We must keep in perspective the historical dimension. On the other hand, we should know that EU contributes to our image in the world; and, through her dynamism in democracy, will contribute to our work to overcome some delays that we have in our democratic process. We should not consider representatives of EU as "inspectors" coming from an alien world to dictate us what is wrong and what is right; but as friends who work with us to contribute to common goals and to shared values.

We are not like any other candidate because we have already covered considerable ground to membership: We have signed a Customs-Union Agreement with EU way back in 1996. Almost no other candidate is even close to signing this crucial Agreement with EU.

***The development of Turkey's relations with Greece has helped Ankara's EU candidacy, but there were some other noteworthy factors that have also played a decisive role. The change of government in Germany, for example...*

A HISTORIC DECISION FOR EU AS WELL: I was recently asked how is it that I am on good terms both with conservatives and socialists. Regardless of whether a right wing or left-wing government is in power, most European countries continue to implement a stable policy towards Turkey. For example, the French President Jacques Chirac is a conservative, Prime Minister Lionel Jospin is a socialist. We have very good relations both with the President and the Prime Minister of France.

Germany, however, is a different case. The change of government in Germany has been a decisive factor in the recognition of Turkey as an EU candidate. Germany has very close relations with

225

Turkey. Two-and-a-half million Turks live in Germany. While the former Helmut Kohl Administration was distant towards Turkey, the new Social Democrat - Green Government gave strong support to Turkey's EU candidacy.

Global strategic trends, which brought to the economic and political forefront the regions where Turkey is a decisive factor (...Caucasus, Central Asia, Balkans, - Eurasia, in a sense) turned Turkey into a precious, vital component for EU to incorporate as "candidate". This reality was enhanced by Turkish policies, which now are conscious of Turkey's historical, cultural assets and her expanding role in this vast geography. All these factors consolidated each other and brought about the Helsinki decision.

But I do give great credit to EU for taking this decision. It took courage, to overcome some old prejudgments, biases, and discriminations, negative sentiments some of which goes as far back as the Crusades. As much as EU candidacy was a historic decision for us, it was more so for the European Union. Europe, too, has decided to change.

Rather than confining itself to a limited geography as a small, ethnically defined club of rich countries, EU has taken a bold step by accepting Turkey a candidate for accession. In doing so, EU now develops into a multi-cultural, multi-religious, multi-ethnic entity. After Helsinki, EU has new horizons full of new challenges and opportunities.

*** *And it would have a much healthier structure...*

Definitely. We have positively contributed to the courageous move of EU by taking steps ourselves in order to support our European friends in having a better assessment of realities.

Without the active participation of Turkey, EU's opening to new worlds and new civilizational dimensions would have been rather limited. Her influence in Central Asia, the Caucus, Balkans even in Middle East will be enhanced by Turkey's participation. Without Turkey, Europe cannot have a multi cultural, multi religious dimension. For a genuine enlargement process, membership of Turkey is a prerequisite. EU has realized this historic reality.

About 10 days before the Helsinki Summit, I participated in several bilateral meetings. Some of these had been planned long in advance and had no connection with the Summit. However,

Helsinki was quite naturally on the agenda. I first traveled to Sweden, and then moved on to Denmark. Although it was not originally scheduled, I met as well Gunter Verheugen, the EU Commissioner responsible for enlargement. Conversing at dinner in Brussels, I was explaining, as it had become a habit by now, how crucial Turkey had become after the emergence of Eurasia, after the signing of the Baku-Tbilisi-Ceyhan Pipeline deal, etc. I was elaborating on the historical perspective of Turkish foreign policy, the coexistence of cultures, the Eurasian dimension and such, when my interlocutor (Verheugen) said, "...*But Minister Cem, that's precisely why we shall make Turkey an EU candidate.*"

In fact, the vision and the particular mission that I was trying to develop for Turkey's foreign policy matched with the global strategic changes taking place at a certain moment in history. This produced a great increase in Turkey's strategic capability and enhanced her role in a very large geography. It is mainly to these factors that Turkey owes her EU candidacy.

***Where does Turkey see itself in geopolitical terms in 10 and 20 years from now?*

A member of the European Union and a pivotal, decisive center of Eurasia.

***Some people think Turkey's head thinks west and its heart beats east?*

No. I believe that Turkey is both European and Asian, and that this is an asset. It is not a contradiction. It reflects two complementary dimensions. This analysis provides a major dynamics for the foreign policy that I am trying to implement.

In my youth we had a strong dissent in our student organizations; some believed we were "Western", others objected that we were "Eastern". We fought each other on those issues. But the reality is that we're both European and Asian. We have both Western and Eastern characteristics. With the Balkans we are European, with the Caucasus we are Caucasian, we are Middle Eastern as well and of course have strong links with Central Asia. Therefore Turkey's identity is not a common one, not like any other country. Turkey has the background of an empire, of a state, which was inter - continental. We still keep these specific traits and we have that multidimensional character.

227

This is one of our strong points, one that I take advantage in formulating our foreign policies. And the policies seem to be successful.

***Is there perhaps a danger of Turkey being pulled in too many directions at once?*

As a country, which for centuries has dealt simultaneously with several continents and geographies, I do not see such a danger.

(Interview given to I. Cevik and Y. Kanli; published in Turkish Daily News, Ankara, December 1999 & Excerpts from statements to the international press, February - June 2000)